Joff Sharpe served for 10 years in the British Army, culminating in a tour as an SAS Troop Commander. His specialisms were anti-terrorism, jungle and amphibious operations. Since then he has forged a 30 year career in business, founding two start-ups and holding corporate roles in a range of international companies as Chairman, CEO, COO and CHRO. In the course of a varied career he has so far lived in ten countries and worked in many more, including a year in the Borneo rainforest.

Sharpe is now an investor and Board member of various technology-based companies in the UK and USA. In addition to *Who Dares Wins in Business* he has freelanced for Newsweek, Huffington Post, and South China Morning Post and appeared on BBC and other media. He is an in-demand public speaker.

Educated at The Royal Military Academy Sandhurst, he is a Fellow of The Royal Geographical Society (& Institute of Geographers), Chartered Fellow of Chartered Institute of Personnel Development and Member of Special Forces Club. With a strong interest in sustainable business, he has participated in expeditions to rainforest, Antarctica and endangered coral reefs.

Who Dares Wins in Business

JOFF SHARPE

LUME BOOKS

LUME BOOKS

This edition published in 2021 by Lume Books

Copyright © Joff Sharpe 2014

The right of Joff Sharpe to be identified as the author of this work has been asserted by them in accordance with the Copyright, Design and Patents Act, 1988.

ISBN 978-1-83901-447-5

Typeset using Atomik ePublisher from Easypress Technologies

www.lumebooks.co.uk

Table of Contents

Introduction

Have you ever fancied the SAS life - even for a heartbeat? Be careful what you wish for. We live in a time of crisis. Fires rage the length of the West Coast of America. They've only just gone out in Australia on the other side of the world. A heat-wave is melting the permafrost in Siberia releasing methane gases that threaten the stability of our atmosphere. There is - quite literally - a burning platform. The decline in biodiversity is unprecedented and, as we collide with other species, we've unleashed a pandemic that has almost brought the global economy to a standstill, threatening any business that didn't have the cash reserves to weather the storm. Unusual climate conditions also spawned the worst locust storm in eighty years, ravaging East Africa. In Spite of - or maybe because of - these things the world is at war with itself with major conflagrations in more than 40 places. In some countries, like Afghanistan, war and its horrors have become a "whole life" experience for most of the population. Worldwide, around 70 million people have been displaced from their homes and nearly half of that number now roam the planet as refugees.

There is no upside. But crises do create opportunities for those who can pivot, leveraging new business models and technologies to create better alternatives. Since business-as-usual isn't working, the time has come for courageous leaders to step up with creative new solutions. They will need to show innovation, humanity, decisiveness, cooperation and many other qualities in abundance. There is much at stake.

What can we learn from the SAS analogy? At the very least, it is an organisation that has confronted the toughest situations imaginable with great daring - and it tends to win.

I'll be brief

The first edition of *Who Dares Wins in Business* ran to 235 pages. My readers bounced between the sections like a hopping bird looking for the fattest worms. I know this because authors can see the consumption of Kindle pages. I don't take it personally. No one reads whole books anymore. We live in a digital world of short attention spans – but also greater customer intimacy. So, I've pruned this Second Edition *'Fighting Back the SAS Way'* to a more manageable 174 and made sure that you'll find at least one big idea for every 2-3 pages. Give it a try – pick a random section and see what you find.

Having thrown down that challenge, I have to say that the first couple of chapters are pretty important if you want to understand the whole SAS approach. And I'm confident that there's something in this book for you, whatever business you're involved in. Since publication I have delivered the book's core messages via public speaking engagements to insurance companies, entrepreneurs, gatherings of finance directors, a recruitment jamboree in Ibiza, a provincial real estate company, university athletes, a school business studies course, a corporate lawyers' shindig in Alicante, Wall Street banks, a PR company specialising in the luxury sector and a regional export hub to name but a cross-section. I published excerpts via an MBA column in the South China Morning Post[1] which spawned a Chinese edition of the book. During the Covid crisis I podcast a version to 450 members of the Global Workspace Association in 23 countries. Without exception, these audiences were quick to connect the lessons of WDWiB (this book) with their everyday lives in business. The SAS analogy works. The data says so. *But it requires thoughtful interpretation.*

---

1   SCMP, Hong Kong's largest circulation English speaking newspaper

Getting to the knowledge

The subject of the SAS seems to appeal to a sort of popular warrior instinct. The SAS craze began when Steve Mitchell - better known as Andy McNab - opened the proverbial SAS kimono with his best-selling book *Bravo Two Zero*[2]. The public lapped up this (possibly embellished) tale of the regiment's least successful mission, in which bravery and resilience far exceeded planning, operational good practice and sound judgement. Fast forward to 2015 and the SAS's selection procedure became the basis for a wildly successful TV programme *Who Dares Wins*. The audience cares little that three of the four instructors weren't in the SAS and the one that was in gets furious with contestants who don't take things seriously enough, oblivious to the irony that he is co-hosting a game show featuring celebrities like ex-glamour model Katie Price and Joey Essex. No one cares that SAS selection is a 6 month long attritional process, not 8 days or that real SAS candidates aren't, in reality, shouted at very much because the whole point is to test the candidate's self-motivation and independence.

Don't get me wrong. I'm not saying these Special Forces media heroes are schmucks. On the contrary. Mitchell went on to become a best-selling author and secured a well-deserved CBE for services to literacy. Ant Middleton and his boys, highly credible members of the SAS's sister organisation the Special Boat Service, have made a fortune from their work. But the world they inhabit doesn't trans-late easily to everyday business life, beyond the simple idea that: if they exhibit qualities like courage and determination, we should do likewise. In fact, one of the *Who Dares* team penned a candid memoir in which he describes just how alien he felt corporate life was for him when he left the military[3]. So to get to the real nuggets

2   Bravo Two Zero, Andy McNab, Bantam Press 1993

3   Battle Scars, A story of War and all that follows, Jason Fox, Penguin Random House 2018

of commercial wisdom we need to sift much more carefully through the muck and bullets.

It all starts with the SAS's creation.

A pocket history of the SAS

The SAS exists because what came before wasn't working. In the course of the wartime North African campaign 1941-43 there were around a million casualties, shared between all sides. One million men. Killed, wounded, captured, lost, bones buried in the sand. That's a lot of dead people and a lot of unhappy families back home. Sometimes the Germans and Italians had the upper hand, sometimes the British and their Commonwealth allies. Both sides believed that the way to win was to concentrate their forces into massive, armoured formations that could smash their way through enemy lines. In one such smash-up my uncle was blown up in his tank and blinded. (He survived, later to become Chairman of the Control Risks Corporation).

C'est la guerre. Or at least that's how most people saw it. But in a hospital bed in Cairo lay an iconoclastic Army officer called David Stirling. He was no poster boy for his regiment, the aristocratic Scots Guards. Before the War his Cambridge University life revolved around betting on horses at nearby Newmarket. From there he flip-flopped from life as an artist in Paris's sleazy Pigalle, to alpine mountaineering and cattle ranching on the North American plains. He was a gambler, a dreamer, a curiosity to his aloof father and most unsuited to military life. But like everyone else, war rounded him up, put him in uniform and flung him into the maelstrom.

Stirling had no love of conventional military discipline but he certainly didn't lack courage. He volunteered for the Commandos, along with his brother. But when there wasn't any action he became quickly bored and was on a charge for malingering when he hit upon the idea of experimenting with some parachutes. The parachutes were supposed to be heading to a unit in India but he confiscated them, jerry-rigged the static-line (rip-cord) to a light aircraft and "caught some air" as parachutists like to say. With little technique, his massive six foot six frame hit the ground on landing like a sack of potatoes, badly injuring his legs. Hence to hospital.

Lying in his bed awaiting court-martial he began to think-outside-the-box. He grabbed a piece of paper, a pencil stub and began to sketch out an audacious plan based on root cause analysis. It seemed to Stirling that the way to defeat the Germans and their Italian friends was not wholesale slaughter but simply to deny them the ammunition, fuel, food and supplies that allowed them to function. This would require disrupting enemy shipping between Italy and Africa. To do this, in turn, required domination of the skies by Allied aircraft. Once again, the way to achieve this was not a bloody air battle but a campaign of clandestine commando raids by small groups on Luftwaffe airfields. Rommel's Heinkel bombers would be sabotaged whilst their pilots slept. To do this effectively he would need to invent a new technology - a time-delay bomb. The plan stood conventional military thinking on its head.

Stirling's first task was to get around the many layers of military hierarchy that would likely do everything in their power to kill off his idea. Let's quickly jump to the Business World for a second. Imagine a young manager of limited experience and no great distinction, currently fielding some sort of Written Warning from Human Resources, whilst simultaneously on sick-leave. In her hand is a strategy proposal scribbled on a scruffy piece of paper, outlining a plan that flies in the face of a well-established business model, competently implemented on a daily basis by layers of tenured executives. She wants to give the proposal an airing with the Group Chief Executive. Good luck with that.

Stirling knew that the "fossilised layers of shit," as he unkindly described the military hierarchy, would not give him the time of day. So he clambered out of his hospital bed and threw his crutches over the barbed wire fence that circled Group HQ in Cairo. Dodging the military police and finally fleeing from an angry adjutant, he burst into the office of supremo General Ritchie and thrust his crazy plan into the startled general's face. To his endless credit, Ritchie knew a great idea when he saw one. Months later 400 of Rommel's aircraft lay in pieces, destroyed by a tiny force that started with no more than around 60 men. The war turned in the Allies' favour. One of the world's most entrepreneurial fighting forces was up and running.

It's better to be a pirate than join the Navy

As someone who's now spent over 30 years in commerce, the application of this story to modern business is painfully obvious. How often do industries cling to conventional business models in the deluded belief that things will eventually get better? It's not that business folk are dumb. Imagine yourself as an Eastman Kodak executive who persuaded the Board to pile money into a new laminate film factory, only to discover that digital photography has rendered the investment redundant a couple of years later. There's not much incentive to 'fess up to your short-sightedness. There are numerous similar examples and they are now multiplying like the plague that is Covid. Interestingly, Kodak is now valiantly trying to reinvent itself as an anti-Covid drug provider.

And maybe it's not surprising that the architects of constructive disruption, like David Stirling, often come from left-field. A young Richard Branson, distributing abortion advice following his girlfiend's unplanned pregancy or cooling his heels in prison for tax evasion on record sales might not have made it to the graduate trainee programme of a company like GE, Mars or PepsiCo. Steve Jobs was famously fired from his own company, Apple. Phil Knight surrounded himself with misfits when he created a company that he wanted to call Dimension Six. One of the misfits suggested the alternative brand name of Nike - because he saw the word in a dream. In his book Shoe Dog[4], Knight has a hilarious term for his government nemesis; "the bureau-kraken"- the equivalent of Stirling's fossilised layer.

Some years ago the parents of a friend of mine attended a dinner party with a work colleague and his wife. The two fathers were senior

---

4   Shoe Dog, A memoir by the creator of Nike, Phil Knight, Simon & Schuster

executives at a well-known oil company and one of them had a loose connection with a young man who was seeking a five hundred dollar investment in his new start-up. As a student, the guy resented having to buy new college books and thought there was an obvious opportunity to recycle. His plan was to provide the platform. One of the executives was persuaded to hand-over five hundred dollars. My friend's father sadly didn't. Why not? Because, compared to the oil executives he was used to dealing with, "the guy came across as *lame*." Name: Jeff Bezos.

'The reasonable man adapts himself to the world, the unreasonable man persists in adapting the world to himself, therefore all progress depends on the unreasonable man'.

George Bernard Shaw, 1905 drama Man & Superman

I wish I had the gift of such men. But you don't have to go "fully pirate" to learn from them. In my own business career I've created two start-ups *inside* large corporations. In different ways, they were painful for the mothership to absorb. At the turn of the Millenium I ran a digital business called Revolver.com inside News International. I worked for Rupert Murdoch's son-in-law, Alasdair Macleod, and at the time the Murdoch family had clashing views on the value of digital businesses. (Have you seen *Succession?*) And I was no friend of the print advertising department whose lunch I was busily eating. Some years later I was part of a more extreme effort to convert the entire 1 billion euro revenue of a multinational Yellow Page business, enjoying 40% margins, to digital. More recently I introduced a flexible workspace business (a bit like WeWork) to an established real estate investment company, whose principal value came from providing long leases on office buildings to big, corporate customers. In the course of these adventures I never met a stupid executive or even one I thought of as particularly dogmatic or short-sighted. But replacing established revenues with new, less-proven solutions is inevitably troublesome. And yet, in hindsight, it's inconceivable that any of these businesses could have opted out and carried on business as usual. Consumer trends, new technologies and even "Black Swans" swoop in, compelling change whether companies like it or not. And it's always better to be on the front foot.

If this book has a specific target market, it is the budding entre-preneur, wondering how to give their boundless energy shape and substance or the *intra*preneur, the change-agent working inside an established business, seeking a better way. It's for students of WHY and HOW, more than the servants of WHAT. And it's for those determined to emerge stronger and perhaps more enlightened post-Covid apocalypse.

A good idea that sticks

The SAS was not the only entrepreneurial force to be spawned by WWII. In fact there were a great many others: Popski's private army, the Chindits of Burma and the Long Range Desert Group to name a few. Axis forces had their equivalents. But unlike these organisations, the SAS survived after the war (except for a brief interlude) and has subsequently gone from strength to strength for nearly eighty years. This is because Stirling's SAS didn't just solve a specific problem at a given point in time. He future-proofed his invention with a whole rucksack full of creative organisational qualities that could be applied in almost any situation imaginable.

I've studied these qualities - and organisations that embrace them - for much of my working life. You could say it's a bit of an obsession. As a young army officer in the 1980s I read every book that had ever been written about the SAS, from Sunday Times journalist Tony Geraghty's ground-breaking work[5] to the adoring memoirs of Suzanne Lassen[6] whose son, Anders, won the SAS's only wartime VC before his death

5   Who Dares Wins, Tony Geraghty, 2nd Edition, 2002 Time Warner Books

6   Anders Lassen VC: the story of a courageous Dane, Suzanne Lassen 1965 Frederick Muller Ltd

in combat aged 25. I even read the collected love letters of Jock Lewes,[7] Stirling's martinet training officer who was killed in the desert by the machine-cannon of a Messerschmitt fighter. I compared and contrasted Alan Hoe's candid biography of his friend David Stirling[8] with Virginia Cowles' 1958 classic *The Phantom Major*[9]. As I read through these works it became clear to me that there was something almost mystical about the curiously named Special Air Service Regiment and the men who served in it. It possessed peculiar, contradictory qualities. There was self-discipline in abundance but scant regard for formality. The founders seemed to be aristocrats but wanted nothing to do with the class system or hierarchy. In the words of one veteran "they were a bunch of misfits who happened to fit together."

My own involvement with the regiment came gradually. After an early baptism of fire in Northern Ireland where I first encountered special forces, I moved to the Far East where I became a jungle warfare instructor. My mentors were two SAS veterans (Bill 1 and Bill 2) who taught me to master the environment and unleashed a new curiosity in me about the post-war campaigns of Borneo and Malaya, in which my father served. All-told, I lived in the rainforest for more than a year, relying on resupply by helicopter and dugout canoe. Amongst other adventures, I met the Iban in their long-houses, famed for their head-hunting but in modern times more focused on family, preserving their culture and the biodiversity they rely upon for sustenance. I explored a lost world of limestone mountains and caves in the Sarawak interior and later, on an operation in Central America, stumbled upon a Mayan temple festooned with creepers and inhabited for the last thousand years by nothing but tarantulas and deadly snakes. Like a great green womb

---

7   Joy Street, a wartime romance in letters, Jock Lewes & Mirren Barford, 1996 Chivers P

8   David Stirling: the Authorised biography of the founder of the SAS, Alan Hoe, Little Brown, 2nd Edition 1992

9   The Phantom Major: The story of David Stirling & the SAS Regiment, Virginia Cowles, Pen & Sword Military 2011

the forest enveloped me, slowed me down to its own pace, playing insect-music to me during long, pitch-black nights. Contemplation time was abundant.

One day I finally asked Bill 1 whether he could imagine me serving in the SAS. "I could imagine you as much as anyone else," came the reply. We had spent months in the jungle together, got on well and yet he offered neither encouragement nor caution. You got the sense it was almost a *personal matter* between me and my Gods. In a strange way his neutrality spurred me on because it played the ball firmly back into my court. Once I decided to apply to SAS selection it became a fixation. I returned to Hong Kong and began a punishing training regime that, by today's standards, was pretty unscientific. In the 1980s there were no Fitbits or protein shakes and lycra was something that went on in the disco. But every day I tried to do at least three or four training sessions; either some form of military fitness, a hill run (there wasn't any other kind of run around Stanley Fort), a swim, cycle, a free weights session or something more fun like a game of tennis. Nor was this solely a physical thing. On occasion, I drove myself to exhaustion and then made a point of reading The Economist or some other dense literature to make sure my brain could still function when I was shattered.

When winter came I moved back to the UK and headed to the Brecon Beacons where I spent three weeks navigating alone amongst the rain-swept hills. No one checked my rucksack to see that I increased the weight I carried each day, no one checked that I maintained a minimum 4 Kph across the mountains or kept off established tracks. If I became lost, disoriented or sprained an ankle I would need to solve the problem for myself. The only encouragement I received the entire time was purely coincidental. One day I decided to replace the hill walking with a long, fast run on a treadmill in the barracks gym, to ensure that I wasn't turning into some kind of plodding Welsh packhorse. Well into the run and soaked in sweat, I was accosted by SAS general Peter de la Billiere who happened to be in camp and in need of exercise. Having no clue who I was, he bellowed; "What are you doing indoors?" above the sound of the crazily whirring conveyor belt. "You should be outside." Believe it or not, I completed the run, showered, had my dinner and set out on an unplanned night march. I was, if nothing else, a dedicated student.

And yet it would be two more years before I finally got to examine the SAS from the inside. We'll come back to that.

What do you stand to learn from this book?

I've dropped a few hints already. The value of this book depends a whole lot on you. If you're simultaneously scrolling twitter, instagramming your latest selfie and hoping that I'm going to reach out of the Kindle and spoon-feed you wisdom, we're in for a *#disappointment*. We need to go at this together. (If you prefer, as they say on the TV programme, we need to "f***ing switch on!")

For the social media addicts amongst you, when I deliver this book as a motivational talk it's quite often accompanied by a live Twitter feed and it's always interesting to see which bits land most readily with people. Some favourite call-outs have included:

> *"If you're not learning you're becoming a liability"*
> *"Companies need strategic versatility"*
> *"Lead, follow or get out of the way"*
> *"Diversity starts with assembling diverse skill-sets"*

You'll forgive me if I recycle some of these phrases as chapter headings. The book is focused on the four main themes below that I believe to be key:

Culture as foundation

Organisational cultures are a popular topic in business books but the SAS has some quirky ingredients. They've learned to reconcile issues like individuality and personal independence with teamwork. They see leadership as something that gets done, not as a demonstration of executive greatness. And the very motto 'Who Dares Wins' has far-reaching consequences, not just in terms of personal courage but around collective mindset and ways of approaching things.

Operational excellence

The SAS was born with negligible resources and continues to be every CFO's wet dream, achieving so much more with less. In SAS parlance the 3 'S's' stand for: Speed, Aggression & Surprise. These are kinetic ingredients with multiple applications. The machinery of business - processes, systems, technologies and procedures - are teased apart and reassembled in ways that bind with the culture.

Evolution

I've already explained that "necessity was the mother of the SAS's invention". SAS soldiers never stop learning and they never stand still. Restlessness is in their nature (even if it plays hell with marriages!). The need to continuously reinvent at both personal and organisational level is a given, the acquisition of diverse skill-sets a prerequisite. Less obviously for an elite independent unit, they also have the humility to seek all kinds of help and support when needed.

Resilience

We'll come back to this topic. But let's just say Who Dares can't *always* Win - by definition. When you take risks you accept the consequences when it goes wrong and you have to be capable of bouncing back.

This is our basic roadmap which I've split out into the ten chapters that follow. You'll also see that I've picked out some of the key points along the way and delivered them via an imaginary SAS coach. Shall we call him BILL? I guess I'm taking a liberty with that but I have also shared WDWiB with numerous SAS veterans and their reaction is pretty universal; they're glad to see that their extraordinary skills have a useful application outside the military. It cuts both ways.

Chapter One: The Man is the Regiment

In this age of individuality, where the Internet allows anyone with a laptop and electricity to express themself to the World, it is interesting to note that Stirling saw his organisation as something that almost had a human personality. This is what he meant when he said; "The Man is the Regiment and the Regiment is the Man." If such expressions existed in 1941, it's doubtful he would have talked about Human Capital. He wouldn't have even said; "people are our most important assets," which suggests that people are key but not the only consideration. He went the whole hog. To Stirling, the person and the organisation were one and the same. Why was he such an extremist? Consider the following example:

As a Boat Troop Commander I once undertook a Royal Navy diving course. We spent many hours running around, jumping into and swimming underwater in a miserable gravel pit with very little to look at apart from the resident eels. My diving partner, however, had recently completed an anti-terrorist operation that spoke to Stirling's Man/Regiment view of life. He was part of a team that had staked out a government building which had been the subject of terrorist reconnaissance. Although standing by, his team were unprepared when the terrorists drove up to the building with an oil drum full of explosives in the bucket of a JCB and detonated it, before opening fire with machine-guns. Concussed and lying on the floor of the half-demolished building was my diving buddy and his colleague. The air was full of swirling dust and bullets took chunks out of the brickwork around them as they both sat up and looked at each other. Without passing a word between them they leapt to their feet and poured fire back at the terrorists. Within moments all eight of them were dead. When confronted by a terrifying situation, two men with a shared value system reacted courageously, consistently with their organisation's principles and in a way that was mutually supportive, without the need for communication. The question is: *how do you build a system so relentlessly reliable?*

From organisation to organism

The founder of the SAS knew that if he wanted to build a truly special organisation he would have to create a kind of living organism that, in a sense, would be capable of making things up as it went along. In Stirling's eyes his unit was made up of a single fabric and you could take a swatch from any part of it and you would find exactly the same thing. Put less esoterically, you could pull up a canvas chair in "L Detachment's" desert camp in Kabrit, with any one of his soldiers, and they would give you an entirely consistent picture of what was going on and what people stood for. They would tell you about the obligations of membership; the endurance required by the long thirsty marches, the bruising parachute exercises and ultimately the sacrifice that might be expected of them in the days to come. On the other hand, they would also enthuse about how much more enjoyable it was to work in a much less formal culture where everyone was focused on creative soldiering rather than petty discipline. Stirling summarised the culture with the five qualities below and I have added a sixth - Courage - because that was enshrined in the motto on the winged dagger[10] cap badge that he designed:

Meritocracy
Humility
Humour
A sense of one family

---

10   Emblem was actually supposed to be a flaming Excalibur but is generally popularised as a Winged Dagger

Self-discipline
+ Courage

Those principles have stood the test of time and do differentiate the regiment from the rest of the army, in areas such as the focus on self-discipline rather than traditional regimentation and the social classlessness of the unit. Interestingly, INSEAD Clinical Professor of Leadership Manfred Kets de Vries often summarises his thoughts on leadership with: *Humanity, Humility and Humour*. Stirling got to the same place in 1941. In the course of Selection instructors constantly scrutinise recruits to see whether they are exhibiting these kinds of qualities. Do they help the other patrol members, conduct themselves quietly and professionally in their daily business and deploy a touch of humour to diffuse the tension when things become difficult? Can they be relied upon to get things done without being reminded and do they turn up to briefings on time with the correct equipment? In the case of young officers, are they comfortable with the more informal relationships that go on in SAS Troops and can they still exert authority in spite of them? If the answer to any of these questions is "*no*" then the chances are the person won't make it in the SAS.

Infectious culture

These principles don't appear on mission statements, websites, displays on the walls of headquarter buildings or any other places that a corporation would typically use to proclaim its way of doing business. Stirling, the Founder, was captured by the Nazis in 1943, stuck in Colditz for the rest of the war and his involvement with the regiment was largely symbolic after that. So this was no personality cult. And yet his cultural legacy spread first to wartime SAS units in France and Belgium and subsequently to the former Rhodesia (Zimbabwe), Australia and New Zealand. In the intervening 80 years SAS Commanding Officers have not seen fit to make speeches about these principles nor have they thought to replace or improve them. Somehow an organisation culture has been created that is greater than the sum of many generations of military coworkers. As journalist Tony Geraghty once wrote, the SAS phenomenon may be best thought of as an "idea."

But what makes such an idea both infectious and enduring? The answer has a lot to do with the "Golden Circle" Simon Sinek describes in his best-selling book '*Start With Why*[11]'. Sinek began his career in advertising and this undoubtedly helped him get under the skin of what makes for effective communication. His Golden Circle comprises three concentric rings with Why in the centre, ebbing outwards through How and on towards What at the periphery. He is clearly a fan of Apple and argues that, to most consumers, the brand has come to represent a series of ideals around challenging the status quo and thinking differently. This is their Why. How they do this is through beautifully designed, innovative products and What they do is make computers. The fact that all this activity is a licence to print money, such that non-founder CEO Tim Cook is now apparently a paper billionaire, is neither here nor there. Sinek says it better. But if Stirling had simply said that he was creating an organisation to blow up aeroplanes (What) using Commando teams (How), it's highly doubtful that the regiment would have survived. And in fact Vladimir Peniakoff's "Popski's Private Army" was specifically set up to destroy Rommel's fuel dumps (What…you get the message) and it folded immediately after the war.

If I were to attempt to distill Stirling's secret sauce into a few ingredients it might look something like this:

We are going to challenge the status quo and think differently (aka Apple) about how to solve military problems.

We are going to assemble an exceptional group of self-starting people who are passionate and capable of innovating in this way. They will be trained, armed and equipped to perform.

Given the exceptional demands we're going to place on people, we will create a family atmosphere to provide mutual support.

---

11   Start with why: How great leaders inspire everyone to take action, Simon Sinek, Penguin 2017

The "Why concept" is really what underpins umbrella brands like Virgin, Easy and Musk Co. Branson started with vinyl records and moved into recording. You could say he got lucky with Mike Oldfield's Tubular Bells. You could say not many people would be innovative enough to back an instrumental piece like that. To Virgin Records he has added Virgin Airways, Virgin Trains, Brides, Holidays, Money, Media, Cosmetics, Mobile phones, Health Clubs and now even space travel. These entities are not vertically integrated, or even particularly synergistic, but together they represent a kind of strategic intent. All of these activities are intertwined with Branson's inimitable style and customers somehow expect to get a little bit of his bearded, cheeky persona each time they purchase his products or services. They may not actually climb into one of his balloons with Branson, but when they sit on one of his trains they half expect him to suddenly appear pushing a drinks trolley, possibly in drag. Virgin departure lounges have pool-tables, their planes serve ice creams and, since some people evidently want to join the Mile High Club, why not provide them with a double bed instead of a police escort at the other end? There's more than a touch of the Charlie Chaplin anti-establishment about Branson.

Virgin employs plenty of marketing people and the different company websites allude to brand virtues. But collectively, the Virgin concept is a little harder to articulate and even harder to separate from the man himself. There are elements of Everyman about it, a social boldness that PLCs typically shy away from (even though they are supposed to be "publicly owned") but more than anything a kind of unwritten guarantee that poor service and rip-off behaviour don't sit with the Richard Branson ethos and therefore shouldn't be encountered anywhere in the Virgin empire. Like Apple, he's never afraid to question the status quo and seek a better alternative.

Another version of the brand umbrella is the "Easy" empire of Stelios Haji-ioannou. Stelios is the son of a successful shipping magnate who gave him a chunk of seed capital (£30 million) to get started with his own entrepreneurial venture. Stelios was inspired by Herb Kelleher of South Western Airlines, the original innovator that stripped the cost and hassle of short-haul flying and replaced it with an ethos of fun, an ingredient, incidentally, that is something quite recognisable to early pioneer passengers of commercial air travel. Stelios built upon the franchise by creating new, vertically integrated businesses like car hire, but in time, like Branson, he migrated away from travel into disparate other businesses that simply carried the same generic customer service promise. Also like Branson, he tested the limits of the Easy franchise with things like Easy Money that stretch beyond his original area of competence. In contrast, Elon Musk sought a range of technological synergies between Tesla, solar power and even Space X and this - typically of him - was described in his biography as 'The Unified Field Theory of Elon Musk.[12]'

What these entities have in common with the SAS is that they are somehow more than the sum of individual operations. They represent a clear statement of intent, which probably boils down to something rather simple; "We promise to deliver against a robust set of values, no matter what the product or service we are offering." The really interesting point is that knights like Sir Richard and Sir Stelios clearly believe that their respective formulas are applicable across all sorts of commercial activities and are likely to generate high returns, even in areas where they have no proven track record. They may be "serial entrepreneurs" but it's not a "win some/lose some" kind of thing (even though there have been hiccups along the way). In common with the SAS, these men have a kind of belief that they can try their hands at almost anything, falling back on a combination of raw talent and unassailable values to win the day.

Cultures that persist tend to have elements of uniqueness and real authenticity. Take Mars Incorporated, the powerhouse that added Wrigley to its home-grown stable of candy, petfood and rice brands. It is a huge company (around $40 Billion revenues) and unusual in

---

12   Elon Musk: How the Billionaire CEO of SpaceX and Tesla is shaping our future, Ashlee Vance, Virgin Books 2015

that it continues to be fully owned by the founding family. Successive generations have resisted the temptation to create unfeasible wealth for themselves by taking the company public. This is because one of the founding principles of the company is *Freedom* and specifically the freedom that comes from private ownership. There are four other company values. *Quality* and *Efficiency*, which you might expect from a large manufacturing company. *Responsibility* reflects the view that all Associates - as Mars calls its coworkers - should be reliable and self-starting. The final value is *Mutuality* to which I will return in a minute. Given family ownership, you might assume that these values were dictated by the founders from on high. In fact the family commissioned a study some decades after the company's formation to figure out which key ingredients had made the business so successful to that point. A large number of Mars veteran Associates were interviewed and 'The Five Principles of Mars' was an attempt to summarise their collective wisdom. So the principles were more an observation rather than a dictate.

When CEOs and HR Directors wrap cold towels around their heads and try to create new or improved principles, they often produce vanilla results. For example, I was once invited to talk to a group of senior leaders from the global cosmetics company L'Oreal, at a conference in Berlin. I was working at telecomm's giant Vodafone at the time and I looked at the L'Oreal website to see how their cultural values compared with ours. What I found was pretty instructive. One company sold phones, the other lipstick but our cultures were surprisingly similar, at least if you took the statements at face value. Both companies made a series of promises to their principal stakeholders. Vodafone had a *passion* for their customers, L'Oreal *respect* for theirs. Vodafone was also *passionate* about employees, L'Oreal similarly *respectful*. Vodafone was passionate about "The World Around Us" and L'Oreal continued to be respectful towards the environment and the law. When I had gone down the list I pointed out to the audience, in passable French, that I found it ironic that a very British company claimed to have a culture based on that Latin quality, *passion*, whereas the French were grounded in *respect*! It got a good laugh. The serious point is not that either company lacked a coherent culture but that only those two words, *passion* and *respect*, were the things that set these two manifestos apart. The rest was pretty much a job description. Mars deals with the need to satisfy stakeholders in their value statements by bundling them into the single quality '*Mutuality*'. That ensures everyone gets a good deal, whether eating or distributing a Mars product, supplying raw materials or whatever their involvement.

Other companies adopt more distinctive tenets but it is not always easy to see how these link to corporate strategy or natural priorities. For example, when experienced CEO Philip Jansen took over at Worldpay in 2013 he found '*Adventurous*' as one of its four principles. Whilst intriguing, and an obvious choice for the Scout movement, Jansen struggled to see how this was a defining attribute and shifted the focus back to more coherent priorities like customer excellence. Most laughable were the values of disgraced Enron: 'Respect, Integrity, Communication, Excellence'! Both the 'Why' - which you could describe as *purpose* - and clear cultural values will be sources of strength for any business as it rides through the Covid storm. A bunch of platitudes on the office wall, on the other hand, won't pass muster.

Eagles flying in formation

How do you stop strong cultures suffocating individual personalities, an occasional criticism of companies like Mars? Steve Jobs' refusal to be put in a corporate box was made famous by his saying; "I'd rather be a pirate than join the Navy." Stirling's piracy began when his men stole an entire camp, including a piano, from a New Zealand unit, when they couldn't secure the resources more conventionally. Some of his key leaders were no lovers of authority. When Paddy Mayne (future Commanding Officer) was hired he was under arrest for driving a senior officer out of the Mess at the point of a bayonet. Stirling called his people "a group of misfits, rogues and rule-breakers. In a sense, they weren't controllable." But this was only partially true. He brought in Welsh

8

Guards officer Jock Lewes to impose a ruthless training regime upon the group and anyone who didn't sign up to it was given short-shrift. Stirling also demanded total discretion from his men when socialising. There was to be no hard partying in Cairo. So a truer picture is probably that of a high-octane mix of characters who knew that they had to operate within a well-defined SAS sandbox. To coin a much-used business phrase, there was freedom within a framework.

Setting aside national differences, most people want to express their individuality in the workplace and to feel that they can make some sort of personal difference. No one wants to be a cog in a machine. But how do you reconcile this with the need for some measure of cultural conformity, especially in complex organisations with multiple stakeholders? This problem was pondered by Wayne Calloway, the late Chairman of PepsiCo. Pepsi had an expression "*Pepsi Pretty*" which it applied to potential new hires and this had nothing to do with physical appearance. *Pepsi Pretty* was short-hand for a kind of stand-out charisma that was expected of executives, if not the whole workforce. In Calloway's view his company was not a place for corporate clones. To square the circle he coined the expression; "We teach eagles to fly in formation." It was a nice concept. He wanted individualists who could gang up into powerful, aligned teams. Even SAS soldiers can't be loners because the special forces existence is pretty intimate. They operate a buddy-buddy system that, at its most basic, involves one man cooking, washing or even defecating whilst another covers him with his rifle. The basic operating unit is a 4-man patrol and when they are not sharing a patch of dirt or snow somewhere they're rattling along in a Land Rover or "hot bunking" in the cramped confines of a diesel-powered submarine. This is not a life for someone who prefers his own company to teamwork, however loosely structured.

Ugly

A test of a culture's robustness is also the willingness of an organisation to dispense with the services of anyone who doesn't fit the pattern. Lewes established a zero tolerance approach. Membership of L Detachment, as the SAS was then known, was entirely voluntary but if a recruit displayed a moment of self-doubt or lost enthusiasm for even a second, they would be shipped straight back to their sending units. During the jungle phase of Selection I remember seeing a Parachute Regiment NCO sobbing into his hands one morning. After months of excruciating effort, he had concluded that the SAS life wasn't for him and it was a profound moment of self-reflection and, presumably, disappointment. The training staff were both sympathetic and supportive. He was an excellent soldier, it was simply that his *aptitude* lay elsewhere. They had him on a helicopter in under an hour.

There were a couple of reasons for this strategy of rapidly returning soldiers to their units. The first is that the SAS makes exceptional demands on its people and you can't afford to have anyone on board who might throw the towel in. Corporal Jack Sillitoe set the standard when he found himself stranded behind enemy lines in Libya in WWII and hiked more than 100 miles through baking desert back to base-camp. The feat was both repeated and extended 50 years later by Colin Armstrong, *nom de plume* Chris Ryan, *"The one that got away*[13] *(from Bravo Two Zero)"* when he walked 200 miles across Iraqi desert to freedom in Syria during Operation Desert Storm. This kind of survival-of-the-fittest approach will be music to the ears of people like ex-GE boss Jack Welch, famous for culling the lowest performing 10% of his management population, as it will to anyone who attracts sobriquets like "Chainsaw" or "Fred The Shred." However, Lewes's approach wasn't about Darwinism. He was acutely conscious of the fact that if the SAS was to become something special, the people who stayed in the unit would need to feel that they belonged to something rather unique and something that attracted significant personal obligations. Jock Lewes' feeling was that, if he allowed dubious recruits to slip through the net, it would somehow dilute the *raison d'etre* of the unit for everybody else.

---

13   The one that got away: My SAS mission behind enemy lines, Chris Ryan, Potomac Books Inc 1998

The Hiring Process

If The Man is, indeed, The Regiment then it stands to reason that the recruitment and onboarding process is going to have to be highly effective. Every recruitment process in the world is really designed to answer the same three simple questions:

Can this person do the job?
Does it fit with their personal motivations?
Can they get along with the rest of us?

But how the SAS addresses these questions is rather interesting and it's different to a lot of industry thinking.

Focus on raw talent, potential

You might assume that the quintessential SAS recruit is a battle-hardened paratrooper looking for an upgrade. There were such men in my own unit, the Para-favouring D Squadron. But this is an incomplete picture, as are TV programmes that focus overly on the physical side of things. The official name for SAS "Selection" is actually the SAS Aptitude Test. The word Aptitude is carefully chosen. It is a word that focuses on the *potential* a soldier may have for this kind of military service. Lowest on the list of SAS requirements is the quality business people might call functional competence. If the regiment wanted explosives experts they would recruit from the Royal Engineers. If they wanted snipers they would go to the Small Arms School Corps. For medics they would go to the Royal Army Medical Corps, for HF radio operators to the Royal Signals and so on. Plenty of people from these regiments do join the SAS, but all of these types of skills are developed in soldiers once they join the regiment and in fact multi-skilling is the norm. However, no one is barred from joining the regiment simply because they arrive at the start of the selection and training process without any of these competencies. When I undertook Selection a member of my patrol was

11

a groom who looked after horses for the Household Cavalry. What the SAS are looking for is raw talent, potential.

The same sentiment was expressed by Herb Kelleher, the famed CEO of Southwest Airlines, when he said; "You don't hire for skills, you hire for attitude. You can always teach skills." But this might seem at odds with today's business career where the average tenure of a salaried worker, in the US for example, barely stands at 4 years. It might seem hard to accomplish when managers often feel overwhelmed by quarterly objectives. But the wartime SAS was a potent force for the 4 years 1941-45 before being briefly disbanded and, however tough our business lives may be, they don't compare with the challenges faced by the Finest Generation. Moreover, the speed of technological change means that legacy knowledge is a diminished currency. But maybe the most potent argument is simply enshrined in this question: can yours ever be a truly great organisation if it's simply a net importer of other people's talent and never an originator? Surely a more statesman-like perspective is called for!

Use realistic simulations to determine potential

There are many ways to determine potential. For example, the SAS are often required to train or work with foreign armies or security forces and many of these people do not speak much English. So an SAS training team may be required to learn the rudiments of a foreign language in a relatively short time frame. As everyone probably remembers from school days, some people have quite an aptitude for languages and somehow find it easy to pick up the vocabulary, grammar and cadence of a new tongue. For others, it's an impenetrable nightmare. The SAS have a simple way to sort the linguists from those who struggle. In the first week of Selection, soldiers are handed a textbook. In my case it was Operational Malay. Our days were full, primarily conducting navigation exercises around Wales but in the evening we were expected to sit on our bunks chanting "*Salamat Pagi!"(Good morning!)* to each other, as well as other phrases that were presumably useful during the 1950's

Emergency such as ; *"Anda telah melihat mana-mana penduduk kampung yang membawa bom tangan?"* (Have you recently seen any villagers carrying hand grenades?). At the end of the week we did an oral exam.

Another feature of SAS service is action behind enemy lines and the likely necessity, once things become a little kinetic, of using other people's weapons to defend yourself. In years past, soldiers undergoing Selection would be given a foreign weapon at one of the checkpoints on a march. An instructor would time the trainee, as they disassembled and reassembled the unfamiliar weapon. Morse code is another skill that can be learnt by all, but some people can achieve much higher speeds than others in a relatively short period, due to their superior aptitude.

There are plenty of jobs that require very specific skills; if a person isn't a chartered accountant, a biochemist or an expert in search engine marketing then there are certain roles they won't be able to fulfil. On the other hand, executives like Ben Legg, the previous COO of Google in Europe, was an ex Royal Engineer with only a passing knowledge of the Internet when he joined that company. (His proven competence was the use of military engineering to help alleviate the siege of Sarajevo). When company Adknowledge later hired Ben they tested his aptitude by presenting him with a complex set of data that he had to juggle and evaluate using Excel pivot tables. He obviously acquitted himself well because Ben took on the role and later became a serial CEO of technology-based start-ups and now mentors aspiring CEOs and gig executives. Provided that the person is a very quick learner it's surprising how low the barriers to entry actually are for some jobs that people might believe are the preserve of the cognoscenti. Addressing this topic Richard Branson once said; "If someone offers you an amazing opportunity and you're not sure you can do it, say yes - then learn how to do it later." Similar encouragement came from Sara Blakely, Founder & CEO of Spanx: "Don't be intimidated by what you don't know. That can be your greatest strength and ensure that you do things differently from everyone else."

Helios Private Equity is a very different business that invests on behalf of its clients in Sub-Saharan Africa. When they recruit Operating

Partners they present them with a whole portfolio of business case studies that the candidate likely knows little about. The person may know about mobile phones, but probably not in conjunction with heavy plant lease-hire, outdoor advertising and vegetable growing. What Helios wants to know is whether the individual can take a look at an unfamiliar business and quickly figure out the Key Performance Indicators (KPIs), strategies and key leverage points that impact the success of such a company. Once again, they don't expect the person to already know about oil exploration in the Niger Delta, but they do expect them to be able to figure things out very quickly for themselves; to have the *aptitude* to do so.

When Four Square, the drinks division of Mars, needed to hire new engineers the line-manager, an ex-submariner called Fraser Geekie, devised an aptitude test. He selected a piece of equipment that rotated in more than one direction using complex gears. Potential recruits were asked to explain what function they thought the machinery might perform and how it could work. In a similar vein, students applying to study Anthropology at Cambridge University are presented with an ancient chalice of some sort and asked to hypothesise about its use and origins.

Just like the SAS, these companies (and colleges) are not concerned with whether potential recruits can cope with a narrow, pre-defined role for which a single set of competencies would suffice. They want people with the horsepower and versatility to apply themselves, not only to a wider range of challenges, but also to those missions that have yet to be determined. They want razor-sharp "Swiss Army knives" that can be brought to bear on short notice, who will improvise and re-invent themselves as the situation demands. This is the essence of the SAS approach to acquiring raw talent, rather than going for pre-formed, but limited solutions to recruitment needs.

Helicopter view

The same sort of thinking is applied when assessing SAS leadership potential. Young officers complete the same physical Selection test as everyone else but then go on to do an additional "Officers' Week". This involves more sleep deprivation, but is primarily designed to evaluate an officer's analytical skills, initiative, planning and team leadership. Each officer is given a number of tasks that might include planning the demolition of a railway or a hostage release scenario. The officer has little money, is not allowed to use their own car and must rely on cunning to complete a series of exercises over a wide geographic area. For example, I had to do a daylight reconnaissance of an isolated farmhouse, miles away in Gloucestershire. I hitched a ride with a lorry to Gloucester and walked on foot some miles to the designated farm complex. I had carried out this kind of work a hundred times in Northern Ireland so I wasn't overly worried. However, when I got to the area, I was dismayed to see that the farm was stuck in the middle of acres of open fields with very little cover to conceal my approach. I had no binoculars or other surveillance devices, so I had to somehow get close, in broad daylight, without being rumbled. I thought for a bit and jogged back to a village a few miles away. An hour later I was back, having spent my precious pennies on a dog lead. I then wandered past the farmhouse, dangling the lead in my hand and nonchalantly calling for my lost – and entirely imaginary – dog! Abandoning my truculent canine, I then huddled in a culvert under a road making copious notes before leaving the area. I managed to get back to Hereford, narrowly avoiding getting run over by a train in the process, and presented my story to an amused (but I like to think impressed) bunch of SAS veterans later that evening.

Recruiting for managerial potential is an important topic. Companies like Shell have a rule of thumb, namely that no one should be recruited unless they have the potential to grow two or more levels further up the company hierarchy in the course of their career. In order to assess this, they used criteria like "Helicopter Quality." Like a real helicopter, a leader needs to be able to hover high above a situation and see it from a strategic perspective, and yet descend rapidly to observe points of detail where relevant. It was a quality that was observed to be lacking when senior military bosses failed to spot the inadequacy of the British Army's standard DMS combat boot during the 1980s Falklands War. Whilst the overall campaign strategy was sound, it might have been foiled by a First World War medical condition known as trench foot. Similarly, Boeing's multi-billion dollar investment in the new Dreamliner 787 aircraft was initially sabotaged by a humble battery pack that kept bursting into flames. These criteria differ slightly from management competencies in that they suggest, once again, not so much a collection of knowledge and skills, as an aptitude, a way of mental functioning that can be applied to almost any situation.

> B *When was the last time you recruited raw talent rather than someone who's done the same job a couple of times before?*
> I *Are you brave enough to hire people who are better than you? How many of your team are promotable or at least lateral movers?*
> L *How strong are graduate trainee & apprentice programmes? Do high-potentials stick with the company or move on?*
> L *Are qualities like Helicopter View understood and valued?*

Metamotivation

Whether people have the ability to become a good SAS soldier and whether they *want* to fulfil that role is, of course, an entirely different question. I've mentioned that my own entry to the SAS was not smooth. I undertook a winter Selection course where the weather was so severe that the final endurance march had to be cut short, after 20 hours of fighting through blizzards. To give some sense of perspective, this last test covers 64 kilometres of mountainous terrain and is conducted after no more than two hours sleep, following the previous day's exertions. And it's a lucky recruit that isn't covered in sores and blisters by this point. It's a bit like embarking on a journey up the length of the M1 when your petrol-tank is empty at the start and there's no chance of a refill. I somehow succeeded and returned yet again to the jungle. All went well with this phase of training until the last day. My instructor, the late *Jock Harris*, told me that I was a great guy. And that one day he'd like to see me in the Regiment. Just not now.

It was a crushing blow and when I reported to Hereford for Day 1, Attempt 2 of Selection a year later it was the most horrific groundhog day imaginable. By then my investment of effort had expanded over several years and, in spite of the exhausting days, I struggled to sleep at night, so great was my fear of failure. Months later I passed the complete selection process but not before one last twist. Having committed some *faux pas* during an escape and evasion exercise, I was subjected to a more severe and protracted interrogation than anyone else on the course. The result was frostnip in my feet and a severe muscle-spasm in my back. More sleep deprivation accompanied the condition. Others have fared less well. At least five people have died whilst undertaking the first phase of Selection.

> We are the Pilgrims, master; we shall go
> Always a little further: it may be
> Beyond the last blue mountain barred with snow,
> Across that angry or that glimmering sea,
> White on a throne or guarded in a cave
> There lives a prophet who can understand
> Why men were born: but surely we are brave,
> Who make the Golden Journey to Samarkand.
> Excerpt SAS Regimental Prayer

What drives people on? Around the time Stirling was being thrown into Colditz, a psychologist called Abraham Maslow was dreaming up his much-quoted motivation theory centered on a "hierarchy of needs". He also coined a less familiar term "metamotivation[14]" which focused on the idea that some people are very driven by the need to "self-actualise" or fulfil their potential. Stirling was rather dismissive

---

14   Goble, F. The Third Force: The Psychology of Abraham Maslow. Richmond, Ca: Maurice Bassett Publishing, 1970.

of the rest of the Army whom he termed "the thundering horde." He wanted to create a group that was special and he wanted people who weren't satisfied with being part of a khaki swarm. When Sir David died in 1990, he was described by Field Marshal Lord Bramall as "a true knight", which he was, although sometimes of the quixotic variety. A bronze statue of Sir David now stands beside a small Scottish country road in Doune looking towards Ben Vorlich, just as he would have wished. The US Army would probably describe all this with their catch-phrase; 'Be all that you can be.' This seems to be the simplest explanation for many people's pursuit of excellence - in the SAS or elsewhere.

The Porridge Factor

Other psychologists believe that the experience of hardship or set-backs early in life are more likely to equip someone to cope with extreme stresses that go with hyper-demanding roles. SAS autobiographies, of which there are now quite a few, often cite difficult and sometimes violent childhoods, early brushes with the law and - in one case - a father who dumped a bowl of porridge on his son's head[15]! Ex-SAS soldier Henry Gow, son of a murdered gangster, has a whole host of facial scars to illustrate the point created by an axe attack, knife slash and a poker driven through his cheek when a young boy in the course of a brutal Glasgow upbringing. He was initially rejected by the Army because he weighed eight stone and had malnutrition. On the face of it, Stirling didn't have much in common with a man like Gow. He was an imposing figure and an aristocrat, born to General Sir Archibald Stirling and mother Margaret, daughter of Lord Lovat. He was raised in an Italianate mansion in Keir in Stirlingshire – a county that bore his family name – and attended to by gardeners, cooks and other servants. It seemed like he was born to greatness and an easily privileged

---

15   Eye of the Storm: 25 years in action with the SAS, Peter Ratcliffe DCM, Michael O'Mara Books, 2003

life. When we look a little more closely at Stirling's early life a different picture emerges.

David was born with a speech impediment that made communication extremely difficult until the age of about four when an operation to his palate resolved the problem. His father had been an orphan himself and was kindly but aloof and struggled, in any case, to relate to his children. Communication was therefore mainly with his mother and his closest sister, also called Margaret. Psychologically, it was not an easy beginning. As David grew, he was far from a robust child and very nearly had to have his leg amputated when an adder bit him whilst he walked through heather on a holiday on the Isle of Mull. This cost the young boy a year of schooling as he convalesced and a further year was subsequently lost when he contracted typhoid. Although he ended up as a tall young man, he initially grew more slowly than his brothers and he became rather taciturn and inward looking as he wrestled with his many challenges. Inevitably, he went to boarding school (Ampleforth) where he was homesick and eventually made it to Cambridge.

It is fair to say that Stirling embraced adulthood with some enthusiasm and he enjoyed a playboy lifestyle that included spending quite a bit of time betting on the horses at nearby Newmarket. Eventually the faculty tired of his lack of application and he was kicked out of university or "sent down". He responded with imagination. David had always enjoyed art (in common with his father) and bought himself some paint, brushes and beret and headed to Paris to engage in a sybaritic and intellectual lifestyle, surrounded by fashionable communists. The reality is that he shared little of their anti-bourgeois anger, although this period in his life may have later contributed to his meritocratic approach to the SAS. However, the simple truth was that he wasn't a very accomplished artist and many years later he confessed to biographer Alan Hoe[16] that it was a very bitter pill to swallow when his tutor gave him this frank assessment. He tried to make the most of the situation and returned

16   David Stirling: the Authorised biography of the founder of the SAS, Alan Hoe, Little Brown, 2nd Edition 1992

to Cambridge to study architecture. He lasted about a year before he was kicked out for a second time.

At this point perhaps Stirling felt that he would have to achieve a more physical form of greatness and he set his sights on Everest. Adventures followed in mountains and on horseback, but it all came to end in 1939 when war was declared. He joined the family regiment, the Scots Guards, and immediately ran into trouble with an organisation that thrived on salutes, polished boots and bureaucracy. Stirling was described by his officers as "an unremarkable soldier" and it was only when he joined the Laycock Commando force that he began to get fully energised. Just at the wrong point, from Stirling's point of view, the force was disbanded and in the Spring of 1941 his beloved brother Hugh was killed in combat. In trouble with senior officers for his endless partying in Cairo, out of a meaningful job and bereaved, he was at a loss when a Commando friend - Jock Lewes - enticed him to start experimenting with some surplus parachutes. As we know, he then got badly injured. His great innovation was born at a time when his morale was rock-bottom.

Businesses have also picked up on this general theme. Surinder Kumar, ex SVP R&D at PepsiCo restaurants, attributed his drive and determination to the fact that he had had to walk barefoot five miles to and from school each day. His parents cut back on family food spending to pay for his education. He repaid them by gaining a Ph.D., an MBA and, incidentally, by specialising in food science. Another senior PepsiCo executive put his success down to a childhood battle with polio. George Buckley, self-made Chairman of Smiths and Stanley Black and Decker, was born into abject poverty, abandoned at four months old by his parents and passed onto lodgers by his grandmother, one of whom was a paedophile. "He did what paedophiles do," commented Buckley with understatement, "so it was a rough and tumble upbringing."

Famously troubled was Steve Jobs[17] who had childhood demons

---

17   Steve Jobs, Walter Isaacson, Little, Brown & Company 2011

to deal with. Whether he was troubled by the fact of his adoption (by working class parents) is a matter of debate. Less debatable is the fact that, at a certain point, he came to realise that he was significantly more intelligent than both of them. He seems to have spent quite a bit of his early life wrestling with his true identity and he wasn't averse to including other people in his wrestling matches. Although he showed promise at school he quickly developed anti-establishment tendencies and this took the form of school pranks, like blowing up his poor teacher, Mrs Thurman, with a firework under her chair, or declaring a "bring a pet to school day" without authorisation. Apparently Mrs Thurman developed a nervous tick. Jobs dropped out of Reed College, joining the ranks of other famous corporate faces who turned their backs on academia like Bill Gates and Mark Zuckerberg. If there is a recurring theme to such people, it is brilliance combined with an impatience to get on and do something with it, instead of biding time in the classroom. In Jobs' case there was an added layer of emotional angst to this whole topic. His birth parents were graduates and they had insisted that his prospective adoptive parents should share the same academic credentials. They didn't but they reassured Jobs' parents that they would make education a high priority for their child and they suffered financially as they delivered on this promise in due course. When Jobs' walked away from school he showed scant regard for either party's wishes.

In 1974 Jobs set out with a friend, Daniel Kottke, for India to study under a yogi called Neem Karoli Baba. When he got there, he discovered that Baba had died the previous September and he seemed to spend a lot of the next six months on bus rides around the areas of Delhi and Uttar Pradesh as he sought enlightenment. You get the sense that he didn't find whatever he was looking for on these adventures, although of course Jobs remained a Buddhist throughout his life. Jobs's adoptive parents were Lutheran, his birth parents of Catholic and Muslim extraction and he later held the view that no one could really relate to him unless, like him, they were somehow living a counter-cultural existence, swimming in the opposite direction to the mainstream.

Of course you can't recruit to these sorts of biographical data but many, if not most highly successful business people can point to a formative period in the earlier part of their lives that somehow helped shape who they are. Gerry Mulvin was at one time responsible for the recruitment of new hires to Bain, the elite management consultancy, and said he always paid particular attention to the early part of a prospective recruit's CV for this very reason. Bain, incidentally, regularly hovers around the top of Glassdoor and other preferred employer lists and exhibits a lot of other WDWiB qualities.

Up against trouble

In 2020 James Dyson was proclaimed UK's richest man by the Sunday Times. As far as we know he was never attacked with a bowl of porridge but his father died when he was a child and this resulted in him being sent to boarding school, where he felt his creative talents were suppressed rather than nurtured. In his own words he learned that; "to change things and be an inventor you are going to come up against trouble all the time." (He would have to be "an unreasonable man" GBS). Dyson worked through 5,127 prototypes of his dual cyclone bagless vacuum cleaner before he came up with a product he thought he could sell. When he started to run out of production capacity he moved manufacturing to Malaysia, even though everyone said he should stick to his base in Malmesbury in Wiltshire and as a result dozens of local jobs were lost. Yet, by taking the potential PR disaster on the chin, Dyson was able to hugely increase his manufacturing capacity at a lower unit cost and better meet the massive surge in orders as the business grew. When he started to run out of customers in the UK and Japan, Dyson decided to tackle America. The naysayers said it would be the death of his business. He forged ahead and quickly enjoyed 35% market share (50% in UK).

How about Kentucky Colonel Harland Sanders? Sanders' father also died when he was only five and as a youth he was endlessly fired from manual jobs for insubordination, bust-ups and - eventually - a gunfight with a rival. He ran a humble motel and gas station for decades and finally sold it to finance his dream of selling fried chicken to America. At the age of 65 he drove around the USA peddling his "secret herbs and spices" recipe and covered 250,000 miles a year in the process. There are now over 15,000 KFC outlets in 100 different markets. I imagine there were many times when both men did literally drop from physical exhaustion.

The conclusion from all these biographical stories is not that setbacks and conflicts are somehow necessary or desirable for people to be successful. But they do present a picture of high achievers having exceptional determination, resilience, stamina and - perhaps most importantly - a *sense of self* in order to achieve their goals. I once had the pleasure of playing a round of golf at Wentworth with its former owner Surinder Arora. Arora's principal business is a chain of airport hotels and he grew his business from humble origins when he supplied lodging to British Airways staff. I asked him about the early days of his empire and he told me that, with each new investment, friends and colleagues would invite him to cash in his chips and be glad that fortune had smiled so favourably upon him. He ignored their advice and built his business, hotel room by hotel room, into a substantial concern. With typical modesty he added that he could always go back to waiting tables if it didn't all work out.

Inescapably, it also seems like none of these people grew up with much in the way of a safety net to catch them if they fell, so they were that much more committed to their life goals. As an aside, I recently asked Sir John Sorell, a powerful figure in the UK Design industry[18], how he had learned to be a successful businessman. Son of a milkman, born in an air-raid, John studied art and design and had no formal business training. He told me that in the early part of his career he voraciously read the biographies of all sorts of successful people and drew wisdom from them. This suggests that, even if you've had a less

18   https://en.wikipedia.org/wiki/John_Sorrell_(designer)

troubled start than these super-achievers, there's plenty to be learned just by listening to their voices.

Industriousness

Industriousness, enthusiasm and raw energy are the bed-fellows of stamina. A curious social phenomenon in the SAS were the crazes that swept through Stirling Lines (the previous headquarters and training centre for the regiment) from time to time. Whether it was motorbikes or computers, SAS wives would be exasperated when their men were swept up in some new frenzy of activity that filled in the small blanks between training and operations. Some soldiers had a particular hobby that they carried through to the *Nth* degree, such as Peter "Billy" Ratcliffe (Porridge casualty) who became one of the best squash players in the Army. Others mounted ambitious expeditions, such as the famous 'Soldiers on Everest' exploits of SNCOs Brummie Stokes and Bronco Lane. Holidays were spent SCUBA diving, parachuting in California or climbing in the Austrian Alps. Not all hobbies were so physical. A member of my patrol called Mac had a keen interest in antique restoration. Even mundane tasks could take on new dimensions. I shared a flat with Ken Hames, who now runs expeditions and makes TV programs. Ken is absurdly strong and I still have visions of him running (yes, *running*) down the road in Hereford with a fridge-freezer on his back. We had sold the appliance to some remote neighbour. The wartime SAS leader Anders Lassen was described by an American medic in the following terms; "He was like a restless dynamo, charged with energy. He had to do something to translate his thoughts into action…..life had become a race against death. He drove his jeep like fury. He drank big gulps, as if he were thirstily trying to find everything there was in life….."[19] There was a sense in the Regiment that every moment was precious and should be jam-packed with activity.

This feeling will be familiar to anyone who has been part of a successful

---

19   Sergeant Porter Jarrell, Supreme Courage, Peter de la Billiere, Littlebrown 2004

start-up or other dynamic business. I mentioned that I ran a digital company, Revolver.com, within News International in 1999, which was in the middle of the heady days of the Internet boom. We were housed in an old storage facility, whilst bowler-hatted Britain (the journo's of The Times) were in more salubrious Wapping offices next door. Everyone was pleased to work long hours, rarely wore shoes indoors and endlessly tweaked the business model of the company as we sought a sweet-spot in what was already a chaotic on-line battle ground. Some years later I saw the same sort of thing going in Silicon Valley as it absorbed new waves of Internet activity. It was pointed out to me that you could gauge the level of excitement in on-line companies by what went on in the car parks. Google had "normalised" and cars were now heading home between 5 and 7pm, whereas Facebook was still humming at 10pm. Other brand new innovators were working through the night, oblivious to personal hygiene, sleep or regular nutritious meals. Such goings on are well-understood by Americans, taken for granted by the Chinese and a total mystery to whoever dreamt up the European Working Time Directive.

B *Are you metamotivated? Do others see your enthusiasm and energy?*

I *What are the big drivers in your organisation? Is the balance right between things like money, camaraderie, potential fulfillment…?*

L *How do you keep your team members committed and energised when job changes every 3-5 years are pretty normal?*

L *Does your organisation and its people have real stamina?*

Do leaders suffer short attention spans?

Monty Python & the psychopaths

Attempts to understand other psychological complexities of SAS volunteering seem to be problematic. In 2014 Steve Mitchell (Andy McNab) cooperated on a book[20] with a psychologist called Dr. Kevin Dutton, who has a preoccupation with psychopathy - but as a potential force for good. The central premise is that the ability to switch on/off emotion and human empathy has value in certain situations. It sounds plausible until you factor in the opinion of Steve's FIVE wives! I was once part of a study to determine why some people volunteer for dangerous work. When I asked the psychologists to share their data with me their patronising reply was; "Don't worry, you've passed", suggesting that I was a moron who shared none of their intellectual curiosity. More bizarre still was a visit to the US Delta Force in Fort Bragg. I was hanging out in their training wing and saw that the walls were decorated with photographs of soldiers undergoing selection and one photo particularly caught my eye. It showed a man in full frock coat, bow tie and dress shirt eating off bone china at a white tablecloth restaurant table – in the middle of a wilderness area. It was vintage Monty Python. Apparently the photo depicted an exercise where recruits were sent off on some vector that caused them to stumble across this fantastical scene. Meanwhile, hidden in a treeline a hundred yards away, was an occupational psychologist equipped with a pair of binoculars. His job was to evaluate the behaviour of the individual as he tried to reconcile this apparition with his assumptions about normality. John Cleese would have loved it!

This is not to say that psychology has no further role to play. The most coherent approach to this broader subject can probably be found in the Israeli Defence Force, which benefits from decades of war experience and the expertise of Nobel Prize-winning psychologist, Daniel Kahneman. Kahneman was an early critic of the IDF's Kaba selection process and helped shape its criteria, adjusted for men and women, according to role and based upon six personality traits; precision, activism, adjustment to frameworks, motivation for combat, sociability and independence. Military psychology seems to work best when applied through this kind of practical lens.

20   The Good Psychopath's guide to success, Andy McNab & Dr Kevin Dutton, Bantam Press 2014

Can you get along with us?

All recruitment boils down to answering three questions. So far we've tackled the first two: *can the candidate do the job and are they motivated to do so?* Leaving aside the recent uptick in home-working, most of us spend more time with our work colleagues than with our spouses or partners. So it's pretty important that we get along with them. Pre-Covid, it's reckoned that one in three entry-level jobs were being secured through work experience - a kind of try-before-you-buy arrangement. On the face of it this is a good way to de-risk and get to know someone before you commit to employment. If the person fits in well enough for six months then it reduces everyone's stress levels, slowly absorbing them into the culture and seeing how comfortable they are with it. In many ways this reflects the SAS Selection procedure in which candidates and 'Directing Staff' (serving SAS members) get to observe each other over a similarly extended period. More senior executives can also be absorbed into the business via preliminary consulting arrangements which give the same sort of exposure.

This doesn't suit every situation. An excellent prospect who is already in a good job, for example, may be unwilling to exchange their current security for such an arrangement. (And of course there's no fair comparison between the in-house and unknown, external candidates). So an alternative method will be needed to assess whether someone will "fit in." This generally means more interviews or the occasional "drink to get to know someone informally". At this stage several things can go wrong. The first - and quite common problem - is that no one decides anything. One of the world's largest and best-known headhunting agencies, that charges fees up-front for its services, has failed to complete about one third of its assignments in recent years. The fault lies as much with the clients as it does with the agency. Quite often the interview process takes too long, the goal-posts move and the ball is dropped. A colleague of mine recently secured a senior Technology position via eleven interviews. This is not an unusual number, particularly for Partnership-based businesses that take a collegiate approach. This can be time-consuming and highly stressful for the candidate (even causing bitterness if the decision doesn't go their way). Curiously, it also hints at some strange dysfunctionalities: why does it take eleven people to make a decision? If there's cultural alignment between them, shouldn't a couple of executives be able to make a representative decision on behalf of their colleagues? Is it fair that all eleven individuals have a right of veto? And if all eleven agree on a hire, is that a powerful consensus in support or a partial abrogation of responsibility because the accountability is so widely shared between them?

As we've established, the SAS have a very thorough selection process but they also tackle the question of social and cultural fit very directly. At the end of Officers' Week, the additional week of Selection for senior recruits, I was summoned to the Officers Mess to have a whisky with the Second-in-command, Arthur Denaro, and Regimental Sergeant-Major (RSM) *Taff Reynolds*. By this stage I was so shattered I doubted my ability to drink anything without falling over. However, the normally terrifying Taff (he was famous for walking off a mountainside in Oman with a bullet in his neck) was relaxed and friendly and it was a pleasant enough chat. The purpose of this little talk was very simple. They wanted to decide whether they liked me. Did they want to share the Mess with me, or the CRW Killing House, or the Iraqi desert? It was no coincidence that this responsibility fell to Arthur and Taff. For the non-military reader, British Army regiments are organised a bit like the parliamentary system. The Sergeants' Mess might be considered a House of Commons, an elected meritocracy that forms the backbone of the unit. The RSM - in this case Taff - is universally accepted as the living personification of the unit's culture. The Officers' Mess is often considered a bit like the House of Lords; a heady mix of extraordinary talent and less-proven, hereditary power with the 2IC - Arthur - as its chief representative. So although the whisky-drinking session was casual, it represented something much more structured. The heads of the "Upper and Lower chambers" were making a judgement on behalf of their constituencies. This seems a more efficient way to make what, in the final analysis, is a subjective call.

B *Do you and your colleagues have a sense of "One Family"?*
How important are team members to you personally?
I *Is the company's culture distinctive and engaging?*
Does it inform how people behave on a daily basis?
L *How important is cultural fit when making recruitment decisions?*
L *How does the company deal with "brilliant jerks" - people who are good at their job but a lousy fit with everybody else?*

10,000 hours of on-boarding

SAS recruits know that, when they finally put the sand-coloured beret on their head, this is only the beginning of an intense learning process. There's a popular theory that to be really world class at something - pretty much anything - requires 10,000 hours of practice. When Malcolm Gladwell first thought about this idea[21] he had in mind 20 hours per week for 10 years (with the occasional vacation). That's an awful lot of golf/tennis/violin/tiddlywinks. My guess is "an SAS year" of pre-training, Selection and specialist troop training in things like parachuting, diving, or mountaineering pretty quickly gets you up to 5,000 hours in a tenth of the time. Deploy with your squadron and you've blown through 10,000 hours in no time.

Business jargon for this kind of work lifestyle is a continuous learning environment. It's hard to achieve. Assume a bright young recruit has already accumulated 2,000 hours of relevant experience before they join a new company. The average EU employee works 40 hours a week and no more than 48 weeks a year, total 1920 hours. Multiply by 4+ years of company tenure and the maths rounds up nicely to 8,000 hours total. The conclusion is that, for this person to become world class within a single company experience, *every waking minute of their working life would need to be developmental in nature.*

This might sound an absurd proposition - but is it really? It might

---

21   Outliers: The Story of Success, Malcolm Gladwell, Penguin 2009

not feel so alien to employees of an exciting Silicon Valley start-up that goes from a blank sheet of paper to Unicorn status in a few years. It might make some sense to Google employees who are encouraged to allocate 20% of their time to their own R&D projects. It certainly *won't* make sense to an employee in a mechanistic role with 3-5 days of training per year. (Interestingly, the companies that provide the *least* training per head are those that employ 250+ people[22]). But it may be more instructive to take a less literal view of the 10,000 hour conundrum and focus instead on a more general mindset. SAS recruits are imbued with the idea that every moment of their career is a potential learning opportunity. The conclusion is that: If we are to believe in the SAS's focus on raw potential, we must accept that it is combined with a hunger for continuous learning. We'll return to this theme in more detail in Chapter 9.

---

22   Statista, D.Clark Aug 2020

The Man is the Regiment		
Quality	SAS approach	Things to watch out for
Raw Talent	Heavy focus on longer term potential and aptitude rather than short-term operational expediency.	Line-manager buys into principle (of nurturing raw talent) but sees own priorities as too pressing to accommodate. Under-recruits to protect self.
Motivation	Exceptional motivation necessary for the accomplishment of stretching goals. Create an atmosphere of excitement where organisation allows people to fulfil their personal potential.	Mixed motivation levels within a work group, leading to confusion as to what is expected. Dysfunctional motivators like money & fear.
Cultural Fit	"Eagles who fly in formation". A culture that encourages individualism but within a clear framework of values.	Indistinct/generic values that don't drive anything or – at the other extreme – a suffocating culture that crushes individualism.
Zero Tolerance	Zero tolerance for the benefit of those who remain in organisation and to emphasise the obligations of membership.	Whether more or less tolerant, using termination as a way to get rid of a problem rather than reinforcing the company's values & attributes.

Chapter Two:
Lead, Follow or Get out of the way!

SAS soldiers know there is a time to lead from the front, a time to chip in and add energy to the team effort and even occasions when the best thing you can do is keep out of the way and let others get on with it. In SAS parlance; "Lead, follow or get out of the way." It's a phrase that conveys a lot of kinetic energy and a bias for action. It suggests that people shouldn't involve themselves in an activity simply because of FOMO (fear of missing out), because they need to be acknowledged or need time to absorb the shock of some small change. They shouldn't insist on finesse-ing things when an 80/20 approach would work well or seek a platform for self-promotion. It puts a premium on speed and mutual belief, things we'll explore in Chapter 6. But Leadership, Followership and even Getting-out-of-the-way-ship are done a little differently in the SAS and it's a source of strength.

May the force be with you

Most people think of 'Leadership' as a good thing, even if it can sometimes be exploited by corrupt and powerful figures. But what if leadership was not something that an individual did but actually a word that describes a complete organisation? What if leadership were a kind of energy source with every employee both contributing to, and feeding off that source? It's an idea that George Lucas captured with his Star Wars franchise where 'The Force' is a kind of benevolent energy source that gives its recipients superhuman powers in pursuit of good.

When you serve in the SAS it does sometimes feel as though there's some kind of Force haunting the corridors of the Training Wing or blowing through the trees in the jungle. You can't see it but you know there's a source of encouragement out there somewhere and you have an obligation to be a net contributor to it. And it may explain why a visiting General once said of SAS soldiers they exhibit "a kind of insolent certainty." Where this life-force comes from is actually not so difficult to understand. To begin with the SAS only hires leaders. Almost everyone on Selection is already either an Officer or NCO. They have proven themselves in their sending units, proven themselves again during Selection and will need to continue proving themselves the minute they arrive in their Squadrons. NCOs become Troopers when they enter the regiment, irrespective of whether their former rank was Corporal or Sergeant. In a non-SAS unit there is a wide gulf between a Lance-corporal and Sergeant. And yet when they join the SAS they become overnight equals. It's a kind of rebirth or baselining. Officers escape this humiliation but they arrive knowing that they will have to work hard to win their soldiers' respect and their first tour of duty with the SAS will only last three years. There is no guarantee of return. For the soldiers it's a career-long commitment. In this 'no passenger' organisation every man is of equal importance and a leader - both on paper and in practice.

If there's a danger with such a construct it's that having "all Chiefs and no Indians" can cause confusion. But SAS service necessitates being comfortable with the idea that you can be both at the same time. What does that feel like? I remember once training in Scotland with the Submarine Service. Over several days the Navy placed its submarines at my disposal, great fun and quite an ego-trip for a young Army officer. But away from the naval base we were billeted with a squad of raw infantry recruits who would have been amazed if they had known our identity. At the end of the training we left the barracks at the same time as the greenhorns and an NCO arrived from somewhere demanding volunteers to mop out the latrines before we went. The recruits began moaning and excuse-making until I quietly seized the mop and bucket. I didn't mind. In fact I quite liked the idea of being an Admiral one minute, a janitor the next, somehow honouring Stirling's demands for humility. (The gesture was, of course, entirely lost on the recruits).

BHAGs - tackling the impossible

If the regiment's "force" has a center of gravity it's probably the idea that almost anything can be achieved with enough determination and a willingness to face the challenge head-on. The very first task any soldier has to perform when they join the SAS is to undergo the Aptitude Test. In Chapter one I described the "Welsh" phase of the test, lasting some four weeks, and this is followed up by a month or so of strenuous jungle training, combat survival, resistance to interrogation, anti-terrorist training and finally parachuting; in all, six months of intense effort and relentless scrutiny by instructors. The pass rate is a single digit percentage and I never met anyone who *expected* to pass. On the contrary, most people expect to fail, either because of physical or psychological shortcomings, but hope against hope they might somehow make the grade. When they do pass, they therefore typically experience the sensation of having accomplished something they previously thought beyond them. Quite often, this is the first time in their life they have felt this way and it rather sets the tone for the rest of their SAS service. The sensation may even be addictive. In 1976 Warrant Officer Brummie Stokes stumbled off the summit of Mount Everest with frostbitten toes. Eight years later I met him at HMS Tamar in Hong Kong on his way back to the Himalayas. This time he broke his neck. More recently, the media reported the controversial case of Danny Nightingale, the Training Wing NCO, who succumbed to heat-stroke whilst subjecting himself to an ultra-marathon in Brazil. If it's easy, it evidently isn't worth doing.

In the bestselling book *Built to Last*[23] Stanford professors Jim Collins and Jerry Porras coined the phrase; Big Hairy Audacious Goals (BHAGs). "Bee-Hag's", as they are now often called, refer to longer term objectives that are ambitious, visionary and something for an organisation to strive towards. David Stirling exhibited all the symptoms of BHAG addiction. His first BHAG was to make an ascent of Everest but this was interrupted by the War. But of course stretching goals don't have to be of the physical variety. The formation and development of the SAS was Stirling's first successful BHAG and he got a taste for this kind of thing. After the war he established a much less well-known body called the Capricorn Africa Society. It was a rather idealised attempt to bring harmony and racial equality to a fractured continent and was described by a contemporary journalist (1956) in the following rather romantic terms; *'While Africa strained under the growing pressure of racial tension, a strange and polychromic group of idealists, white, black and brown, gathered last week on the southern shore of Nyasaland's windy and beautiful Lake Nyasa. From every corner of east and central Africa, by every means of transportation, they travelled to a wooded rise perched above the surf-tossed shores where lions and gazelles had roamed only a few weeks before. With them they brought an idea that they hope will change all Africa into a land without racial barriers or bitterness.*[24] It was a grand but unachievable BHAG and had to be abandoned. Then later in life he established another quixotic body, Great Britain 75. The 1970s was a difficult political period in Britain and he had an idea to create a kind of "government-in-waiting" in case law and order broke down. Again it was rather unrealistic but once a person has accomplished something they thought was probably impossible, it's hard to go back.

Elon Musk is the ultimate BHAG exponent. His visionary objectives include embedding mobile-enabled software in the human brain, creating new underground transportation systems with his ironically

23   Built to Last: Successful habits of visionary companies, Jim Collins and Jerry Porras, Random House Business Books, 1994

24   Time Magazine, July 1956

named Boring Company and of course Space X. His projects tend to have a "Genius of the And" aspect to them - the achievement of more than one objective (like high performance and price) that others would see as a trade-off. Fellow space entrepreneur Richard Branson summarised it perfectly; "My interest in life comes from setting myself huge, apparently unachievable challenges and trying to rise above them….." His justification for attempting to circumnavigate the earth in a hot balloon was; "From the perspective of wanting to live life to the full, I felt that I had to attempt it."

We shouldn't let Branson and Musk corner the BHAG market. Another exponent of the "SAS approach" might be Simon Murray, himself an ex Foreign Legionnaire. Variously Chairman of Deutsche Bank and a host of other investments and directorships across Asia worthy of any Shogun, he began his career hunting FLN guerrillas in Algeria as a Corporal with a Legion parachute battalion. He was occasionally known to chop the odd terrorist head off and stuff it into his knapsack for subsequent identification purposes[25]. He rediscovered his youth when, aged 60, he ran the Marathon des Sables (presumably reminiscing the Beau Geste days), and three years later became the oldest man to walk unaided to the South Pole. Somewhere along the way he fit in Vodafone Board meetings, dramas at commodities trader Glencore and his latest venture, a company that provides paramilitary protection to vessels in waters infested with Somali pirates. Andrew Partridge, Simon's HR Director many years ago, describes daily conversations with him that were fast, vigorous and punctuated with onomatopoeic sounds. He was a man on a mission. Not to be outdone, his wife flew around the planet in a helicopter, the first woman to accomplish this particular BHAG.

Whilst in the Silicon Valley I had the great pleasure of meeting Scott Cook. With a degree from University of Southern California and a Harvard MBA, he is quietly spoken and unassuming. Scott created Intuit, a $81Bn company that provides accounting software for SMEs.

25   Legionnaire, An Englishman in the French Foreign Legion, Simon Murray, Sidgwick & Jackson 1980

His business was based on a BHAG. He wanted to provide SMEs with an accounting package that was more intuitive and easier to use than a pad and pencil. By the time he achieved that goal his company had passed the first billion dollar mark. He is also passionate about his people, nurturing talent and the company's culture. These days he is somewhat removed from daily operations at Intuit but, when we met he had a team working on a project to spread educational materials to the Third World via mobile devices. From behind the steel-rimmed spectacles you could detect all the signs of a man locked onto a new BHAG with a fiery passion and an intellectual commitment to make it happen.

Ambitious goal-setting might seem an obvious enough point in business. Conventional wisdom has it that objectives should be *stretching but achievable*. However, people like these aren't really interested in *stretching but achievable* goals. What actually stimulates them is that their goals are at the limit of finger-tip reach, an elusive prize that, if achieved, will take them to a whole new level. It's worth pointing out that this, in turn, requires a very hands-on type of leadership because no leader can possibly set such an objective and then sit back and delegate, expecting others to have a burning passion that isn't evident in the leader himself. Of course the achievement of such a BHAG delivers a huge jolt of kinetic energy through every single person involved and establishes the desire for the next impossible mission.

Before we leave BHAGs, one small word of caution: it is a fact of commercial life that leaders change from time to time and there is nothing more debilitating for an organisation than to be told that yesterday's BHAG is being replaced by a new one and, with it, a new leadership approach, a whole new culture and most probably a new cadre of managers. In fact Sheryl Sandberg, COO Facebook, said; "Leadership is about making others better as a result of your presence - and making sure that impact lasts in your absence." If the machinery is broken – so be it. But leaders should think carefully before assuming that their own BHAG is more important than their predecessor's. When Stirling was captured, leadership of the SAS was taken over by Paddy (Blair) Mayne. Mayne was an ex-rugby international and 1936 Irish

Universities heavyweight boxing champion. He went on to collect 4 Distinguished Service Orders (DSOs) and pretty much did for Axis forces in North Africa what Lassen did in the Hellenic Mediterranean. Whether one of those DSOs was more properly a VC was still being debated in parliament in 2005. Descended from the man who led the legendary Scots Greys charge at The Battle of Waterloo, he personally destroyed dozens of grounded Luftwaffe aircraft and on one famous occasion, when he ran out of ammunition in the course of an airfield raid, clambered into the cockpit of a Messerschmitt and ripped the instrument panel out with his bare hands. His forays were legend and, like Lassen, he wasn't afraid to go on solo rampages, freelance. In the early days of SAS raiding, Mayne was personally more successful than Stirling and it would have been very easy for him to claim the unit as his own and set some new direction as soon as his predecessor was safely incarcerated in Colditz. Lassen might have done the same with his SBS off-shoot in Greece and conceivably also David Lloyd-Owen of the Long Range Desert Group who partnered with the SAS. All of these men subordinated their ego to the pursuit of a vision established by another man. Had they not done so, the SAS would have mutated, been subsumed into another unit or disappeared altogether. The value of this behaviour should not be underestimated.

Leaders Eat Last

'*Leaders Eat Last*'[26] is the title of another Sinek book, which heavily features the US Marine Corps. But actually this is a principle that's taught at Royal Military Academy Sandhurst and a lot of other elite military establishments. The basic idea is that officers can have quite a cushy life back in barracks but when an army deploys it's the leader's job to put themselves last in the field kitchen dinner queue. This might seem a bit high-minded. But think about it. Would you follow

---

26   Leaders Eat Last: Why some teams pull together and others don't, Simon Sinek, Penguin

an officer into battle if you knew that he had just tucked into a hearty meal whilst letting you go hungry? Or that he had slept better, was warmer, drier and safer than you. To hell with that.

Many business leaders don't appear to buy into the idea of self-sacrifice as a leadership obligation. There have been many studies into CEO/median worker pay ratios and the figure is generally in the 120-300:1 range, depending on country and year. But how about this quote from a report by Britain's CIPD[27]: *'The highest paid CEO in the financial year ending 2018 was Jeff Fairburn of Persimmon plc, who received £38.97 million. This is 1,318 times the median salary of a full-time UK worker. At this rate, it would take an average full-time worker nearly three working days to earn what Jeff Fairburn could earn in one minute'.*

But maybe these kinds of fearless leaders don't care about the troops because they believe they are really the servants of shareholders who are the true judges of their worth? Wrong again. Sunday Times journalist Oliver Shah recently pointed out that the CEOs of four of the UK's largest real estate companies paid themselves £93m over the same 10 year period that their companies lost a combined market value of around £5.45Bn. Their mistake, according to Shah, was to harvest millions whilst "missing the retail crisis," namely the dramatic shift from bricks-n-mortar to on-line shopping. But Shah tells us in his book *'Damaged Goods: The Inside Story of Sir Philip Green*[28]*'* that we shouldn't be surprised that retailers like super-CEO Sir Philip struggled with technology because he was in the habit of asking his secretary to print off emails. As for his valued employees, he allegedly once said to a female buyer; "You're absolutely f***ing useless. I should throw you out of the window but you're so fat you'd probably bounce back in again". When BHS, his clothing business, collapsed irate workers pointed out that their paltry redundancy payments would not cover the cost of wife Tina's Chanel handbag as she climbed aboard Green's

---

27   FTSE executive pay report 2018, Chartered Institute of Personnel Development

28   *Damaged Goods: The Inside Story of Sir Philip Green, the Collapse of BHS and the Death of the High Street by Oliver Shah (Portfolio Penguin*

£100m yacht, safely harbored in a tax haven. If such people were military leaders you could imagine them not only standing at the front of the lunch queue but holding everyone else back until they had got to the after dinner mints.

Of course not every CEO is a bloated fat cat sitting in their corner office/ship's cabin, counting their stock options. When Mark Sebba retired as Chief Executive of Net-a-Porter he was described by founder Natalie Massenet as 'the World's most loved CEO.' Judging by the Youtube video[29] of his last day in the office, in which thousands of coworkers danced and sang along to Aloe Blacc's song 'The Man', she may not have been exaggerating. Multi-talented, a trustee of the V&A museum, supporter of many entrepreneurial ventures he was also modest. So much so that Massenet orchestrated his farewell gig to ensure that the credit for Net-a-Porter's stellar success was properly shared with him. When he died at 69 in his Cretian home she said; "he was described by everyone as elegant, charming, kind, funny, generous, inspiring and humble." Personally, I'm proud to say that I once leased an office to him on a hand-shake.

It's interesting how often humility pops up in discussion with the best leaders. Intuit's Scott Cook said the following; "Be humble about your importance, about how many answers you know and about how much you don't know (which is always more than you think), humble about the need to engage with and learn from people around you, humble about customers, humble about learning. Please understand that I'm saying behave humbly; I don't think you can actually will yourself to be humble, but you can behave humbly. Which means saying, often, 'I was wrong.' Which you'll discover is the moment when the real insights and breakthroughs occur. And when it's hard to behave humbly because you're afraid people won't value you, just remember: People already know, they can see through you. They know what you're good at and what you're not, so don't pretend. Instead, try being true. Be human, and vulnerable the way you really are. And you'll find that

---

29   https://www.youtube.com/watch?v=4u5VQlBENB8

by admitting you're not good at stuff you build a bridge to people. You give them room to contribute."[30]

Scott's advice sounds almost religious but it is deeply rooted in commercial experiences. Intuit nearly failed in the early days and the key to its success was Scott's absolute determination to listen to what customers wanted from his products and to deliver accordingly.

Less Green more Sebba

Why are leaders like Mark Sebba and Scott Cook so rare in business? There's no great mystery. Some explanations include:

A lack of higher purpose and values
A lack of training
A lack of mentoring and role-modeling
A lack of governance

In the first chapter we talked about the higher purpose of organisations like the SAS and Apple and how they transcend daily objectives. "Making the world a better place" has become an inside joke in Silicon Valley because all the would-be Unicorn breeders know that there has to be more to life than producing an App' and becoming a billionaire. Maybe if Bernard Looney can switch an oil company like BP to green energy in a couple of decades he really will have made the world a better place. But the key is that the purpose is authentic rather than grandiose. The Mars family have a Mormon-inspired work ethic and are notorious for showing up at offices around the globe in cheap hire cars rather than the limousines they can easily afford. They believe that Mars products should be high quality, everyday good value and the proof is that the Mars Bar was seen as a sort of consumer benchmark for many years. At the other end of the spectrum was Gianni Versace who, before his murder in 1997, lived in an ostentatious

---

30   America's most fascinating 25 entrepreneurs, Inc. Magazine 2004

Italiante palazzo on Miami Beach. But Versace conducted his life in the spirit of the brand that he sold to other people. Neither candy bars nor gaudy shirts will necessarily change the world but leaders are credible when they believe in some overall direction of travel that other people can relate to.

Serve to lead

Let's be honest, military leaders aren't all perfect. In fact I'm not claiming that military leaders are necessarily better than business leaders. But they definitely have a better chance of making the grade, for a couple of reasons. Firstly, when people volunteer for the military they know they will be expected to demonstrate leadership and, from this group of hopefuls, only a few will be picked to go to officer school. Secondly, when they get there, they will receive 2-3,000 hours of leadership training before they are allowed anywhere near a group of servicemen. They will make mistakes in front of their peers and they will get direct feedback.

The most ambitious leadership programmes in business stretch to about 10% of this figure. More often, the figure for executives is nearer 1% or zero. There is simply no presumption that a person has to be trained to take on a leadership role in commerce. Functional skills are often deemed sufficient.

At Sandhurst Leadership theory is less important than practical experimentation. However, Officer Cadets are given a small, hardback book on the topic of leadership entitled 'Serve to Lead[31].' This contains some basic principles that are designed to support a lifelong career as servant-leader, including a very simple leadership model which I have never forgotten. This is one of very few pieces of pure theory that you will find in this book and it was devised by Professor John Adair who, now in his eighties, still lectures all over the world. John's 'Action

31   Serve to Lead: the British Army's anthology on leadership, RMAS, available Blackwells/Amazon

Centred Leadership[32]' model model is pretty simple and hard to argue with. I've paraphrased it here:

Leaders exist to tackle tasks. That could be something concrete like "take that hill" or something more esoteric like "uphold traditions". You can't have leadership without a purpose - and a good leader is passionate about its achievement.

Leaders require followers. Again, this could mean a platoon or something more vague like a community but a leader without followers is a lone contributor. A good leader will harness the potential of this group so that they achieve much more than they could as individuals.

Finally, sooner or later the members of this group will ask themselves the question; "What's in it for me?" They may not be seeking material rewards but they will want recognition, fun, security, useful experience - something that adds value to their lives. They want their humanity to be acknowledged. A leader with no interest in their followers will soon find the indifference is reciprocated.

Obvious, right? Some business leaders fail because they are heavily task focused, at the expense of their people - the archetypal taskmaster. An improved, but still inadequate leader is task focused, enjoys making charismatic speeches and rallying the team but who ultimately has little patience for the daily lives of their subordinates. This is typical of high achievers who enjoy spending time with other Alphas but find the occupants of the proverbial Clapham Omnibus rather uninteresting. Being self-interested doesn't preclude thinking about what motivates others. Many years ago I had the strange job of being HR Director for media personality Piers Morgan. At the time he was Editor of *The Mirror* newspaper. We got on quite well. Piers thought it hilarious that an ex-SAS man was his HR partner and I thought Piers was..... well, hilarious. Not known for his self-effacing style (his autobiography is entitled: 'Misadventures of a Big Mouth Brit[33]'), it was nonetheless instructive to see him in action late one afternoon on the editing

32   Action Centred Leadership, John Adair, 1973 The Industrial Society

33   Misadventures of a Big Mouth Brit, Piers Morgan, Ebury Press, April 2010

floor. At the time *The Mirror* was campaigning on the issue of Gurkha pensions and one of the journalists had filed a report from Nepal. By this time she was already asleep in her hotel room but Piers rang her in person to tell her that she had made the front page of the next day's papers, a first for this aspiring reporter. Although removed from the conversation, I could sense the palpable excitement at the other end of the line in Kathmandu. I Imagine she went back to bed with a pounding heart and it cost Piers no more than a few minutes. My point is that it's OK for leaders to have an ego provided it doesn't make them blind to everybody else's.

One of the most dysfunctional styles of leadership I have personally experienced occurs where a leader is focused on the task and also individual team members but is lousy at managing the group as a whole. This leadership style feels a bit like living in a Medieval Royal Court where you have to know exactly who's saying what to whom to survive. Finally, there may be leaders who take care of their people, both as individuals and as a team, but lack the necessary drive or focus to accomplish the task. When we look at these patterns of behaviour, it's obvious why Adair insisted that all three requirements of leadership be met.

Fighting back-to-back

Having laid out an effective model of leadership, it is now relatively easy to identify the ingredients of effective followership. An effective follower is one who understands the task, why it is important and the role they will play in its accomplishment. They also understand the purpose and value of the team, its way of working and feel a sense of belonging. They will know what contribution they are expected to make and which special skills and attributes they can bring to the party. Finally, in order to be fully effective, they will feel as though the task, team and its leader are all helping them to accomplish some personal goals, whatever they may be. Simple enough to understand on paper, these are the rudiments of leading and following.

That "sense of belonging" has a practical application. When an SAS soldier bursts into a room, confronts a terrorist and hears the "dead man's click" of a jammed weapon, he needs to know that his buddy will have fired two rounds over his shoulder at the target before he can even yell; "Stoppage!" This is only possible in an organization where its members feel a mutuality of obligation or, to put it more simply, people are loyal to each other and can be trusted. Why does this matter so much? Consider the following comments from Ari Emmanuel, CEO of Talent Agency William Morris Endeavor;

> *"Loyalty was a huge component in the success of Endeavor. When I broke away from the comforts of an established agency to start my own venture, I got a real sense of who had my back. A handful of agents took the leap of faith, leaving steady paychecks and 401k's for the great unknown. The same goes for my clients, who took a huge gamble following me (often against the advice of their managers). But they all knew that I would do the same for them in a heartbeat. Four years ago, loyalty came into play again when Endeavor merged with William Morris. But this time, hundreds of staffers were asked to put their trust into WME. And you know what? Every one of them rose to the occasion and had faith that our new company would thrive. Loyalty is what makes businesses strong and I have no doubt that it's been responsible for the continued success of WME."*[34]

It's only possible to ask for help if you work in a business that has a general understanding of the critical importance of loyalty, not only at the top of organisations but right across them. As a young army officer, I was taught what loyalty means as a concept and the reasons why it matters so much. It's worth taking a moment to explain. I learned that leaders should take ownership of instructions passed down from bosses and present them as their own, or at least as orders with which they agreed. There are two reasons for this. The first is that your subordinates

---

34   Ari Emmanuel, LinkedIn blog April 2013

will execute poorly if you tell them; "Sorry, we have to do this even though (as your immediate line-manager) I don't believe in it." The second is that, if you take this approach, you establish the principle that insubordination towards *you* is also OK. Loyalty downwards means taking ownership of your team's outputs, whether they are good or bad. Even if a leader has been badly let down by a subordinate, they should "take the flak" and then follow-up with the team member. Never manage a boss's ire by off-loading blame in a downward direction. This buffer is essential for trust between a boss and their team members. The third form of loyalty concerns the relationship between colleagues and also other teams or functions. Businesses often wrestle with the "Silo mentality" that sees functions exert mutual blame whilst simultaneously ducking responsibility for the overall task. A major building block of organizational effectiveness, is to recognize the mutuality of obligation that exists in any self-respecting business. This is what enables people to ask for help, whether seeking sponsors, partners, allies or expertise.

Judas Priest and the baptism of fire

Even if business leaders don't have time to be trained they can at least find a mentor, coach or even just someone in their circle who sets a great example. When I look back on my career I've had support and advice from all sorts of people but a handful stick out in my mind. These were people who helped me transition through different phases of my life. In every case they were intelligent, non-judgemental, example-setters and with no agenda other than to be helpful. But of all the people who've helped me develop leadership skills, top prize goes to my first Platoon Sergeant called Terry Cooper. Terry had been the drummer of heavy metal group Judas Priest before joining the Army and he personified the qualities of humanity, humility and humour – not necessarily qualities you associate with a metal group whose song titles include: 'Beyond the realms of Death, Eat me alive'. My platoon was the regiment's Corps of Drums; infantry soldiers who are also expected to play a drum, bugle or flute on ceremonial occasions. Terry was the backbone of the platoon.

He was immaculate on the parade ground, relaxed and professional on operations and on the odd occasion I saw him on a drum kit a sight to behold. When drugs started to creep into the regiment he drew on his "Real World" experience to nip the problem in the bud.

His qualities shone through many times during our two year tour of Northern Ireland and never more than on the night of 6 December 1982. I guess the Irish National Liberation Army (INLA) would have called the bombers an Active Service Unit but to me that gives too much credence to a pair of middle-aged women, a giddy daughter and a couple of hanger-on boyfriends out on a killing spree.

It was late in the evening and I was lying on my bunk in the Guard Room in Shackleton Barracks, Ballykelly, in full dress uniform. Suddenly there was a loud CRUMP from down the road. I leapt up, grabbed a pistol and ran off in the direction of the noise. Two hundred yards down the road I came to the Droppin Well disco and was confronted by a walking, smouldering nightmare. From out of the burning ruins of the bar about 100 people – the living – were staggering out into the night air, their clothes burnt and still smouldering like something out of the Michael Jackson Thriller video. A soldier approached me, his torso naked, his arms outstretched in a crucifix position. The blast had picked him up and bodily flung him through a door and into the kitchen where he landed on his back on the boiling hob. All around me people were collapsing onto the grass. "Can you make it to the sick bay?" I asked him. "Yessir!" came the resolute reply and he walked, still in cruciform, along the road back to the barracks. As he set out, a woman in a torn red dress literally grabbed me by the throat and screamed in my face; "My hair's going to grow back again! Tell me my hair's gonna' grow!" Her eyebrows and hair were singed. She'd be OK. I gently unlaced her fingers from around my trachea and passed her to Corporal Rich Amery and his wife, a trained nurse, who now stood by my side offering help.

It was a night of horrors. As I advanced into the rubble I gingerly stepped over human remains but in many ways the more disturbing scene was created by the fallen roof. The bomb consisted of only a couple of pounds of explosive but it had been placed in such a way that the main supporting pillar of the disco was blown away, causing the concrete roof to collapse on top of the dancing throng. This had killed a number of people whose feet and ankles now protruded from the slab. They had been crushed to death. I turned my attention to the living. One soldier had been having a shit and was a little surprised when another man flew through the air, smashed through the cubicle door and landed on his lap. Both would be OK but the first man now had six feet of copper piping driven through his foot.

A little later we lined up about ten bodies on a grassy bank, ready for the ambulances, and covered them with whatever we could find. Just when I thought things couldn't get any worse, a young soldier I knew quite well arrived on the scene, frantic to find his missing wife. He asked me if he could inspect the bodies. It was not an easy decision. Some of the bodies were in very poor condition and I didn't want him to see his wife looking like that. What should I say? I looked him hard in the eye for several seconds and said; "It's your decision." He nodded, understanding the gravity of what I was saying. He checked, She wasn't there. Thank Christ.

I spent the night as "Incident Control Point Commander," directing police, ambulances and helicopters with their searchlights. Distraught locals appeared and at one point, close to dawn as I recall, an Ulster Defence Regiment Warrant Officer suddenly appeared with white tape and a bullhorn, adding to the general confusion. Inevitably, senior officers also appeared, amongst them Bob Stewart, the man who would become known as "Bosnia Bob", now a Conservative MP. In due course it was Bob's job to comfort the families of the murdered soldiers who came from his Rifle Company. I suspect it gave Bob a certain perspective when the Army of Republika Srpska went on a genocidal rampage through Ahmici ten years later. Bob had had enough and stepped in with his UN infantry. He won the DSO for his actions.

Terry, meanwhile, had an innate sense of the practical. Whilst this terrible circus went on around him, he immediately headed into the rubble to look for survivors, with little regard for his own safety. The whole area was a mass of blood-spattered broken concrete, twisted metal and human remains. Terry probed further into the darkness until he found what he was looking for; the living. Trapped under tons of concrete, captured in a void, was an injured woman. Terry lay in the dust and debris and reached down as far as his arm would allow into the darkness. A hand grabbed his and hung on to it for the next two hours. With years of experience under his belt, he knew that the simple act of talking constantly to a person staring death in the face was the strongest lifeline he could offer before the JCB finally arrived to lift away the concrete. The woman survived and Terry received a Queen's Commendation. That, my friends, is leadership on the front-line.

Jam in the sandwich

The benefit of having a partner like Terry was that I become comfortable, at the very start of my career, with the idea that it's OK to take advice from people who are junior to you on paper. In fact, it suggests self-confidence. I also learnt that organisations tend not to be run by the top brass or, at the other end, the troops but rather by a managerial class, the jam in the sandwich. For the Army that means the Sergeants' Mess. When I joined Mars I discovered such people were called Area Sales Managers and Factory Shift Managers. At Pizza Hut we did a detailed study of unit profitability, restaurant by restaurant. What we discovered, with unnerving consistency, was that profits were determined in large part by the experience of the Restaurant General Manager (RGM) and, moreover by the amount of time these people had spent leading specific units. Over time, the RGMs learnt to fine-tune issues like manning according to local dining habits and this made a material difference to the bottom line.

Leveraging the strength of this managerial group is a key leadership skill. This was enshrined in the corporate culture when YUM brands CEO David Novak declared "The RGM is Number One!" This was no empty gesture. Each week the highest performing RGM in the USA would be flown to the YUM Headquarters in Louisville Kentucky, together with his or her family. They would be chauffeured from the airport to the HQ building, which consisted of a Southern style house with white clapperboard fasciae and, inside, a large atrium surrounded by three levels of internal verandas. Before they entered the building every last member of the HQ group, without exception and numbering several hundred, would be positioned along the verandas to welcome them. At a pre-arranged time, the RGM and their family walked down a 'Hall of Fame' corridor festooned with the pictures of former RGM heroes and into the atrium. At this moment the assembled staff would burst into a noisy ticker tape parade and yell their approval. Imagine the impact on the RGM and, for example, their small children who suddenly saw their parents in an entirely new and heroic light! Later the family would visit the Kentucky Derby and KFC museums and enjoy a night at a fish restaurant on the Ohio River.

All of this cost very little but achieved a couple of useful objectives. The first was that the RGM would feel ten feet tall, for some months to come. They would also enjoy the full support of their family as they put that little extra effort into their daily work back in the home restaurant. The second, more subversive benefit was that the HQ staff would receive a weekly reminder that the front line stores and supervisors were the *raison d'etre* of the company. It was also for this reason that the HQ was re-labelled the Restaurant Support Centre. Ivory tower thinking was strictly frowned upon, a theme to which I will return a little in the last section of this chapter.

    B *Is Leadership a shared resource in the company or something that sits with a few big egos?*
    I *Does the company have a BHAG that everyone knows about? Do you personally? Does it make you feel excited?*
    L *Are you the go-to-guy with special skills that other people value (beyond simply fulfilling your job description)?*
    L *Are the front-line leaders the heroes of the company? Is their experience adequately drawn upon?*

Faster following

If it is important to have leaders with ambitious goals and a passion to match, it is no less important to have a followership that is able and willing to rise to the challenge. The first requirement is for the team members to understand their task and this is where the "All chiefs no Indians" factor plays to the SAS's advantage. An infantry unit may be called upon to "Take The Hill" but a Special Forces unit will often receive more ambiguous instructions; "Go and have a look at The Hill, see who's there and decide what to do about it." Rather than attacking The Hill, it may be better to build an irrigation system for the locals and receive The Hill as a Christmas present from the village chief. This principle - first explored in places like Oman in the 1970s - spawned a good many initiatives to build new wells in Afghanistan some years later. To make such judgements it is clearly necessary for even the most junior SAS soldier to appreciate the bigger picture and how their particular assignment fits with it. Equipped with the knowledge, nous and autonomy to interpret their task in this way, no time is lost by having to report back to HQ with the new information and request new instructions. The team just gets on with it. This improvisational approach is a major source of momentum and it translates directly into business.

The second ingredient of effective followership is a strong sense of team belonging and this begins with making a contribution that everyone else appreciates. Over time SAS soldiers develop multiple skills but fundamentally each is assigned a major area of competence. Within the standard four-man SAS patrol one man is a medic. This person is expected to develop quite advanced combat medical skills and will typically spend some weeks training in the A&E department of a major London hospital. Understandably, the other team members are pleased to have such a person in their group when bullets start to fly. (Incidentally, if you are ever in A&E and a large bloke with airborne tattoos and a Burt Reynolds moustache offers to stitch you up, I should ask to see a female nurse ☺). A second man will be the signaller, another vital contributor since communications provide security, coordination and logistical support. A third man may be a linguist and, as such, the bridge to friendly local forces or the indigenous population. Other skills include sniping, demolitions or scouting. All are critical to accomplishing the task and protecting the group, for example from ambush or booby-trap.

The need to have a major personal competence or "strong suit" is just as critical in business. Managers, in particular, should be seen as the "go-to-guy" for some definable area of expertise. When Vodafone built a Marketing University it quickly identified specific individuals who had a reputation for excellence in a critical area of the marketing mix; communications, market segmentation, product development and so forth. The majority of CEOs (not just Vodafone) have a background in finance, marketing or some other major discipline that shapes their contribution. Of course general management can also constitute a robust skillset but verbs like coordinating, consulting, business partnering, supporting, and committee membership look weak on job descriptions and sound curiously like someone else is doing the work. They can also absorb energy that is better spent on things like customers.

A third important team attribute is to have a way of working that everyone understands and buys into. In the SAS this has several important ingredients, beginning with a set of routines and procedures that everyone adheres to, which we will cover in more depth in Chapter Six. This saves an enormous amount of time because, for example, if a Troop is setting up a patrol base, ambush position or even conducting a routine communications stop each member of the team goes into a well-drilled routine without the need for a lot of instructions and chat. On the other hand, any member of an SAS team can assume temporary control if they are best positioned to do so, either by virtue of their competence or circumstances. The demolition expert might issue orders whilst the team lays charges, or a junior Trooper might give directions to others in a confused counter-terrorist situation where he may see what the bad guys are doing better than anybody else. This is a much faster way of working than having to coordinate all decisions through a formal chain of command. Of course the consequence of this interchangeable approach to leadership is that those in formal positions of authority must make every effort to brief other members of the group on what is going on. All members of a patrol will be informed of geographical location and developing plans, unlike an infantryman who, for example, may trudge along in line with minimal awareness. If you want people to behave more like leaders you have to make more effort to inform them and involve them in decisions.

A theme that recurs in this chapter is that speed and energy can come as much from what you *don't do*, as what you do. Fast moving organisations have little patience for long, tedious set-piece meetings. In the Special Forces Club in Knightsbridge there hangs an amusing painting by David Rowlands. It depicts a full Sergeants' Mess meeting held behind enemy lines in Iraq during Operation Desert Storm, the first Gulf War. For the uninitiated, a Mess meeting is an administrative event that covers such vital topics as whether the table-mats need renewing or what date should be selected for the next dinner-dance. Since such meetings had no chance of ever making it into anyone's calendar, Billy Ratcliffe decided that the middle of the war was both the ideal place and time for such an occasion, since no one could escape! (I suspect it also appealed to his zany sense of humour).

A few years after these bizarre events I was in Portugal and met up with an Irish couple. In time I asked the gentleman what he did for a living. "Grocer!" came the firm reply. We chatted amicably enough but at some point his wife took me to one side and explained that he was a little more than a grocer. As I now know, Feargal Quinn was an Irish senator and proprietor of an enormously successful grocery chain, Superquinn. The conversation suddenly became a lot more interesting and I particularly remember one anecdote. Feargal explained that he ran all management meetings standing up. Neither chairs nor tables were provided for these senior management events. As far as he was concerned, this was the best way to keep the conversation brief and remind everyone that they were, after all, glorified shopkeepers who should be capable of standing on their own two feet. Less is often more and that's the theme of this next section. (He is also, incidentally, author of *'Crowning the customer*[35]*'*, a self-explanatory title and former presenter of the RTE show Retail Therapy that helps independent firms get their shop in order).

Learning to get out of the way

The hardest thing for any motivated person to do is to accept that their most useful contribution in a given situation may be simply to cease obstructing others. A colleague of mine runs a very successful international training business employing about twenty-five people. He once attended a conference for leaders of similar-sized businesses hosted by a UK Government minister. At the end of the speech-making the minister asked his audience what he could do to make their life easier. Their answer was as unanimous as it was unwelcome to the minister; "we want to see less of you" (i.e. government intervention). The expression "get out of the way" has negative connotations but, expressed more positively, most people would recognise the merits of effective delegation, operating a lean headquarters and minimising red tape. This is the SAS approach.

The most obvious form of obstruction in any organisation is a towering office block full of Vice Presidents. The VPs need Directors who in turn need executives, managers, co-workers, secretaries, mail men and car park attendants. Busy people create busy work. The technical term in the Army applied to such people is a REMF. This stands for Rear Echelon Mother and I'll leave you to work out the fourth letter. Being a REMF is clearly not a good thing, at least not in the eyes of someone who isn't one. But this is not personal. It's just a job description and it casts a kind of automatic suspicion over any role that is removed from the business or front-line warfare or in the case of commerce that of buying, making or selling - which is not entirely a bad thing. Praising the work of a headquarters, any headquarters, is anathema to most organisations. Somehow in the collective psychology

---

35   Crowning the Customer, Feargal Quinn, O'Brien Press, 1990

of front line units is a presumption of incompetence in those who sit in over-sized office buildings. The conclusion is obvious; HQs should be kept lean and high value-adding.

The SAS HQ, sometimes referred to as the 'Head Shed' or 'Kremlin', is kept to the bare minimum and staffed for the most part by battle hardened veterans. There is a small command group, a Training Wing that manages Selection, a small group of counter-terrorist experts and a couple who experiment with new weapons and technologies. There is also a kind of out-sourced ingredient in areas like communications, intelligence staff and parachuting. That's about it. From this run-down, we can see that the HQ fulfils a number of functions:

Keeping top brass away from soldiers trying to go about their daily business
Allocating operational tasks and informing them with intelligence
Guardianship of recruitment and training standards
Research & development
Logistics
Provision of expert support in non-core areas

When you look at this list it is pretty clear that the prime purpose of the HQ is to help the Sabre Squadrons to operate more freely and effectively. Only rarely does the SAS deploy as a complete regiment, necessitating a full command structure. More often, deployments occur in rotating squadrons or discreet teams. Not a lot of paper gets shuffled.

This approach is analogous to M&M Mars, famous for its understated HQ in Maclean, Virginia. Although the company does have a number of staff officers, they are co-located with operating units and even the Mars brothers themselves managed their empire by relentlessly travelling, rather than sitting in oak-panelled offices. The HQ itself is restricted to a limited cadre, mainly comprising functions like treasury, legal and a couple in HR. However, most notable about the Mars approach is not so much the real estate as the devolution of decision-making. As owners of an entirely privately held company, John and Forrest Mars were at liberty to do pretty much whatever they liked with their empire without reference to public shareholders or anybody else. Not only did they fiercely resist this temptation but according to the former head of HR in Europe, Neil Donnan; "they rarely get their way". In other words, nine times out of ten they allowed their senior business leaders to make the major judgement calls, even when they disagreed with them. This is a more telling data point than the size of the Maclean parking lot.

HQs also need to resist the temptation to keep recalling front-line leaders, up to their elbows in Taliban, to keep reporting back with plans, updates and status reports. Most infuriating of all is when HQ staff ask field units to produce roughly the same data but in twelve different formats, according to each staff officer's agenda. As we've already seen with the SAS, one of the best ways to avoid these kinds of problems is to staff an HQ with high quality people who have front-line experience. They have a better understanding of what's needed and are consequently economic and yet firm with their demands.

Lead, Follow or Get out of the way		
Quality	SAS approach	Things To watch out for
Leadership	Leaders set the example, go the extra mile themselves & inspire with audacious goals.	Leaders focused on checks & balances rather than giving direction and encouragement.
	Leadership is what you do, not a badge of rank. Local responsibility moves to where it's needed to get stuff done.	Hierarchy-based decision-making and inflexibility.

	95% of leadership productivity comes from the managerial layer, not the top brass. Unit must be fully staffed & lever-aged accordingly.	Middle management weak or caught in no-man's-land between dictatorial bosses and unhappy troops.
Followership	Flexible, modular & multi-skilled teams to allow organisa-tion to be constantly reformed to meet task needs.	Functional silos, rigid organograms, empire-building.
Getting out of the way	Lean HQ, devolved decision-making.	Cumbersome HQ & inappropriate top-down decision-making, red tape.
	HQ staff amongst the most experi-enced operators. High value-adding when involved.	HQ people with low understanding of field operations.

Chapter Three: Be Courageous. If you don't dare, how can you possibly win?

We all know bravery when we see it. There are currently nine living recipients of the Victoria Cross. Three served with the SAS. Australian Mark Donaldson was sixteen when his father, a Vietnam veteran, died suddenly of a heart attack. Three years later his mother was murdered by a boyfriend-turned-stalker. He quit art school, joined the Army and in 2008 found himself in Afghanistan on the receiving end of a ferocious Taliban ambush. As his patrol withdrew with multiple casualties, Donaldson realised his interpreter was wounded and had been left behind in open ground at the mercy of the Taliban. He ran back a hundred yards through a hail of bullets, picked the man up and carried him to safety[36].

The stories of Ben Roberts-Smith and Willie Apiata, the other SAS VCs, are no less awe-inspiring. When Stirling chose to put *Who Dares Wins* on the regimental cap-badge it wasn't just bravado. He realized that courage was going to be the most important weapon in the unit's armoury and it was an attribute that was going to have to be mastered by every member of the team. Coupled with the element of surprise, this is where the unit would get its strength and compensate for its small scale. But - as we've already discussed in Chapter 1 - he also had the courage to think about strategic problems differently, to recruit and

---

36   https://www.sasresourcesfund.org.au/static/uploads/files/citation-mdonaldson-wfxzqajvasvs.pdf

organise differently and to build a culture that was totally alien to the British Army of the 1940s. In the decades that followed the regiment has shown courage in different ways. There have been "back-against-the-wall" episodes, cheeky commando raids that caught the enemy with their pants down and outright gambling for a big prize. In this chapter we will explore these themes and their application to business. We will discover that courage is a versatile quality, a facilitator for many other things.

"Courage is rightly esteemed the finest of human qualities because it is the quality that guarantees all others."

Winston Churchill

If you're reading this book - and especially now that you've got to Chapter 3 - you're almost certainly a leader. You might not have a huge following just yet but chances are you're working on an idea that's going to need the support of other people. That means you're going to have to demonstrate leadership. Some business leaders are seen as kind and compassionate, others as ruthless and egotistical. None, I suspect, would be comfortable with the idea that they are seen as lacking courage. As Churchill said - it's the cornerstone.

Facing fear - a leader's responsibility

Put yourself in the muddy boots of a nineteen year-old infantry second-lieutenant in command of forty soldiers, on operations in a rural part of Ulster called South Tyrone. In common with every counter-insurgency operation, practiced by every nation since time began, we spent our days gathering random low-level intelligence whilst attempting to create some sort of impression that law and order prevailed. The French did it in Indochina, the US took over where they left off, the British/Russians/Americans/British did it in Afghanistan - the tragi-comedy continues. The main difference was that in Northern Ireland we were constantly wet. For two years.

In the middle of one of these three day walk-abouts we were given the task of laying an overnight ambush on a disused border crossing-point favored by terrorists. The whole point of an ambush is that it's deeply unfair. The ambushers tool up, lie in wait and slaughter their unsuspecting prey when they stroll unawares into the trap, just as they did to Mark Donaldson and his companions. *If only.* It was a pitch-black night, visibility no more than a few yards, and the rain came pouring down. We lay in a ditch behind a hedgerow and as the long, cold night wore on I could see the soldiers beside me, one after the other, curling up and turning in upon themselves as they fought hypothermia. I could not blame them. This was the hundredth night we had spent this way, supported by negligible intelligence. The sapping cold and numbing boredom were not our only disadvantages. Since we were peace-keepers, not war-mongers, our weapons were loaded with a magazine of live rounds but not cocked; a noisy, cumbersome action that puts a bullet into the breach of the weapon. Without performing this action, no weapon can be fired. In addition, we had no licence to spring an ambush in the normal, violent sense. The "law of minimum force" required us to give an enemy up to three warnings to surrender before opening fire. In the highly unlikely event that a terrorist showed up, their disposition would be very different. They would be buzzing with adrenaline, weapons loaded, cocked and nervously fingering their safety catches en route to a certain killing. Like so many counter-insurgency operations before us, we had the firepower and technology to blow our enemy to kingdom come and yet somehow passed all the advantages to them.

By the early hours of the morning the rain had turned into a cold, clinging mist that soaked into our wrinkled fingers and numbed our brains. An occasional grunt or snore broke the silence along the line. Suddenly two silhouettes lurched out of the gloom. They were carrying what looked like weapons and in three strides they were practically standing on top of me. I glanced to my left and right and saw soldiers huddled against the cold, muddy bank, barely aware of their surroundings, far less these two visitors. I considered my options – none of them very attractive:

Option A: Shoot them. But this would be difficult. I would have to noisily cock the weapon, shout a warning, bring the rifle to the shoulder and release the safety-catch, hoping that they didn't react by riddling me with bullets. Assuming they didn't, I would then have to justify the killing of two men to a coroner and quite likely a court of law. If that went badly I could be facing a lengthy prison sentence, my adult life over before it started.

Option B: I could bluff it out by shouting a warning and pretending that my weapon was ready to fire and hope that they would be shocked into surrender. If they didn't buy it, and someone like local maniac "Mad Dog" McGlinchy definitely wouldn't, I'd be hamburger.

Option C: Crawl around waking people up, gathering reinforcements but also probably allowing the terrorists to get away. This would have its own risks. The preceding year a similarly inexperienced Parachute Regiment subaltern and his signaller had been in the same situation and attempted to rouse their men. In the darkness and confusion their own soldiers shot them both dead. Assuming I could avoid this fate, there would be no deaths, no prison sentences - just a mild reprimand for incompetence from my boss who, as it happened, was a very understanding person. Whilst this option had its attractions, the main "opportunity cost" would be the death of whomever it was they were en route to murder. At the very least I would be passing the responsibility of catching them to someone else.

Executive summary:

A. Get shot and/or go to prison.
B. Get shot.
C. Get shot accidentally and/or allow terrorists to kill somebody else.

When you look at it that way, B. does look like the strongest option.

I lunged forward so that the terrorists would be shocked by my proximity and the fact that the muzzle of my SLR rifle, lethal range officially 875 yards, was four feet from one of their noses.

"Freeze! Move and you're f***ing dead!" (Not just dead but with

61

your head likely sailing through the mist back into Eire).

They screamed back; "Don't shoot!" One of them added helpfully; "We're unarmed."

They threw their hands up, dropping the heavy objects onto the road with a metallic clatter. Strictly speaking, they weren't freezing as instructed but it seemed a fair interpretation. And, anyway, it was too cold to be pedantic. Groggy soldiers came to instant alertness as we advanced cautiously, mindful that others might still be lurking in the darkness. But it turned out that the heavy objects were electronic components, the men were smugglers and they were, indeed, unarmed. Whew! (As my good Irish friend Gerry remarked; "They were more concerned with the *spirit* of the law than the letter of the law".) The one alternative that didn't occur to me (Option D) was to cower behind the bank and let the men pass, unseen, unremarked by my soldiers.

The point of this story is not to suggest I'm brave. Ironically, the older I become the less inclined to risk-taking I am. But in my very first leadership role, now forty years ago (which is probably before you were born), I learnt that leadership carries certain obligations, not just in terms of courage but also moral responsibility. (Courage + Morality = Moral Courage).

Trouble will find you

James Dyson described himself as 'Up against trouble.' Peter de la Billiere, my fitness center companion, went a step further when he wrote an autobiography called: 'Looking for trouble'[37]. And I guess that was pretty much my attitude when I volunteered for the SAS. But 'trouble' has a habit of doing things on its own terms. As a Cold War soldier I saw limited action beyond early exposure to Northern Irish terrorism like the events I've described. My brother, a career soldier, had little interest in such things but experienced the horrors of war alongside

---

37   Looking for trouble: SAS to Gulf Command, Peter de la Billiere, Harper Collins 1995

SAS troops in both Bosnia and Iraq. During his six month tour of Iraq he was mortared almost every night and his greatest fear was the daily drive between two Baghdad HQs, running a gauntlet of suicide bombers. The atrocities he witnessed in Bosnia were beyond obscene. My grandfather was essentially a school teacher in the Army Education Corps. At the height of the First World War he was transferred to the Artists Rifles, a unit that would morph into 21 SAS. Latin grammar probably didn't count for much when he was plunged into the bloody quagmire of Passchendaele where he was badly wounded.

Conclusion: trouble tends to go looking for you, not the other way around. And when it finds you, how you behave says a lot about you - especially if you are in a leadership position.

Where were you during 9/11 Daddy?

Unless conducting business in a conflict zone, commercial leaders rarely have to confront physical danger. But when they do, how they react will be closely observed. It was an unfortunate coincidence that a major European multi-national corporation had organized a leadership conference, for a couple of hundred of its top people, the day after 9/11. This was no ordinary conference. The business was going through a series of major changes concerning its brands and company culture and, not to put too fine a point on it, this was a meeting to define what it meant to be a leader in this business in 2001. The participants would be flying into London from all over Europe. They had even called in a prominent academic and expert on leadership from a top business school. As Mao Tse Tung pointed out, the purpose of terrorism is to *kill one and frighten a thousand* and that is exactly the impact 9/11 had on the public psyche. One minute people were travelling between meetings in comfortable jets or sitting at boardroom tables in office blocks, the next minute those very things were blazing, deadly infernos. Suddenly people felt very vulnerable. At that moment airplanes and even office blocks were uncomfortable places to be for an awful lot of people, and not just the faint of heart.

The first decision lay with the Group Chief Executive. Should he go ahead with the meeting? If he didn't, that would be giving in to terrorism. If he went ahead with it he would be requiring all his top people to clamber onto commercial airlines and fly to London. This would be quite an onerous demand under the circumstances and he couldn't even lead by example since he was already safely positioned in London himself. The decision was made instantly easier for him when several of the market CEOs informed him, unhesitatingly, that they would be coming to London as planned. Supported in this way the Group CEO declared that the meeting would go ahead. He would like everybody to be there but it was not mandatory. The CEOs who had volunteered to come had already secured the buy-in of their management teams and would be coming as a unit. Those who hadn't decided quite so quickly now had to sit down with their management and navigate their own leadership dilemmas.

First, the local CEOs had to confront their own fears. If they weren't willing to fly they certainly couldn't expect their subordinates to do so and they might lose their respect. On the other hand if they declared that they were flying their subordinates would feel some obligation to follow their example and might not thank them for it. So it would be hard to disguise any decision as "group-think". Exactly what transpired in those meetings is a private matter. However, the result was that the vast majority of leaders attended the conference. But not all. The point of this story is not to shame those who declined to travel. Each person must make their own decision, based on their own values. However, one thing is for sure; a lot of people learned something about courageous leadership in the course of forty-eight hours and it wasn't because a leadership professor was in attendance. (Interestingly, the first market CEO to make his positive intentions clear subsequently became the Group CEO).

Backs against the wall

Who would imagine that twenty years later aeroplanes and office blocks would again be subject to an airborne terror but this time a virus that probably came from bats rather than kamikaze hijackers? Air travel came to a standstill prompting TUI's CEO Fritz Joussen to say; "It's hard to run a business with no revenue," later conceding that tourist figures for 2020 might be in the order of 15% of normal. Easyjet has offered "seasonal" contracts to its pilots to keep them on the books, if only semi-employed. Ryanair has been flying empty jets around the sky because it's cheaper than mothballing them. Richard Branson has offered Necker island as collateral for Virgin Airways. Some pundits believe that most major airlines can only survive through partial or complete nationalisation.

Offices haven't fared much better. Tech companies like Google, Microsoft, Facebook and Salesforce have extended home-working for a year - if not indefinitely - and even banks like Morgan Stanley and JP Morgan have made similar concessions. The move towards urban densification has been thrown into reverse. Architects' desire to build ever taller skyscrapers has been foreshortened by the humble elevator, an enclosed space that doesn't sit well with a rampant virus. Sandwich and coffee shops like Pret a Manger that feed office life have been ruined. Subway trains run half-empty, containing mostly low-paid workers. Already suffering: 'Fine particles of dust, metal, skin and clothing fibre that have built up in the tunnels over a century of use, leaving a toxic miasma that is stirred up by passing trains and inhaled by passengers[38],' they are now having to contend with Covid.

Of course offices and aeroplanes have no monopoly on heartache. Many other businesses have been threatened or destroyed. Some of them - like sketchy retailers - weren't very good anyway and Covid simply accelerated their downfall. Others were of a high quality but were powerless against the shut-down. And when business folk trudge home, their livelihoods under threat, they are having to cope with ruined weddings, funerals, school timetables and myriad other things that we normally take for granted. It could be worse. Lebanese readers of this

---

38   FT 5 Nov 2019. London underground, the dirtiest place in the City.

book (welcome) have just had their capital city accidentally levelled by 2,750 tonnes of ammonium nitrate.

Enough of that.

The question is:

How will you, as a leader, deal with the situation?

Courageous leadership presents a series of dilemmas that go beyond simply facing up to a given danger. Before Covid, British business leaders were confronted with Brexit. Some CEOs, like JD Wetherspoons' Tim Martin, were vocal supporters. Many were strongly against and in some cases saw their share prices quickly hammered as the likely implications of Brexit became apparent. But no CEO would be respected if she stood up in front of her employees, the morning after the Brexit decision, bemoaning the nation's democratic decision and expressing fear for the company's future. On such occasions leaders have to walk a difficult tightrope, maintaining openness and honesty but showing a way forward, however tough that journey may be. Here are a couple of ideas from military life:

Soldiers hate to be lied to. No matter how terrible the odds, they'd rather know what they're up against and give it their best shot. Understating the danger wins no leadership prizes.

It's best to focus your energy on the things you can control. Complaining about things you can't influence is debilitating for both leader and follower.

Empower your people to solve what they can solve.

Don't horde the crisis for yourself. Dying is bad - dying because you wouldn't let them have a say is worse.

Some leaders are already starting to set out their stall for the tough years ahead - maybe even relishing the challenge. Even before Covid, the flexible office space company WeWork had engineered a crisis for itself. It embarked on a massive land grab that created commercial rent liabilities of around $50Bn and operating losses of $2Bn. This might sound like standard Unicorn behaviour. But then-CEO Adam Neumann lost all touch with reality when he attempted to IPO the company. The prospectus offered no clear path to future profitability whilst drawing attention to the hard-partying founder himself 169 times (compare with founders of Zoom 38, Uber 29, Lyft 28, Slack 18). The result was a failed IPO and ousted CEO. In stepped Sandeep Mathrani, a man who had already performed a conjuring trick by turning a huge profit on an over-expanded shopping mall business GGP. Far from being fazed by the challenge he remarked; "I find it invigorating to find solutions. I like the adrenaline, like when you are running a marathon and the endorphins kick in." At the time of writing, he is busy dialling through every one of WeWork's 828 locations, scrutinising their business models.

In the UK the much-loved John Lewis partnership has seen profits dip from £370m to £123m in three years and the company's famous employee bonus pay-out shrink to its lowest level ever at 2%. Into the breach steps new Chairman Sharon White, a non-retailer who won't be able to lean on the previous, more seasoned CEOs of John Lewis and Waitrose because they both quit. Hers is an unenviable task given the havoc that Covid has caused to retail. But as the daughter of two immigrants who left school at 11 and 15, she doesn't expect life to be an easy ride. However, John Lewis is a home-centric kind of business and she's been quick to realise that Covid has focussed minds on the home like never before. With the right products, marketing and technology perhaps the stay-at-home crisis can be turned to her advantage? The oil industry has taken a pounding of late. Oil prices tanked and with it the share prices of companies like BP. Within months of taking over CEO Bernard Looney found himself with asset write-downs, multi-billion dollar losses and - most painful of all - having to lay off 10,000 colleagues. It's hard to imagine a more testing time for a leader. In spite of these things Looney remains committed to totally overhauling the company to be net carbon neutral by 2050, a brave vision that seeks to address what many believe to be the biggest challenge of all, namely the threat to human existence posed by climate change.

In this woke era, in which CEOs can take a mental health break with no shame, we still need leaders to be leaders. We need to be given a direction, to be part of an *esprit de corps* and to be acknowledged individually. That's the essence of leadership.

B *Given current economic challenges, have you thought about how much courage you may need to come out on top? What reserves will you draw upon?*

I *Do you behave courageously as a leader in spite of your own worries? Are you a source of encouragement to others?*

L *Do you support other people when they demonstrate courage - or keep your head down and play it safe? Can they count on you?*

L *Following the 'Churchill principle', what bold moves might you consider based on a more courageous approach?*

Sharing the leadership burden

The good news is that leaders don't need to go it alone. When things go wrong or get tough it's often a leader's instinct to take control, give orders and generally exert their authority. In fact it's the standard leadership response to a crisis. But this only works when the leader is present, able to communicate and is appraised of the key facts. It also assumes that the hierarchical leader is most knowledgeable, experienced and generally best equipped to make the relevant judgements. It's a notion that tends to be reinforced when generals and CEOs write their memoirs. But is that always the case, particularly in a world in which experience and comfort with the latest technology can have an inverse relationship? The good news is that leaders don't always have to shoulder the complete leadership burden on their own.

The SAS has had its fair share of "back-against-the-wall moments" and one of its most famous is a great example of the principle of shared leadership in action. It took place in a small coastal town in the lee of the Jebel Ali in Oman in the early 1970s. An SAS team commanded by an officer called Mike Kealy were holed up in a house beside a Beau Geste-style mudbrick fort supporting the local Dhofar gendarmerie. They found themselves surrounded by over three hundred communist rebels (nicknamed Adoo) and were subject to a ferocious attack. Kealey acquitted himself well in the battle that followed and in fact received the DSO in recognition. But the greatest credit must go to two Fijian SAS soldiers.

I once served with a Fijian officer called Philip Brown. The perfect gentleman, he was a force on the rugby field and had an aging picture of a relative in full warrior regalia on his living room wall. This ancestor was the last man officially on record to eat a white missionary! This is no urban myth. Philip's grandfather was so upset by this inheritance that he built a small church in memory of his ancestor's meal, the unfortunate Reverend Baker. Fijians are, quite simply, a race genetically designed for warfare and this fact did not escape the attention of the SAS. In the 1970s Philip and other Fijians were approached by the regiment and asked if they would consider joining. Philip politely declined but several accepted, most prominent amongst them Talaiasi Labalaba and Sekonaia Takavesi.

The communist rebels began by shooting-up a small outpost beyond the perimeter wire of the fort. This was swiftly followed up by a mortar bombardment that sent mud and shrapnel raining down on the soldiers and the thirty gendarmes. At first Kealy thought this might be a stand-off attack; essentially a bombardment to inflict casualties followed by a withdrawal. He soon learnt the terrifying truth as he saw wave upon wave of rebels swarming up and over the perimeter wire. They were clearly intent on a wholesale massacre. Inside the fort some thirty to forty gendarmerie locked themselves in and concentrated on survival, as well they might. If captured they would suffer mightily at the hands of the rebels.

The SAS soldiers returned fire with everything they had. Suddenly Kealy looked around; "Where's Laba?" Corporal Bob Bradshaw looked up from his mortar and pointed. Outside the fort was a sandbag gun-pit containing an old twenty-five pounder, a WWII artillery piece. Laba (Corporal Talaiasi Labalaba) had quickly realized that the gun was their best chance of survival and, equally, the final nail in their coffin if captured by the Adoo. Although the gun was designed to be operated by a team of at least four men, he set to with a single Omani gunner and blasted shell after shell into the enemy mass. They returned fire and before long a Kalashnikov bullet tore through Laba's lower jaw, another the gunner's stomach. Laba dressed their wounds and continued firing at a furious rate, ignoring the blood that poured down his throat and chest.

When "Tak" heard that his fellow Fijian was wounded he didn't hesitate. Weaving like the fine rugby player he was, he sprinted across seven hundred meters of open ground with a medical kit, bullets kicking up the dust all around him. Moments later a group of twenty Adoo appeared right beside the fort and the SAS team in the fort could only watch in horror as it all but disappeared in a cloud of fire and dust. By now Laba, the Omani and Tak were blasting away at point-blank range. Then it was Tak's turn to be shot in the back but, in spite of the heavy blood loss, he too continued to fight covering the left side of the fort. There was a brief lull in the firefight and now Kealy and another man Tobin dashed across the open space to join the Fijians. Laba traversed the gun to the right, slammed a round into the breach and fell soundlessly forward, his final, gallant act. The Adoo flung grenades at the gun pit and at least one landed amongst the SAS but mercifully didn't explode. Tobin was mortally wounded by another as he re-loaded his weapon. Kealy radioed the remaining men at the fort and told them to pour machine-gun fire and mortar rounds as close to the gun-pit as possible since by now the situation was becoming almost untenable. The soldiers did so with deadly accuracy, buying just enough time for an Omani Strikemaster jet to arrive and strafe the Adoo. A second jet appeared and dumped a large black bomb amongst a cluster of Adoo sheltering in a shallow wadi. By now the battle had been ranging for two and half hours and over a hundred men lay dead.

The military philosopher Von Clausewitz wrote 'War is the province of chance' and luck certainly played its part that morning. Only the previous day a second SAS Squadron had arrived in Oman and happened to be carrying a huge amount of firepower in the form of nine GPMGs and four M79 grenade launchers. When they heard about the unfolding battle at Mirbat they scrambled into helicopters and dashed to the scene. The melee was far from over but the reinforcements took control and beat the remaining Adoo back. After some minutes one of the G Squadron relief party, a Geordie, walked into the gun-pit and stared open-mouthed at a scene of total carnage; hundreds of empty shell cases, dead, wounded, bandages, blackened sandbags and blood everywhere. "Jesus wept," he whispered with incredulity[39].

Courageous Organisation

For some reason the West has always romanced a desperate battle story in the desert; Beau Geste, Lawrence of Arabia, Ice Cold in Alex and modern equivalents like Bravo Two Zero and The One That Got Away. The battle of Mirbat could be considered to be of the same genre. But it says so much about the no passenger organisation that Stirling originally created. To understand just how different an organization he created, it's worth listening to the voice of (then) Captain Charlie Beckwith of the US Army. Beckwith was a veteran Ranger of both Korea and Vietnam Wars and found himself assigned to the SAS in 1962; "I couldn't make heads nor tails of this situation. The officers were so professional, so well-read, so articulate, so experienced. Why were they serving with this organisation of non-regimented and apparently poorly disciplined troops? The troops resembled no military organisation I had ever known."[40] Just about everything struck a discordant note with Beckwith. The culture was alien to his conventional military mind, in which concepts like democracy and meritocracy seemed to have run riot at the expense of discipline and obedience. Officers were called "Boss" instead of "Sir", soldiers wore rakish dress and brewed up mugs of tea whenever and wherever they felt like it, headquarters personnel were scarcely acknowledged and the subunits of the regiment seemed to form and reform according to the needs of the moment. It was all

---

39   SAS Operation Oman, Tony Jeapes, William Kimber 1980

40   Delta Force, Colonel Charlie A Beckwith, Arms & Armour Press 1984

very unlike West Point. In time Beckwith tuned in to his new environment and was ultimately so inspired that he returned home creating the USA's most secretive and deadly fighting unit, Delta Force. With the possible exception of the Monty Python dining arrangement, just about everything that now goes on at Delta's Fort Bragg home can be traced to Beckwith's experience with the SAS.

By modern standards, the informality, delegation, meritocracy and classlessness of the SAS might seem fairly normal. Not so in 1940's Britain and particularly not in the military. The culture was genuinely innovative and would have felt novel to the wartime recruits. On the other hand, Stirling gave due credit to his original home regiment, the Scots Guards, by saying that both units should share the same regard for professional excellence, however manifest. His strategic reliance on concealment, aggression and street cunning was at odds with where the rest of the Army was going and he populated his new team with many buccaneering characters like the pugilistic Paddy Mayne that no one else would touch with a barge pole. However, the group quickly acquired a pronounced sense of mission focus and *esprit de corps*. Before long it achieved great success.

There are many examples in Industry of companies that have "dared and won", when it comes to organizing their businesses differently. The Netflix HR strategy[41] is an unlikely hero of the internet but it's been viewed on Youtube over five million times. They broke ranks with most companies when they declared that employees could take vacation as and when needed, provided that employees accomplished assigned tasks. And they explicitly require courage of their co-workers:

> *You say what you think even if it's controversial*
> *You make tough decisions without agonizing*
> *You take smart risks*
> *You question actions inconsistent with our values*

---

41   https://hbr.org/2014/01/how-netflix-reinvented-hr

The book 'Maverick' by Brazilian Ricardo Semler[42] had battalions of executives from blue chip companies flocking to Sao Paulo to see how his SemCo engineering company, which manufactures a wide range of products from food mixers to oil tanker pumps, could possibly be so successful given its anarchic culture. Recruitment is done by peers, shift rosters organized democratically and, perhaps most bizarrely of all, pay determined by individuals themselves! The moderating influence on this last point is the fact that everyone's individual pay level is publicly displayed on the canteen wall so that each employee has to be able to justify his or her salary to colleagues. It has proven an astonishingly effective mechanism of self-regulation. The personnel policy document is called a 'Survival manual,' containing key behaviours and values expected of employees and hierarchy is palpably absent. To conventional business minds it is all very odd and yet SemCo has gone relentlessly from strength to strength.

It would all have made perfect sense to Bill and Vieve Gore of WL Gore, manufacturers of Goretex breathable outdoor fabric and many other polymer innovations. This company turns over about $4 billion in sales and has distinguished itself by being in Fortune's '100 Best Companies To Work For' for many years. Like SemCo, Gore has no organization charts or chains of command. Multi-disciplinary teams are created around particular projects or business opportunities and, just as we will see with the SAS in the next chapter, the role of team leader moves around according to the needs of the moment. Later in the book we will also discuss 'Team Tasks' where ad-hoc groups of SAS soldiers are brought together based on their skills and experience, for instance to provide a training cadre to a friendly foreign government. Gore behaves in the same way. Gore calls their people *Associates* (like Mars) and each Associate is assigned to a general work area. There are no formal bosses but Associates do have 'Sponsors' or mentors who encourage them towards particular opportunities within the overall

42   Maverick! The Success Story Behind the World's most unusual workplace. Random House Business, September 2001

scope of operations. Bill Gore's four founding principles are very simple and transparent:

Fairness to each other and everyone with whom we come into contact
Freedom to encourage, help and allow other associates to grow in knowledge, skill and scope of responsibility
The ability to make one's own commitments and keep them
Consultation with other associates before undertaking actions that could impact the reputation of the company

It is interesting to note that Stirling, Semler and Gore all focused on a small number of very people-centric values as the basis for cohesion in organisations that were designed to function with limited structure. As we know, the SAS was founded on these kinds of principles in 1941 and Gore in 1958 in Delaware. SemCo was founded in 1953 but its innovative culture came later to the party when Ricardo took over as CEO from his father in 1980 and, aged 21, shook things up. At about the same time (1980) Whole Foods was established in Austin, Texas and it now has a turnover of some $16 Billion with 91,000 employees (it was around $3 Bn and 25,000 at the time of the First Edition of WDWiB). As the name suggests it sells organic and natural foods. Once again, authority is highly devolved and employees are clustered into specialist teams within the stores; grocery, cheese, prepared foods and so forth. Rather like John Lewis Partners in the UK they share ownership of the company and have a reputation for happy people and excellent customer service. Participation in the fortunes of the company is a feature of employment in all these businesses and it extends beyond token 'All Employee Share' schemes that typically have more symbolic than financial significance.

It's tempting to think of industrial democracy and cultural innovation as something that came out of the West Coast of the USA or Internet-based businesses in the New Millennium. As we've seen, this is not the case. Long before Google employees started wandering round Mountain View in shorts and sneakers, a whole range of organisations were finding new ways of working, driving both productivity and employee satisfaction. It doesn't matter that much whether an organization employs 300 or 30,000, whether it makes machines, polymers, muesli or, for that matter, commando raids. Running through all these examples is a strong sense of employee ownership, of personal accountability, teamwork and trust. People like Stirling and (recently deceased) Bob Gore were able to found their organisations on such principles, whereas Ricardo Semler had to stage a sort of bloodless *coup d'etat* to accede from his father and then drove through the changes in a company that was accustomed to a more traditional approach. In every case what it took was a little courage to organize things differently, to relinquish the reins of power, to throw away the organisation charts, rip up the rule-books and replace them with a belief in people's ability and desire to work effectively together.

B *Would people put your company in the same organisation bucket as Netflix, SemCo and so on (ignoring scale)? What would it take?*

I *Do you put trust in people and believe in positive intentions - and hire good enough people to make this work - or apply Theory X?*

L *On the flip-side, do you accept "passengers" or expect everyone to share in the leadership burden and involve them accordingly?*

L *Has the Work-from-home phenomenon made you think more broadly about effective ways of getting stuff done?*

Courage as a core competence

There aren't many professions that expect an employee to walk around all day wearing a hat with a word or phrase written on the front that declares what the person stands for - but that is often the case with the military. Look for military unit mottos on Wiki and there's quite a collection. Courage, loyalty and fortitude feature prominently. Occasionally there are entire job descriptions like the Brazilian Action

Commando whose Portugese motto translates to: 'Maximum of confusion, death and destruction behind enemy lines.' More subtle are those that focus more on the Why/How side of things (Sinek) such as the SAS's sister unit, the SBS: 'By strength and guile' or one of the early SAS suggestions 'Descend to Ascend[43]'. In reality, anyone in a military uniform is expected to display courage - it's part of the job description. But a handful of units focus explicitly on daring as a key attribute. Stirling chose Who Dares Wins and the French SAS legacy lives on with *Qui Ose Gagne*, the emblem of the 1st Marine Infantry Parachute Regiment. The Israeli Sayeret Matkal, an SAS type unit whose alumni include ex Prime Minister Benjamin Netanyahu, have the hebrew equivalent *Mi Sheme'ez, Menatze'ah*. Why such a premium on daring?

Required returns

Risk-taking in business sometimes feels a bit like the opposite. Accountants have a term - the Required Rate of Return - which is defined as the minimum return an investor will accept as compensation for a given level of risk. In simple terms, you can buy a bond and the government guarantees a rate of return (not much at the moment) and so investors require an upside if they're to invest in something less certain. It's a curious phrase that suggests some level of entitlement to the risk-taker and also that risk itself can be measured and managed. David Stirling was always scathing about accountants; "Accountants have always made me furious. Utterly cautious and utterly pedantic they have a total lack of imagination. Did you ever see an accountant at the racecourse? Of course not, a horse would have to have at least five legs and a turbocharger under its tail before he would place a bet, and then it would be each way." In fairness, I know some hugely successful business people who are accountants and Shoe Dog himself, Nike's Phil Knight, began his career teaching accounting at

---

43   SAS: Rogue Heroes, Ben Macintyre, Viking 2017

Portland State University. But Phil Knight never suffered from the "analysis paralysis" that afflicts other businesses as they wrestle with life's unpredictabilities. It's true that if you roll a dice you have a one in six chance of rolling a three. However, it's also true that you can roll the dice countless times and each time your chances of getting that three does not improve. Risk is fickle. Thinking Fast and Slow[44] is a great book for exploring this topic in more detail. What Stirling was getting at was that no one is *entitled* to rewards but great profits can come when genuine risk is embraced. Consider the following, my all-time favourite SAS story:

In October 1944, German forces were being pushed out of Greece and Danish VC winner Anders Lassen found himself on the way to the port of Salonika. The area was still occupied by a German battalion at full strength and the surrounding countryside by nervous ELAS guerrillas. Lassen's orders were to make a tentative reconnaissance. After all, he only had 40 men and a Volkswagen jeep he had liberated from the enemy some months before, whereas the occupying German force comprised 600 men in fortified positions.

The ELAS communists stared in disbelief as Lassen and his posse hurtled into the town and demanded that the German garrison surrender immediately to "encircling British forces". The Nazis sheepishly asked for a forty-eight hour truce at which point Anders and his men commandeered three fire engines and staged an instant victory parade down the waterfront. The people of Salonika rushed to their side, crying with joy and hurling flowers at the men, giving the impression of a huge advancing multitude. When the procession reached the Germans it met with nervous opposition. The SAS men jumped off the fire engines and, as civilians ran for cover, rushed forward cutting down two dozen of the enemy. The remainder of them fled for their lives, believing themselves to be hopelessly outnumbered.

Anders established himself in the Hotel Mediterranean as a benevolent dictator. He was tall, blond, athletic, strikingly handsome and fearless.

---

44   Thinking Fast and Slow, Daniel Kahneman, Penguin Books

We can rest assured the women folk of Salonika expressed their appreciation. The movers and shakers of the area plied him with Ouzo and for a week or so he ran the town as his private fiefdom.

Liar dice in the Hotel Mediterranean

What might a Solinika-style *coup-de-main* look like in business? I have spent quite a lot of my career working in Germany, first with a Mars confectionery company, later with mobile phones and finally with Grohe, a traditional manufacturing concern in the Ruhr Valley that makes high-end bathroom fittings. I have found the German business community to be unfailingly pleasant and courteous. Nevertheless, over the years my work has necessitated many taxi rides through Duesseldorf and one of the most enjoyable ways to lighten up such a journey is to engage the driver in a conversation about Vodafone's audacious capture of industrial giant Mannesmann. Within a matter of minutes they are reminding you of the bombing atrocities of the wartime RAF over the industrial German heartland which they see as highly analogous.

Vodafone began as an off-shoot of a rather unglamorous player in the military electronics space called Racal. Racal developed military radios and in fact the ability to send "packets" of data, that forms the basis of modern mobile telephony, partly owes its origins to the burst-transmission technology developed for the SAS and other Special Forces in the past. Racal called its cellular business Vodafone and the first mobile call was famously made in 1985 by Chris Gent from St. Catherine's dock using a device the size of a house brick. Within five years Vodafone was the largest cellular network in the world. In 1991 Racal and Vodafone de-merged and when the latter made its first roaming agreement with a Finnish company it signalled its global intent. In 1997 Chris Gent took the helm as CEO and two years later merged the company with Airtouch Inc. The company's ambitions had taken on a new dimension.

If you look at the total history of Vodafone's share price you could place a straight edged ruler from one end to the other and you would see a pattern of steady, incremental growth. That is, except for a giant mountain of a spike that straddled the Millennium, extending a couple of years either side. In the late 1990s people began to realize the awesome potential of the Internet and technology in general. Telecommunications, Media and Technology (TMT) stocks exploded and Vodafone was no exception. In the course of two years its share price quadrupled so that by 1997 it stood at four hundred pence and sat atop the FTSE 100. Chris Gent and his CFO, Ken Hydon, had some serious financial firepower at their disposal. Perhaps David Stirling would have appreciated Ken - in spite of being an accountant - because he not only paid for the Vodafone Derby from company coffers but ritually enjoyed a game of early morning liar-dice with Chris Gent before every Shareholders Meeting in London. Hydon and Gent were highly entrepreneurial and operated from a nondescript office building behind a curry house in Newbury. Neither man has a university degree, far less an MBA, but they shared street smarts and an impeccable sense of timing, key attributes for any businessman.

Mannesmann was an odd prize for a UK-based mobile phone company. The company was founded in 1885 and centered on a steel business. It was seen by many Germans as the quintessence of teutonic industry, a flagship of the nation's industrial might. But hidden in its portfolio of assets were a couple of highly desirable items. Mannesmann had purchased an outstanding mobile business in Italy from Olivetti called Omnitel and it also had Germany's second major mobile operator D2. The only way Vodafone could get at these assets was to make a bid for the entire consortium. Hydon raked around in his drawers and came up with £112 billion. It was enough money to overcome all but the most ardent objectors. Crucially, the purchase was not made with cash but with Vodafone stock or "paper".

Vodafone seized control and immediately began disposing of unwanted assets. This included chunky items like the steel business, which now trades happily on its own, but also more emotive objects like the oak panelling in BoardRooms and the oil paintings that hung from them.

Cash proceeds were quickly recycled into nasty things like shops and acquisitions of other foreign businesses. German newspaper headlines were full of things like; 'The end of Rheinish Capitalism' and 'Fortress Germany falls.' For many people in Duesseldorf, where Mannesmann was headquartered, it was a dent in national pride. Worse was to come.

Shortly after the acquisition the Internet bubble burst and TMT stocks plummeted. Mannesmann shareholders, who formerly held stock in a business with robust, tangible assets like steel mills, found themselves clutching armfuls of Vodafone paper like latter-day inhabitants of the Weimar Republic. There were all sorts of recriminations and we should take no pleasure in the discomfort of German shareholders. Vodafone shareholders were no more pleased to see their shares eventually plunge to an all time low of seventy pence before steadily getting back on track. But the simple fact is that Gent and Hydon had played the situation beautifully, captured a gargantuan prize and were already charging down the road with new projects like 3G licenses and bolt-on acquisitions. All the different subsidiary brands were consolidated into the single mega-brand Vodafone, creating a vast new mobile empire. The mission, at least as far as Gent and Hydon were concerned, had been accomplished and they were well rewarded for it.

Of course Anders Lassen and the Vodafone boys never met. Lassen was killed at Lake Comacchio in 1945 when Ken Hydon was only 6 months old and Chris Gent wasn't yet born. But I like to think that if they had walked into the Hotel Mediterranean they would have pulled up a chair, accepted a glass from Anders and settled down to a game of liar-dice.

Betting the house

Some business people not only tolerate risk but positively enjoy the gamble. The Chinese are famous for it. Take the late Sir David Tang who once said; "If you can afford to lose you're not really gambling." His tale begins on a night when the young Mr Tang was left alone in his flat to ponder upon the fact he had just gambled his inheritance away, the proceeds of the Kowloon Bus Company, established by his grandfather in 1933. Specifically, he had lost his London flat, most of its contents and his sports car and his creditors would be closing in within a matter of hours. Then, in a moment of clarity, he suddenly realized the seriousness of his situation. His grandfather, who was still very much alive, had dispatched a retainer to London to check on his grandson and, in particular to see that he had invested his money wisely in suitable accommodation. Abruptly, David picked up the phone. At the other end his friend dragged himself out of bed and listened to David's insane request. He agreed, it was simply too bizarre to argue, a true "Talented Mr. Ripley" moment. In due course David arrived at the man's flat in a taxi, carrying armfuls of family photographs and other memorabilia. When the retainer from Hong Kong arrived he would find David comfortably ensconced in "his" quarters, surrounded by his possessions. His report would be favourable. But Tang had literally bet the house.....and lost.

Not long after, David took new risks with the creation of Shanghai Tang, the stylish retailer and made a hefty profit when he sold a stake to Richemont in 1998 and then again in 2006. In the course of doing so he decided that he never wanted to be part of a large corporation with all its paraphernalia. He invested the cash in restaurants in Beijing, Hong Kong and London's Dorchester, founded China Clubs and bought sole distribution rights for Cuban cigars in Asia through his company Pacific Cigars. By now a Knight of the Realm, Honorary Consul of Cuba, Chevalier D'Ordre des Artes et Lettres, critic and bon viveur, his next venture was a bizarre piece of cyberspace called ICorrect. For only £618 a year celebrity subscribers could fight back against salacious gossip (if they're not generating it themselves) and everyone else can observe with amazement. Tang had an extraordinary network and no patience for political correctness; ""I've met many people. I gave Mugabe lunch once - that was before he went mad. What can you say? Does it mean that every time you meet someone you have to think first about whether he's going to be a world pariah in the future? Hindsight is a wonderful thing." He was equally combative on the subjects of

Newcastle, Feng Shui and women in boardrooms. He died before he managed to organise a final farewell bash at the Dorchester.

Analysis Paralysis

None of these stories are designed to advocate recklessness. In fact when people like *Rogue Trader*[45] Nick Leeson was quizzed about why he took such extreme risks with his bank's money, he explained that it's because the risk was asymmetric. If he got lucky he stood to make crazy money. Get it wrong and at worst he would lose his job and try again somewhere else. (He just went way too far, which is why he wound up in prison). But sometimes *not taking action* is just as dangerous as taking the plunge. Too often in my career I've experienced procrastination in both businesses and individuals. One company I was involved with had an ambition to expand into a new area of business. For *seven years* executives traded Powerpoints, "unable to make the numbers work" before finally sighting a potential acquisition. The due diligence process resembled a bather, shuffling nervously up to their kneecaps in a cold sea before dashing back to the beach, scarcely wet. As far as I know, the acquisition never happened, the Powerpoints continue and the share price is sliding. I've seen equivalents at the level of the individual employee. Whilst working for a media company, I was co-responsible for the recruitment of a couple of new managers in the Strategy department. We were going through a heavy digital transformation and this was a clear "no passenger" situation. It soon became obvious who was up for the challenge and who kept hiding behind requests for more information in the hope that the decision would somehow be made for them. In the first chapter I talked about recruiting for potential - it cuts both ways.

> B   *What bold strategies or tactics are you considering to break out*
> *of the current economic difficulties?*

---

45   Rogue Trader: How I brought down Barings Bank and shook the financial world, Nick Leeson, Little, Brown & Company 1996

I *How do you spot "analysis paralysis" in your business? How*
   hard are you prepared to push to clear the logjam?
L *Is risk and reward in balance in your organisation?*
L *When was the last time you unleashed your Inner Viking?*
   (Do you even have an Inner Viking or is it lost in Legoland
   somewhere?)

The big guarantee

What we've learnt in this chapter is that courage isn't just about pulling on a squirrel suit and base-jumping off El Capitan. It's about drawing on the personal resources necessary to cope when the Black Swans start to fly in formation. This in turn requires resilience, stamina, industriousness and staying power. It's about accepting painful responsibilities, example setting but also having the courage to share the burden with others, putting trust in them when a lot is at stake and the leader can't control the detail of what's happening. To this end, it's having the courage to believe in other people's positive intentions, to hire for raw talent, to organise in innovative ways, to contemplate bold moves and ultimately execute without being paralysed by fear of failure. As Churchill said, it's the Big Guarantee.

Reprising The Foundations

As we come to the end of this first section of the book, we've covered a huge amount of ground and it's worth pausing to re-cap. In the first chapter we established that you can't make a great product unless you begin with high quality materials. In my experience, it is entirely a false economy to think that you can make money faster by cutting corners with talent and organisational capability. On the contrary, the more excellent you are, the faster the profits will flow. In the second chapter we recognised that exceptional outcomes demand exceptional leadership. We sought kinetic energy through the mantra "Lead, follow or get out of the way!" We broke this down into some simple imperatives like strong middle management, lean headquarters and fluid teamwork. We did away with low value added activities like lengthy meetings and duplication. Finally we came to realise that courage, as Churchill pointed out, guarantees all other qualities and is really the start point for any journey that includes things like BHAGs, tough competitors and uncertain markets. With all this great stuff in our kitbag we are now going to move onto Section Two, which looks at how the SAS approaches Execution of its varied missions. Without spoiling the surprise, the answer is: *Cheaper, faster, better!*

Be Courageous – if you don't dare, how can you possibly win?		
Quality	SAS approach	Things To watch out for
Organisation	An organisation built around its people & belonging to them; meritocracy, delegation, team-work, informality & professionalism. An optimistic perspective on employees & their desire to excel.	An organisation into which people are slotted. Organograms, hierarchy, rules & regulations that assume employees will under-perform unless guided. (Theory X versus Theory Y, to the cognoscenti).
Defence	Smaller organisations will always come under pressure from big competitors so they have to come out fighting, relying on speed, courage & agility to win.	Allow the bigger competitor to dictate the "rules of the game" or assume moral supremacy. Focus on their strengths rather than their weaknesses.

Offence	Luck & timing is key but you have to spot the opportunity & really go for it. Don't wait for every last "duck" to be "in a row" if that means missing the moment.	Hesitation. A lack of street smarts or commercial acumen within the business.
Risk	Approach holistically, identifying both good & bad possible outcomes & manage accordingly.	Operate at either extreme; seeing risk as inherently bad or being reckless. Confuse/obfuscate decisions concerning risk with circuitous decision-making.

Chapter Four: Big Bangs, Small Bucks

When I do motivational talks I begin by showing a picture of a special forces soldier in their black ninja gear and asking the audience if they could imagine their business being run by the SAS. It always gets a smile. The idea is ridiculous if you take things literally. But as we learnt from the first section of WDWiB, no one's suggesting that business people start attacking airfields or embassies. This book is more WHY/HOW than WHAT. However, some aspects of the SAS translate more directly to business than you might imagine. Some topics we'll explore are:

Disruptive business model
Creative use of limited resources to create big, strategic outcomes
A "capital light" model
Maximum asset utilisation
Tight headcount control (quality & quantity)
Repurposing of resources
Customer focus
Guerilla marketing incorporating Hi and Low Tech solutions
Disruption - finding a better way

In the introduction I explained that Stirling created the SAS because he thought there was a more efficient way to win the North African war than piling bodies up in the desert. Think about it from an accountant's perspective. In the course of the whole war the Luftwaffe lost about 40,000 aircraft through Allied action. At its manpower peak, the wartime

RAF had around 1.2M men and women in uniform and USAF had 2.6M. So that equates to 95 staff, working for up to six years, for each downed enemy aircraft in the course of hostilities. These people had to be housed, fed, clothed, trained, disciplined and entertained with concert parties and dinner-dances. They put aircraft into the sky that needed to be first manufactured in huge warehouse factories and then serviced, fuelled, replenished with ammunition and directed to their targets. Mess halls had to be catered, radars invented, codes broken, runways swept and casualties bandaged. In short, the destruction of a single enemy aircraft was a huge undertaking that absorbed massive resources. And I've not yet mentioned the cost in human lives. For every single Junkers or Messerschmitt that was destroyed, a stricken RAF or USAF family somewhere would bury a cherished relative or friend, sometimes more than one.

How does that compare with what Stirling was up to? On a single summer night in 1942 50 SAS soldiers in 18 jeeps trundled into an extended line in the North African desert and came to a halt. It was eerily quiet and it seemed somehow improbable that less than a mile away was the Nazi Fuka airfield packed with Junkers 52 transport aircraft, Messerschmitts and Stukas. But Corporal Sadler, the team navigator, was rarely wrong about such things. Stirling gave the order and the vehicles rumbled forward in the darkness, line abreast. Suddenly the whole area before them was bathed in yellow light. They were practically on top of the airfield, but it had remained dark and lifeless until a returning German plane had required the landing runway lights to be switched on. Stirling didn't hesitate and Heaven knows what the incoming pilot must have thought. Sixty-four Vickers machine-guns simultaneously erupted, blowing the airfield defences to pieces, sending red tracers streaking in all directions. A green flare arched across the sky and now the drivers roared forward onto the airfield in two columns, their machine-guns pointing outwards. The procession moved steadily down the centre of the asphalt, pouring thousands of rounds into the surrounding aircraft, causing them to explode, one after the other. In minutes, over 40 aircraft were ablaze and the heat was so intense that the soldiers felt their dusty beards and eyebrows being singed. When the carnage was complete, Stirling pulled his tall frame out of his own jeep, which itself was peppered with German machine-gun bullets, clambered into another and led his men away from the scene of mayhem. He had only one criticism for his men - they had used too much ammunition.

It's a bit trite to reduce precious lives, of any nationality, to a game of statistics. But if you follow the arithmetic logic, 50 SAS men achieved in a single night what 3800 conventional staff would have taken six years to achieve whilst incurring losses to men and material. In addition to the destruction of aircraft, his soldiers blew up vehicles, railways and supply dumps, drawing vital front-line troops back into rear-echelon guard duties and creating a sense of uncertainty for German leaders. As the campaign progressed the SAS destroyed a total of 400 enemy aircraft with no more than about 200 men. So the same sort of ratio was maintained.

Stirling's new "business model" proved so successful that it was still being used 40 years after the Fuka raid. In 1982 Soldiers from my own Troop, Boat Troop D Squadron, paddled ashore in Klepper canoes onto an island to the north of West Falkland where an Argentine invading force had established a forward airstrip. The men spent three days reconnoitring the airfield and established useful intelligence, including the less obvious point that strong prevailing winds would slow down the helicopter deployment that was to come and this, in turn, would shorten "time on target" from the planned 90 minutes to only 30. In due course Mountain Troop boarded HMS Hermes' Sea King helicopters and rendezvoused with the Boat Troop boys who guided them on a gruelling march burdened with mortar bombs to the target area. Led by Captain John Hamilton, they crept onto the airfield undetected and laid explosive charges on seven aircraft, retreated and then opened fire with M16s, M203 grenade-launchers and 66mm disposable rockets. In thirty minutes, six Pucara aircraft, four T-34C Mentors and a Skyvan were in flames, along with fuel and ammunition dumps. That's 11 aircraft for a few hours work. When the Argentine defenders popped their heads up their officer was immediately shot and the priority returned to self-preservation when a combination of mortar-fire and HMS Glamorgan's guns showered them with shrapnel. Two SAS soldiers were lightly wounded but dragged back to the helicopter pick-up point. (Sadly, John was later killed near Port Howard under heroic circumstances and was awarded the Military Cross). As with Fuka, about 50 men were involved in the Pebble Island raid, suffering light casualties and expending modest military resources in relation to the gains achieved. Once again, it was a strategic rather than tactical operation. The Pucara aircraft, in particular, were highly effective ground attack planes and would have inflicted horrific casualties on the infantry landings at San Carlos Water, when the ground offensive began in earnest a few days later. Unfortunately, good ideas can also be copied. In September 2012 a group of Taliban insurgents staged a similar attack on what was supposedly an impenetrable fortress at Bagram air base in Afghanistan.

B *Is your business model working - will it continue to do so?*
I *What out-of-the-box strategies and tactics have you considered?*
L *What sort of disruptive forces are bearing down on you? How can you get around or overcome them?*
L *What is your "Big Bangs for Small Bucks" equivalent?*

Headcount is tightly controlled to maintain both the quality of SAS soldiers and the focus of tasking. Although SF soldiers receive a little more pay (not enough to cover a CEO's cocktail party) they work 24/7 for months at a time in unimaginable working conditions and yet motivation is exceptional and satisfaction high as we discussed in Chapter one. Even more impressive than all of this is the fact that the SAS as a "mission factory" has remained true to its core purpose whilst proving itself capable of producing a wide range of "products" to meet divergent needs in the arctic, desert, urban or jungle, creating military value for some 80 years. There is arguably also a greater sense of customer focus and stakeholder management in the SAS than elsewhere in the military for a couple of reasons. On occasions - such as the famed Iranian Embassy siege in 1980 - the SAS are called upon to release VIP hostages who are pretty pleased to be liberated, unscathed. More routinely, special forces carry out tasks that are more political in nature giving soldiers a much more direct sense of the 'Big Picture' objectives that others are trying to accomplish. Pound for pound SAS soldiers provide incredible value to the taxpayer.

Travel light

The 'Asset Light' business model has grown enormously in importance in recent years. Since the building of the pyramids people have always equated wealth with tangible assets - skyscrapers, shopping centers, aeroplanes, factories; big chunks of glass and steel that cost a lot to assemble and represent stored wealth. And profits have been the way to assess how successful they were in the long term. Not anymore. The world's biggest taxi company - Uber - doesn't actually own any cars. The world's biggest hotel company - AirBnb - doesn't own any real estate. Many of the world's biggest high street banks, like Monzo and Starling, don't have any branches. And yet these companies have multi-billion dollar market capitalisations. The value lies in the brands, customers, data lakes and operating platforms they have assembled, not in tangible assets. They also have cash reserves, like Booking.com, that allow them a couple of years runway during the Covid crisis whilst airlines burn through theirs at terrifying speed. So far, so obvious. But what is less well known is that even those companies that you might assume are so deeply grounded in real assets that they couldn't contemplate this kind of virtual, crowd-funded world are headed that way too.

Very few real estate companies can claim to have established a B2C brand but one that can is Westfield, the Australian shopping mall operator that joined with Unibail in 2018. Before the Lowy family took a strategic decision to divest assets, the company owned many of the shopping centers that it operated. But in more recent years it has sold out of its real estate, leased back the assets from their new owners and focused all their efforts onto customer experience. Other shopping center owner-operators like Intu and Hammerson in the UK or GGP in US, that hung onto their assets, have been turned into car crashes by the upsurge in on-line shopping - even before the added impact of Covid. Major hotel chains like Hilton and Marriott no longer own their buildings. The vast majority of their properties are owned and operated by third parties, under a brand franchise arrangement. Ownership of office buildings is also starting to look vulnerable as the Covid pandemic has established WFH (work from home) as a norm, rather than an exception. And although accounting laws changed, forcing companies to recognise their lease commitments on their balance sheets, the UK government was quite happy for tenants to ignore their payment obligations as Covid started to bite. Neither lawyers, accountants nor landlords were happy as ministers threw conventions out of the window.

None of this is to say that real assets don't matter any more. But it does suggest that you accumulate them because you need them, not because they are always a good way to store value. Elon Musk may have a strange interpretation of reality but it's nevertheless interesting that he recently spent $5Bn on a Nevada Gigafactory to support his Tesla empire but at the personal level declared that he was selling nearly all his personal belongings and wouldn't own a house in the future.

Get Capital Working

When assets are unavoidable it's well understood that they should be "sweated" or at least well-used if they are not to be an encumbrance. During 10 years of warfare in both Iraq and Afghanistan the SAS operated a series of rolling night raids, each one leveraging the intelligence that had been gleaned from previous operations[46]. If you think of an SAS squadron as a unit of working capital, it was in continual usage with maximum output and minimal downtime or wastage. The business equivalent might be the rapid turn-around airline concept, pioneered by Southwest and copied by other budget carriers like Ryanair and Easyjet.

Through superior intelligence SAS units are also able to focus resources

---

46   Task Force Black, Mark Urban, Abacus 2011

effectively, for instance through raiding the bases of specific, named individuals and killing them, either with the famed "double-tap" (two rounds of ammunition) or drone strike. Even when the SAS blow up aircraft, vehicles or railways they only use the resources they need. After all, whatever SAS soldiers use they will generally end up carrying on their backs at some point. You will not find battalions of SAS soldiers manning outposts or patrolling around with some nebulous goal of establishing the peace. In the business world, as the global environmental agenda becomes ever more front-of-mind, it also makes sense that shared economy, recycling/upcycling and footprint minimisation are asset-light trends that will only grow in importance.

...and move fast

When you travel light you move faster - and that's a good thing when markets and technologies change exponentially. Movies were something that you saw at the cinema until the invention of the VHS video recorder enabled us to watch them at leisure through our television sets. Videotapes were distributed via retailers like the variety store Woolworths until specialist and premium shops helped push Woolworths to the wall. The slack in the DVD market was taken up by HMV and a Texan company called Blockbuster, but they didn't have the market to themselves for long. Simon Calver, an ex PepsiCo colleague and then CEO of Lovefilm, figured out all the things customers hated about the Blockbuster model, like the late charges they levied, and produced an alternative mail-order model. HMV entered administration - twice - and Blockbuster now has two die-hard stores. One of them is in Alaska. Simon, meanwhile, is a wealthy man having sold to Amazon. Under Amazon ownership, Lovefilm morphed from mail-order to a combined subscription service but by 2017 the model had lost its relevance altogether and been replaced by Amazon Prime Instant. At the time of writing, Netflix had pulled ahead of Amazon Prime with slightly more subscribers. You can be sure other businesses are knocking at their doors.

Technology is a great disrupter but also vulnerable to attacks by new solutions - sometimes even launched by kids from the same colleges. Jerry Yang could now be considered an elder statesman of the Internet world. He founded Yahoo! with fellow Stanford graduate, David Filo in 1995 and pretty much had the market to himself. At the turn of the Millenium, around the time of the great dotcom implosion, Yahoo! had 42% market share. Meanwhile, a couple of other Stanford alumni, Larry Page and Sergey Brin, were cooking up a new search engine called Google. They had 1% of the search market. Within about three years the Google/Yahoo battle was won and lost. Fast forward twenty years and Yahoo! has had a turbulent time but is still the third most popular search engine. Market share? 1.6%. Google completely dominates with nearly 92%[47]. During the melee unholy alliances were formed between people like AOL and Time Warner in a bid to see off the upstart, but that didn't make a dent in Google's armour either. Quite the opposite. Facebook and Google now have a c.70% duopoly of internet Ad spending. When Google decided to take an interest in local commercial search, the entire Yellow Page industry was crushed in a few years. Android and iPhones have relegated once dominant Nokia to the minor league of handsets. Big Tech giants FANG (combined $4 trillion) have their own tussles. Facebook is launching on-line stores, Microsoft is buying a media company and Apple is apparently developing a search engine. Change will never stop or even slow.

Sitting below FANG is a chaotic battlefield of local vertical websites, starting with pioneers like Lastminute.com, but proliferating into specialist sites covering just about everything. Some of these sites built in new business propositions based on a brokerage and recommendation service like Rated People, Myhammer in German-speaking countries and Werkspot in Holland. These sites created a marketplace for buyers and sellers of home improvement work and match specialist tradespeople with jobs. Other sites have focussed on community or gossip, such as Mumsnet in the UK. Wikipedia quickly reached critical mass and Encyclopaedia Britannica became something you find in

---

47   WebFX July 13, 2020

antiquarian bookshops. Groupon sprang up overnight like an epidemic and conquered half the world with a coupon discount model. The owners IPO'd and sold up before a better idea came along to kick them into the long grass. Evolving social media concepts reflect ever shorter attention spans. Even Facebook is now too much like hard work for Instagram-ers or TikTok-ers. Business leaders today have to anticipate that they will come under attack from some form of disruptive business model, product or technology as a normal part of commercial life. Any form of complacency is highly dangerous.

Some of these business names now read like ancient history - but Woolworths only folded in 2009. So the breathless changes I've just described have taken place within about a decade. If you're reading this book in your twenties a decade might seem like a long time. But the world of real assets sometimes moves at a glacial pace. London landlords pulling together Master Plans for investment in areas like Kings Cross, Canada Water or Greenwich Peninsula have waited between five and fifteen years to get the necessary permissions and local buy-in before they even put a spade into the ground and started construction. Once construction commences it is not quick. Leadenhall's "Cheesegrater" building employed the latest construction technology and took four years to build. Other big projects dragged on so long they floundered altogether, mid construction. The physical manufacture time for commercial airliners has decreased significantly but in 2015 Boeing and Airbus had a combined order backlog that would take eight to ten years to clear. It's probably why Warren Buffet once said; "There is no worse business of size that I can think of than the airline business. Since it began in 1903, the industry has had an overall net loss. If there had been a capitalist at Kitty Hawk, the guy should have shot Orville down! I mean…one small step for mankind, and one huge step backwards for capitalism[48]." And he said this long before Covid grounded the entire industry, a pandemic, incidentally, that was well signposted by Bill Gates in 2015. Google's cash war chest,

---

48   Remarks to Berkshire Hathaway shareholders, 2007

meanwhile, is now a similar size to the combined market capitalisation of those two companies.

If the SAS really were a business, it wouldn't be burdened with long lead times, cumbersome assets or inflexible technologies. The overladen infantry are sometimes referred to as "Plodding donkeys" by the Taliban who, of course, are happy to conduct warfare with nothing more than a kalashnikov and a pair of flip-flops. Much more likely is that "an SAS business" would sell a disruptive product or service that sought to take advantage of these types of weaknesses in a competitor. It would be staffed by a group of young innovators, focusing on a customer need and figuring out a way to satisfy it in an agile, future-proofed way. Personally, I have an aversion to encumbrance but I think it runs more deeply than ten years of "yomping" with heavy gear. As an Army child and then an Army officer I moved house on average every two years from ages zero to thirty. After that it took civilian work rotations through Germany, the former Czechoslovakia and Texas before I "settled" - somewhat uncertainly - back in the UK. Each move involved packing, unpacking and a whole bunch of administration. So when I go on holiday now it's whatever I can fit in a rucksack. For a long holiday, make that a big rucksack.

Targeted resources

The frugality of SAS operations comes partly from its preference for using the element of surprise in lieu of scale, but it also comes from the highly targeted and discriminatory nature of what they do. They do not blanket-bomb, scatter cluster-munitions or mines, or accept collateral damage as an inevitable by-product of their work. On the contrary. When the SAS were preparing to assault the Iranian Embassy in 1980 they entered the next door building and quietly drilled a hole through the wall. Through this hole they inserted a fibre-optic cable with a fish-eye lens on the end of it allowing the soldiers to see how many terrorists there were, where they were located and what weapons they carried. They could also see where the hostages were. When the attack went in they used framed-charges to blow in windows that wouldn't kill all the hostages by knifing them with glass fragments, stunned everyone with non-lethal flash-bangs and picked off the terrorists one by one. Only a single hostage lost his life. It was all done with clinical precision.

In the last twenty years people have become accustomed to watching video footage from drones or aircraft documenting the destruction of buildings or even cars in places like Iraq or Syria. Before the era of drones, Special Forces would pin-point specific targets by "painting them" with a laser target marker (LTM). This is a thing a bit like a pair of binoculars that projects a marker beam onto an object, which is then picked up by the sensors of munitions released by fighter ground attack aircraft. This technology is still used, but we now truly live in the era of drones, which have the great advantage of being operated remotely. Like all other technologies, drones are becoming miniaturised. The larger Reaper and Hermes drones are about ten foot long, there's then a three foot Desert Hawk but every boy will want an eight-inch Black Hornet in their Christmas stocking. This hand-controlled gizmo is used in conjunction with a thing like an iPad. This little Nanocopter can be flown into a building, around corners, up stairwells and into the homes of terrorists. It can relay images of faces, number-plates or other details. With miniaturisation will come facial and even retinal recognition technology. A variation on this product will carry a small explosive payload enabling it to buzz up to some unsuspecting terrorist, take a look at his face and, once satisfied of his identity, detonate and quite literally blow his head off or perhaps lance him with a flechette, which for the uninitiated is a nasty metal dart. Similarly, the larger drones will launch a missile at a car that will utterly pulverise it, but leave the vehicles either side almost unscathed. It's horrific but very, very specific.

The world of marketing has become so specific that everyone worries - rightly - about personal privacy. A friend of mine once claimed that he casually mentioned Liverpool Football Club in front of Alexa, the living room stooge, and received promotional merchandising through his mailbox the next day. Pretty much everyone sees their internet browsing played out in banner advertising, junk email and the like. Your on-line purchasing activities create a wealth of data and if you venture into real bricks 'n mortar shops, car park number plate and facial recognition systems are more ways to tell people where you are and what you're doing, even before you reach the EPOS till system. Research firms like CACI stitch the data together, linking your wealth, home location and spending habits. Emergency services like the police have long been able to triangulate people's whereabouts with mobile phones and IP addresses but Covid has brought "track & trace" into the mainstream. The government wants to know where you are and who you've been with - even if it is for health reasons. (Talking of which, think twice if you have a villain in your extended family before you submit DNA to genealogy websites. Your DNA identifies you but plenty of other people as well). Of course you can also drop mapping pins to help people find you when that's what you want or use self-reporting Apps like Foursquare to share with friends. You can also combine location with dating requirements via Tinder or simply ask someone out to lunch via OfficeApp, a platform designed to make office life a little less tedious. Your social ramblings on Facebook, Twitter, Instagram, TikTok are an advertiser's gold mine. And bodily implants of the cyborg variety are going mainstream. It's no longer weird to have a chip in the back of the hand or wrist to allow electronic door access. More controversial is Elon Musk's plan to put an AI powered Fitbit equivalent directly into the brain. No wonder the Smart Fridge is the laughing stock of the Silicon Valley. It's all a million miles away from Lord Leverhulme's famous complaint; "Half the money I spend on advertising is wasted and the trouble is I don't know which half." Every individual consumer is now a potential target.

Guerrilla tactics

When I was growing up Army families didn't have much money. Hand-me-downs, improvisation and making do was the norm. With technology playing such a pervasive part of modern life, it's easy to forget that great results can also sometimes be achieved by low-tech guerrilla tactics. The word "guerrilla" simply means "small war" in Spanish and it was probably first used in the Eighteenth Century. What it has come to mean is a form of cheap-'n-cheerful warfare where small groups of irregulars have to rely on cunning and improvisation to get the better of a superior armed opposition. SAS exploits in North Africa would be a case in point. As we will see in Chapter eight, the SAS have always been skilful at combining with other guerrilla elements such as the French Resistance or Marquis in wartime France, but guerrilla warfare is not the preserve of any one nation or army. When the French tried to move back into post-War Indochina they were defeated by the Viet Minh. In time, the French army was replaced by an American force and the Viet Minh had morphed into the Viet Cong. Amongst the cheapest and most effective of their weapons was a punji trap. It was a ridiculously simple device. They would dig a hole in the ground on a footpath, line it with razor-sharp bamboo stakes covered in buffalo dung and conceal it. A hapless GI would step into the hole, piercing the sole of their boot and then being further harpooned when they tried to yank it out and got stabbed by downward pointing barbs. Neither the bamboo nor cow shit had retail value. On the other hand you can be sure the Americans spent a small fortune on hospitalisation and the evacuation of that man on a Huey. These cunning fighters finally met their match in the Australian and New Zealand SAS. Interestingly, these Commonwealth soldiers had no interest in "Body count", which had by then become the index of American military competence, because they didn't see it as strategically important. Instead they leveraged their own brand of guerrilla tactics to gather intelligence, disrupt enemy supply lines and kill key players. What characterises guerrilla warfare are a couple of things; stealing an unexpected advantage over the enemy/competition and doing so with very limited resources. It works equally well in business.

In many respects, it's never been a better time for smash-n-grab behaviour in business and raids can come in all shapes and sizes. At the tactical level you could hire a talking, smoking-jacket wearing meerkat to advertise your insurance company and bring you a personal fortune of £420 million or thereabouts. You could even build a tree-house.

Yellow.co.nz in New Zealand ran a competition in which an attractive young accordion player called Tracey Collins was commissioned to build a restaurant in a tree near Warkworth, north of Auckland. The restaurant was designed as a futuristic pod, 10 metres off the ground, with seating for 30. There was just one catch; she could only utilise resources that were advertised through Yellow.co.nz for the task. As the project grew day-by-day, so the young Kiwi's popularity grew in cyberspace, with half the population watching as she blogged about her exploits and adventures. In parallel, there was a dramatic rise in the number of unique users on the Yellow website and sales rose accordingly. New Zealand has always been a fun place for guerrilla marketing. A few years before people dined in trees, a man stripped naked, painted his body with the Vodafone logo and streaked across the pitch at a rugby international between the home country and Australia. Some people liked it, some people hated it. Everyone talked about it, including the national news and Vodafone NZ did rather well that year. For out-of-this-World advertising, you could even sponsor the Mars One space mission, as Adknowledge did, under the leadership of Ben Legg (whom we met in Chapter One).

B *How well targeted are your resources? How do you make trade-offs between very different activities - is it a case of "he who shouts loudest"?*

I *Is your organisation a "Plodding Donkey" or an asset-light, fast moving entrepreneurial business? How do you measure that?*

L *Do you have a guerrilla mindset? What tactics have you used?*

L *Are you a disruptor or The Disrupted?*

Guerrilla tactics can be employed just as effectively in the world of employee engagement. As far as I know, David Novak is the only person to ring the bell of the NYSE with his head encased in a large slice of plastic pizza. His trademark, however, was the rubber chicken. The CEO of YUM, whose brands include Pizza Hut and Taco Bell, was obsessed by fun and was, in part, inspired by Herb Kelleher of SouthWest

Airlines fame. Like Kelleher, David Novak was determined to found a culture that brought a smile to people's faces. David created a unique environment that was perhaps best personified by a rubber chicken[49]. Early in his career he had come to two important conclusions: the first was that recognition had a very important role to play in motivating the business community. The second, very practical, observation was that people valued the sentiments behind recognition rather than any material gain that accompanied it. As a consequence, he deliberately chose a recognition vehicle that could not possibly be construed as anything other than symbolic. His choice of a life-sized rubber chicken came naturally since he was then CEO of KFC, the worldwide legacy of Colonel Sanders.

Typically, an employee would find himself sitting quietly at his desk or workstation when his door would burst open and a large, handsome man would step inside, accompanied by a group of employees who purported to play instruments taken from the brass section of a band. As the musical cacophony filled the room, David would thrust a rubber chicken into the victim's hand, on which he had written a short description of the individual's achievement. Each chicken was individually numbered and inscribed and so, for instance, one might receive: '#106. To Fred – great job fixin' the customer survey! Best wishes, David'. Whatever one's temperament or nationality, it was hard not to be caught up in his infectious enthusiasm and copycat objects proliferated around the company. Pizza Hut awarded similarly inscribed plastic pizza slices and Taco Bell created an entire investiture ceremony in which outstanding individuals received The Order of the Chilli Pepper.

In individual markets local variations of the rubber chicken appeared such as the Potjiekos awards in the South African business; it is a miniature version of the bulbous three-legged cooking pot that forms an almost sacred role in traditional cuisine. In Bangkok, YUM's highly charismatic boss Hester Chew distributed playing cards as rewards. The packs were

49   Taking People With You: The Only Way to Make Big Things Happen, David Novak, Portfolio (1st edition) 2013

printed with Hester's crowned likeness where the king of Clubs, Hearts, Diamonds and Spades would normally appear! The Novak Blitzkrieg reached its zenith when he declared; "The Year of Customer Mania" and re-christened his entire 500,000 employee workforce "Customer Maniacs". In Puerto Rico one of these maniacs earned a Rubber Chicken by running three blocks after a customer to hand back a wallet that they had inadvertently left in their restaurant. More latex poultry followed when another helped a stranded customer re-start their car. All over the world Maniacs were having fun trying to outdo each other in the customer service stakes. And it was all costing very little money.

Big Bangs, Small Bucks		
Quality	SAS approach	Things To watch out for
Assets	Assets work for you - not the other way around. Keep nimble, able to pivot as market and Tech scenarios change. Work capital, recycle, upcycle, shared economy - keep it lean & sustainable	Investment horizons that are at odds with speed of market change, with risk of in-built redundancy. Trying to get market to fit your legacy structure
Disruption	Disruption is the new normal. Constantly look for new/better ways to win and expect the competition to do likewise.	Go into a state of denial & hope the good old days return.

Targeted Resources	Technology allows very detailed targeting of communication resources.	Accept the old saying; "I know I'm wasting half of my marketing money, I just don't know which half."
Guerrilla Tactics	When cash is tight, guerrilla tactics are a great way to have impact with both customers & employees. The internet provides many new opportunities.	Fail to tune into the market zeitgeist or the power of the Internet.

Chapter Five: S.A.S. = Speed, Aggression, Surprise

Brand names can have curious origins. I mentioned that Nike's Phil Knight was rescued from Dimension Six by a colleague. Google was originally called Backrub. (Imagine "Backrubbing" for sneakers and choosing a pair from Dimension Six). Generally, people try to create brand names that convey meaning. Storey, the flexible workspace brand, was a play on the double meaning of storeys in buildings but also the *stories* of their entrepreneurial customers. (It was nearly *Forty Bob* - but that's another story). The choice of Special Air Service, on the other hand, was deliberate disinformation. Unlike the Royal Engineers, Royal Signals etc. that do what they say on the tin, the S.A.S. was labelled a much larger brigade (2-5,000 soldiers rather than the actual number of 60) and the Air Service part suggested that it was a glider unit of some sort. The aim was to confuse the Germans rather than celebrate the unit's purpose. So whilst 'SAS' has entered the lexicon of street-speak, the label itself really doesn't mean anything. However, SAS soldiers have taken this empty acronym and given it their own interpretation: *Speed, Aggression, Surprise.*

Contact Drill

Without speed SAS soldiers would have a short life-expectancy. The basic building block of SAS tactics is something called a Contact Drill. Whether intentional or unintentional, a "contact" occurs when an SAS patrol collides with an enemy and how it reacts will determine whether it lives or dies. The technique was developed in the jungles of Borneo and Malaya. When the SAS bump into an enemy, such as an Indonesian unit in 1960s Kalimantan, it is a safe bet that it is massively outnumbered and out-gunned. But the enemy doesn't know that. An alert SAS scout spots the advancing enemy through the dense jungle foliage and that may mean at a range of less than ten yards. In the early days the scout carried a shotgun and then later an M16 Armalite rifle but the drill was the same; a large dose of lead would be instantly blasted straight into the midst of the enemy. "Contact front!" yells the scout as he goes to ground and the other three members pour fire in the direction of the enemy. If they have automatic weapons two may fire bursts on automatic, the other two double-taps to ensure that not everyone runs out of ammo at the same time. Moments later, the group fires and manoeuvres backwards into dead ground and then races away from the contact area, being careful not to leave any sign which would allow the enemy to follow them. By now the enemy are lying flat on the jungle soil, reeling from the shock of what felt like a tidal wave of bullets slicing through the forest around them, felling saplings and splintering the trunks of established trees. In their midst a couple of men are screaming from gunshot wounds and someone is yelling for a medic. The officer and NCOs are shouting and blowing whistles to regain control. It is a scene of apparent devastation and confusion. The less experienced soldiers are convinced they have been hit by a company of infantry, at least. By the time they realise they have been conned the SAS patrol is miles away and has probably booby-trapped their escape route for good measure. Four men have out-manoeuvred four hundred using *speed, aggression and surprise*. It happened in Malaya, it happened in Borneo and it was graphically described in the book Bravo Two Zero when Steve Mitchell's unit ploughed into Iraqi infantry in 1990.

How fast is fast?

Every right-thinking person in business values speed. The question is: how fast is fast? We may both agree that 100 is a good speed but perhaps

I am talking Kph and you are talking Mph. The production cycle for new cars is typically weeks or even months with most US auto manufacturers. With Toyota it is four hours. I mentioned that the "Cheesegrater" took four years to build, using prefabrication in Germany to allow it to be assembled in a confined space in the City area of London. It has 56 storeys. A chinese construction company called 'Broad Sustainable Building' erected a 57 storey towerblook in Changsha in 19 days (with an interruption for bad weather). They claim that the building, Mini Sky City, complies with all the usual international standards. Dubai, meanwhile, has announced its intention to 3D print 25% of all new buildings by 2030. How about whole companies? The fastest unicorn on record is currently US retail site Jet.com that reached a $1Bn valuation 4 months after launching, before selling to Walmart in 2016. In Silicon Valley six months is long enough to dream up a digital company, staff it, run it, fine-tune the business model and then either begin the scale-up or the wind-down depending on the prognosis.

None of this suggests that all business should be conducted at the speed of a contact drill. Like risk, speed needs to be weighed up against other factors. You want faster car production? Be prepared to carry more component inventory. But it is interesting that companies sometimes carry out similar tasks with very different expectations. Consider the following micro example: on my very first day in PepsiCo my boss, Jim Lawler, asked me to take care of a small piece of HR process work. My colleagues were some interesting characters like Simon Calver and Tim Davie who many years later would become the new Director General of the BBC. After five years in Mars, another terrific US company, I was well drilled in how to tackle a task like this. First, I would identify key stakeholders, draw up a list and arrange a series of meetings to gain their input. Based on their ideas I would develop my process and tools and then cycle back with each of them in turn, to ensure that they felt their views had been adequately addressed. After this pre-sell, I would call a meeting for all the stakeholders where the new process would be socialised and, if necessary, further debated. By having everyone in the room at the same time no one could claim that they were somehow confused by the final decision. The outcome would be a high quality process with total support. I reckoned I could accomplish that in four to six weeks, allowing for diaries. Alternatively, I could just do it.

I decided on the latter course of action, just to test the water and see "how things get done around here." I already had experience of designing such a process so, in truth, I really didn't need to spend hours asking for advice just for the sake of getting buy-in. When Jim swung by my office at four o'clock that afternoon I had nearly finished. "How are you getting on with that process?" asked Jim. "Nearly done," I responded. He didn't blink. Interesting. At the risk of inviting ridicule (through comparison), Ashlee Vance's biography of Elon Musk[50] frequently references his imposition of outrageous timescales on his teams but also plants the thought that maybe mainstream business has simply become accustomed to luxuriating in flabby ways of working.

The Need for Speed

Customers expect speed - it's become a hygiene factor. In the USA you can order a Tesla car on-line and it will arrive within a fortnight. (Add a month if you need it in some other country). When not paralysed by Covid, Yoox Net-a-porter will deliver a dress or suit of your choice on the same day. Contact Deliveroo and they will have a meal at your door in 32 minutes on average. Walk into a McDonalds and they will have a hamburger in your hands in 112 seconds. You can transact with Monzo bank in 24 seconds (double for Barclays). When I wrote the first edition of WDWiB a website homepage needed to land in about 7 seconds if it wasn't to irritate a customer and risk them clicking away. Since then expectations have shortened and measurement has become more sophisticated. The equivalent speed is now around 4.7 seconds, 11.4 for mobile but with 'Time to First Byte' (TTFB) more like 1.28

50   Elon Musk: How the billionaire CEO of SpaceX and Tesla is shaping our future, Ashlee Vance, Virgin Books 2015

and 2.5 seconds respectively. It's a crazy world when you press a button and bristle if your command doesn't receive a first response faster than the speed of light travelling from the Moon to Earth!

Speed is an enormously important competence in business for all sorts of reasons. High Tech companies race to develop new products ahead of their competitors. Today's mobile App' has lost its youth appeal by tomorrow. Clothing and accessories change with the seasons and a retail operation that isn't fully tuned in is soon sitting on a pile of worthless inventory. Conversely, if retailers can't replenish popular stock quickly they miss crucial sales. In the "War for Talent", a recruitment process that lasts more than thirty days, or ninety for senior hires, will lose the best candidates to more eager competitors. Customer complaints that go unresolved are a problem because each day that disgruntled customer is telling her friends about her lousy experience, it multiplies the negative impact on sales. Invoices that are not paid on time hurt key suppliers. Equally, receivables that wash around in no man's land for months can bankrupt even robust companies. Employees get fed up when management takes an age to review their ideas or respond to concerns. Speed is the life-blood of modern business and, like any blood, it can drain away with fatal consequences.

In fact, there are surprisingly few exceptions in business to the *need for speed* mantra. When Vodafone fine-tuned its call centre operations some of the Southern European markets defended their longer call duration times because they felt it was culturally appropriate to be a little more chatty. They were persuaded by less garrulous northerners to take a brisker approach to see what would happen. They did so. Call times and hence costs went down. Customer satisfaction, to the surprise of many, went up. In a world in which transistors halve in size and double in computing power every twelve months, it's hard to imagine that any industry is going to slow down. On the contrary, the opposite will certainly be true. So whether we look at speed through a Mph or a Kph lens, speed is becoming more rather than less important to all of us.

The 7P Model

It's easy to equate speed with a sense of urgency or the natural talents of sportsmen like Lewis Hamilton or Usain Bolt. Such qualities certainly help. Training also plays a key role - 10,000 hours of 'Wax On, Wax Off' practice, Karate Kid style. When SAS squadrons rotate through Counter-Revolutionary Warfare (CRW) duties they spend three or more hours a day in the "Killing House", an indoor range that simulates hostage release scenarios. The soldiers fire up to four hundred rounds per morning, frequently engaging targets within touching distance of colleagues. The most skilled soldiers can fire a double-tap with a pistol or MP5 and the two holes overlap on the target. To give some sense of perspective, a firearms trained policeman might fire one hundred rounds per year. After Killing House training the team will go into the gym and do two hours of circuit training – wearing SR6 respirators. But a lot of speed comes from building organisational machinery to deliver. Management consultants love alliterative organisational models, especially when the components all begin with the letter S such as the Kaizen model of 'Sort, Set in Order, Shine, Standardise, Sustain' or the famed McKinsey 7S's: 'Strategy, Systems, Structure, Staff, Skills, Style and Shared Goals.'[51] The Army has a less grandiose 7P equivalent: 'Prior Preparation & Planning Prevents Piss-poor Performance'.

When Iranian dissidents murdered press attaché Abbas Lavasani in the embassy in Knightsbridge in the spring of 1980, their fate was sealed. For five days they had negotiated with the police in an attempt to secure the release of political prisoners held by the regime of Ayatollah Khomeini. The police negotiator made every effort to meet some of their demands, such as the provision of particular brands of cigarettes, but it has always been the position of the British government that it doesn't cave in to blackmail. The group of six terrorists decided to press their point and Lavasani paid with his life. Shortly afterwards the

---

51   In Search of Excellence: Lessons from America's best run companies, Tom Peters & Robert Waterman, Profile Books 2004

Home Secretary William Whitelaw took the gloves off. The terrorist leader was still arguing with the negotiator when SAS troops blew the embassy windows in with framed charges. Seventeen minutes later all but one of the hostages was rescued, all but one of the terrorists killed.

The siege of Peterhead prison in Aberdeenshire took only six minutes. Less complicated, it involved members of D Squadron releasing Jackie Stewart (the prison officer, not the race driver) from the custody of some hardened criminals led by Sammy "The Bear" Ralston. Peterhead was a Victorian red brick building stuffed to the gunnels with three hundred angry inmates and appropriately known by them as "The Hate Factory". Ralston and two murderous colleagues, Jack Devine and Malcolm Leggart, took Stewart hostage and dragged him on a chain leash onto the roof of D Hall. This was seven years after the Iranian Embassy assault but Margaret Thatcher was still on the Prime Ministerial throne and was having none of it. She called in 22 SAS. The next day half a dozen SAS troops walked along a dizzyingly high building edge and dropped down through a skylight onto The Bear and friends in D Hall. It was a short argument and the villains returned to their cells wishing they had stuck to Ping-Pong.

It's easy to imagine that operations like these were spontaneous acts of brilliance. Nothing could be further from the truth. It was the culmination of meticulous planning, rehearsal and an extended regime of training that prepared those who participated – and many who didn't because they were deployed elsewhere – for these kinds of eventualities. In fact the Iranian Embassy terrorists couldn't have timed things any worse. B Squadron was physically en route to conduct a CRW training exercise in Scotland, fully tooled up and ready to go when they were diverted back to London. They didn't even have to change their trousers.

What happened at the Embassy?

In London, further layers of preparation were unfolding. The Cabinet's emergency committee COBRA had practiced many scenarios, particularly the seizure of North Sea oil rigs, and quickly established effective crisis management at government level. In Number 14 Princes Gate, next door to the embassy, Scotland Yard's C13 anti-terrorist command under John Dellow set up an operations room and regular police cordoned off the area. Ambulances were put on standby and brought closer. The SAS arrived at Regents Park Barracks and discussed an "Immediate Action Plan". In essence, if the terrorists started killing all the hostages the SAS would literally blow the windows and doors and charge in, saving whoever they could. This necessitated moving in with C13 next door. Meanwhile, new information was flowing in thick and fast. A BBC cameraman, Chris Cramer, was released with severe stomach pains and was interviewed to determine the number of terrorists and weapons (6 men, 2 submachine-guns, 2 pistols and a grenade). The Foreign office had located six visa applications which gave names, faces and limited histories to the terrorists which were then placed on a pin board for the team to study. Someone also managed to track down the embassy caretaker in his humble bedsit. His information was the most critical of all. He knew that both ground and first floor windows were constructed of bullet-proof glass. If the assault team had used sledge-hammers instead of explosives to break in they would still be pounding away now, or handing over to someone of less pensionable age. The caretaker also looked at architects' drawings and fleshed out more vital detail. There is another Army expression beyond the '7 Ps', namely; *"Time spent in reconnaissance is rarely wasted."* When night fell members of the team climbed up onto the embassy roof, discovering a large glass dome and a skylight. Gingerly, they opened the skylight and looked down. Beneath them was a toilet and bathroom; the perfect entry point.

If you want to know what happened next, look it up on YouTube. An iconic BBC newsreel captures the moment when two soldiers jump between first floor balconies the next day and blast their way into the building through a window, (thanks to the caretaker). But let me tell you what didn't happen. When the night-time recce group discovered the open hatch they reported straight back to the Operations Room and explained what they had discovered. The terrorists and hostages appeared to be largely asleep and in darkness. The team could put on passive night goggles (PNGs), which you often now see in places like Iraq and Afghanistan, providing infra-red night vision. They would then attach silencers to their Heckler Koch MP5 weapons and slip quietly into the building. There would be no stun grenades, no "Harvey wall-banger" framed charges blowing in windows, no loud staccato bursts of machine-gun fire, no yelling. They would advance through the building like black-clad spectres (with apologies to Harry Potter) and silently eliminate the terrorists one by one. The hostages would wake up to find it had all been a very bad dream. The terrorists would not wake up.

In today's post 9/11 era perhaps the go-ahead would be given for such a "Silent Attack" as these things are referred to. But in 1980 it was somehow considered unconstitutional and things had to deteriorate further before the more conventional assault went in. The point of all this detail is that, in a sense, the terrorists did not die in Knightsbridge at all. They died months before in the Killing House, in COBRA meetings, in C13 Operations Rooms. Seventeen minutes of lightning fast assaulting was merely the visible tip of an iceberg of preparation and alignment along the chain of command. When the Arabistan separatists chose London as the venue for their terrorist operation they came up against an organisation that was equipped to deliver a speedy and decisive response.

The New Zealand Way

As COO of a large company I was once responsible for Crisis Management and set up a whole infrastructure with the help of a security company, S-RM, led by Ed Butler, winner of the DSO and 3 Bars and a former SAS colleague. We established a 'War Room', rehearsed various scenarios and even had two trial Work-from-home days - although WFH seemed a remote possibility at the time, given that we had a choice of buildings to operate from. In all honesty, a global pandemic wasn't something we spent a lot of time on. Now, with Covid-related deaths approaching 1 million, Crisis Management has become an everyday required competence for businesses all over the world. Strange concepts like Social Distancing and Furlough (previously more familiar to soldiers and prisoners) have suddenly gone mainstream. Some businesses will fare better than others. But one thing that has already become evident is that countries like New Zealand that reacted quickly and decisively to the pandemic have been cited as best practice. Those that dithered or flip-flopped have run into difficulties. The same applies in business and there are two well-known case studies that illustrate the point.

Tylenol - take the hit and recover

Some years ago a lunatic in the Chicago area launched a random murder spree by lacing Tylenol pain-killers with potassium cyanide. Seven people, including two children, suffered terrible deaths. Although apparently not politically motivated, it was a classic act of terrorism because suddenly every family in America was living in fear of instant death from the consumption of head-ache tablets or even other innocuous consumables. To its owners, Johnson and Johnson, Tylenol was a hugely important product, accounting for nearly twenty percent of profits. J&J heard about the unfolding crisis from the media. Chairman James Burke instantly took control and immediately identified the two priorities: 1. Protect the people (consumers). 2. Save the product. This clarity of direction set the tone for all that followed. In the same way that Thatcher took ownership of the Embassy crisis, Burke made sure that no senior executives would be second-guessing what the leaders of the company wanted to happen.

You will remember that the SAS established an 'Immediate Action' Plan and put this in place whilst they figured out a more comprehensive approach. In the same way, J&J immediately notified consumers via the media that they should cease all consumption of Tylenol products and not resume until the company notified them that it was safe to do so. Tylenol had a 37% market share and who knows what went through the minds of others selling competitor products Anacin, Bayer, Bufferin, and Excedrin. Sales slammed to a halt whilst new cases of product tampering were discovered.

The next action was to create a J&J COBRA, a seven-man crisis committee that determined how the overall situation should be handled. At the heart of their decision-making was the realisation that J&J's strategic purpose was to provide palliative support and care to consumers. They began by withdrawing all capsules from the shelves of drug stores in the Chicago area and then expanded the policy nationwide. In the same way that C13 and the SAS got on with their respective jobs, there was no squabbling between J&J customer care staff, pulling product off the shelves, and sales folk wondering how this would impact their commission and bonus programs. Clear top-down leadership negated this possibility. Rather than cowering from negative publicity, the company launched a pro-active media campaign. A 1-800 help line was established and Burke appeared on *60 Minutes* and the *Donahue Show*, telling the public what was going on and how they should safely respond. Work immediately began on tamper-proof packaging and within six months Tylenol had set a new industry standard with products that had new triple safety seal packaging; a glued box, a plastic sear over the neck of the bottle and a foil seal over the mouth of the bottle. They announced the product via a press conference at the manufacturer's headquarters.

In the wake of the crisis Tylenol sales nose-dived but within a year they had resumed to historic market share levels. Meanwhile, the entire way Burke and his people had managed the crisis reinforced in consumers' minds that patient safety was paramount to J&J, a vital piece of brand reinforcement. Firm, speedy action and absolute transparency won the day and when a second incident occurred four years later lessons had been learned and the response was refined further. The same couldn't be said of Perrier, the French mineral water manufacturer.

Fizzy water gone flat

A substance called Benzene was found in unacceptable quantities in bottles of Perrier in North Carolina. Benzene is a natural component of crude oil and is carcinogenic. Unlike the Tylenol poisonings, the Benzene contamination was not a life-threatening situation but nevertheless the Federal Environmental Protection Agency stipulates safe levels of 5 parts per billion and Perrier bottles contained between 12.3 and 19.9. The President of the Perrier Group of America Inc., then Ron Davis, played down the health risks to the public but gave few details of how the product recall would work. Consumers were left confused, no doubt asking themselves; "If my Perrier is safe how come the FEPA don't want me to drink it? If you're recalling product now, why didn't you recall it immediately when the contaminated sample was first identified? And if at last you are recalling all product nation-wide, doesn't that suggest that your product is, after all, potentially dangerous when you said it wasn't?" A relatively containable problem was made more serious by dithering and hesitant communication. You get the sense Davis and his people were making it up as they went along. In due course this venerable old French company was taken over by Swiss giant Nestle.

B *Is speed an important feature of your business? Do people get on with things?*

I *Is the organisation actually built for speed?*

L *What prizes can you capture by moving fast?*

L *Did your business react quickly to Covid and other crises? What did you learn and decide to do better next time?*

'A' – the middle letter of S.A.S.

We are now somewhere around the middle of the book and that's not a bad place to stop to consider the whole topic of *aggression*, perhaps the most controversial ingredient in the SAS analogy. SAS operations are, by nature, aggressive but how does this usefully translate to business life? Do we really need to be tough or ruthless or even *kill* the competition? Are capitalism and combat interchangeable - or have we all been spending too much time on our Xbox 360s? It would be very easy to deal with this whole topic by offering a few politically correct platitudes about obnoxious behaviour in the workplace and drawing a line under the subject. We could escape from awkward debate by pointing out that analogies are, in any case, not supposed to be taken literally. If this book was about life in the Circus rather than the SAS, I wouldn't be suggesting that everyone dresses for the office as Coco the Clown and brings their lions to work. But I think we should be a little braver.

Aggression Discretion

Warfare, in general, is an undiscriminating business. Bombs and bullets do not care who they kill. Mines are sown into the ground and neither know who they will kill or even when. (All too often the answer is innocent civilians, trying to live their lives on what was formerly a battlefield). Soldiers cannot afford to be any more compassionate. If soldiers appraised the lives of each individual enemy before pulling the trigger they would hesitate and, if that hesitation were not reciprocated, they would die. That is the "him or me" conundrum. The SAS are unusual in that quite often they know precisely who they will kill and why. At the Iranian Embassy and Peterhead Prison they studied the profiles of each of the protagonists. In Iraq they raided the houses of specific Al Qaeda members and built up an intelligence picture based on the data they found in their homes. The same is true of the Taliban in Afghanistan. Of overwhelming importance, of course, is who they *don't* kill. The SAS go to enormous lengths to ensure that they don't kill hostages or even family members of terrorists. The SAS have been likened to a surgeon's knife, carefully removing diseased tissue but avoiding damaging healthy organs.

In the Sunday Times journalist Andrew Roberts published an article entitled: 'With its hands tied the SAS loses[52]'. It was a "pro SAS" article and in general we should be glad that people like Roberts want to make life easier for our forces in contrast, for example, to ambulance chasing lawyers looking to capitalise on battlefield mistakes. But I have to say I didn't agree with some of what he said. The background was

---

52   Sunday Times, 9th August 2020, Andrew Roberts

that SAS soldiers in both Australia and the UK had been accused of killing unarmed civilians in the course of the type of rolling night raids I described previously. Allegations included placing weapons in the hands of the deceased to justify the killings. Whilst Roberts didn't condone law-breaking, the thrust of his article was that "war is hell" and we should allow SF soldiers sufficient freedom of action without them having to worry unduly about prosecution.

To an extent he had a point. From the comfort of our Sunday breakfast tables we're not having to put our lives on the line. The first SAS casualty of the Iraq war was Sergeant John Hollinsworth, already recipient of the Queen's Gallantry Medal for heroism in Northern Ireland. Every night, for months on end, his Task Force Black team would storm buildings in Basra and elsewhere in an attempt to harry terrorists and gather intelligence. Domestic homes in Iraq often conform to a fairly standard lay-out; a front-door and then a corridor leading to a T-junction with rooms to left and right. Generally speaking, a night-time raid would find the occupants of the house in one of these rooms but probably not both. The question was which one? If the SAS troops couldn't answer this question through prior surveillance they would have to charge down that corridor knowing full-well that there was a fifty percent chance that they would barrel into an empty room and risk being shot in the back by the occupants of the other. After a while the terrorists shortened the odds by blocking doors with something like a fridge or even a barricade of sandbags.

On the night of 23rd November 2006 this is exactly what happened to Hollingsworth. Jon's bravery had already been recognised when, in a previous raid in Iraq, he had been shot in the neck whilst dealing with six terrorists, returned to the UK for treatment and been nominated for a Conspicuous Gallantry Cross for his trouble. The bullet had missed his carotid artery by millimetres. A lesser man might have called it a day. Wounded, twice decorated for gallantry and universally respected, he could easily have lingered in the UK without recrimination. But after only two weeks he re-joined his troop and was assaulting a block of flats in Basra when he was shot from behind with what appears to have been a captured NATO weapon by an unseen enemy (there is no evidence for a "blue-on-blue"). His colleague was attempting to batter his way through an obstructed door and asked for Jon's help when he turned and saw that he had been shot in the ribs. He died in a military hospital shortly afterwards.

Given the risks of such an operation, men like Hollingsworth should know that the public "have their back". And when Taliban, Al Qaeda or ISIS complain that yet another "wedding party" has been taken out by drone strike the public don't see the secret satellite footage that makes a mockery of their claim of innocence. There are other more complicated situations. In the books *Bravo Two Zero* and *The One That Got Away* we hear about patrol members deciding whether to kill Iraqi farmers and goatherds who, whilst being innocent civilians, are doubtless loyal to the Iraqi state and will hand them over to Saddam's troops if they get the chance. Does that make them combatants? And if the goatherd is not a tough, ex soldier but a wide-eyed child, does that change things? These are terrible decisions for anyone to have to make. But the SAS do not have a "Double 0" James Bond style licence to kill nor even the kind of "Shoot to kill" mandate claimed by Irish terrorists at the height of The Troubles. When I conducted CRW training in the SAS, one of the very first lectures we received was by a lawyer. Far from hinting at some Double O dispensation, we were reminded of our responsibilities towards the law and of the Rules of Engagement in places like Northern Ireland. The thrust of the talk was that the nature of our work made it far more likely that we would put ourselves in difficult situations and the only concession was that there was a dedicated Army lawyer who would spring into action on our behalf when necessary. So you could argue that we should respect Jon Hollingsworth's sacrifice by upholding the law. Otherwise, why even take the risk of assaulting the building? Why not just obliterate it with a smart bomb? We shouldn't take this discrimination for granted. When Russian Special Forces assaulted Moscow's Dubrovka theatre held by Chechen separatists in 2002 they paid insufficient attention to hostage safety and gassed one hundred and thirty of them to death in the course of the assault.

Kick them in the shins

When is it right to behave "aggressively" in business? That can't be sensibly answered with a simple set of rules. There are too many variables. But I once did a basic negotiation skills course that gave me one useful idea about the topic of 'aggression discretion'. Negotiation, it turns out, is not about stating your position. The traditional barter where I say £50, you say £100 and we settle on £75 is a bit limited. Better is to ask questions: "you're suggesting £100 - how did you arrive at that figure? How does that compare with your competitors' offerings? What cost components are you including? What sort of profit margin would you consider reasonable on a deal like this?" The idea is to reel the opposition in towards your £50 goal but without having to be confrontational or lay all your cards on the table. As your opponent answers your questions they find themselves giving ground because they're not really able to justify the £100 ask. Maybe you settle on £65 - a decent result for you but hopefully also one that makes the other guy feel like he's been treated fairly. However, my negotiation teacher conceded that at some point you may need to lay down a marker or draw a line. When this happens, having soothed your opponent with probing questions, there is a moment to "kick them hard in the shins" (his analogy not mine). Warren Buffett is credited with saying; "Never be afraid to ask for too much when selling or offer too little when buying." Sage advice from the Sage of Omaha. So - a bit like the SAS - be sparing with aggression in negotiation but when it's required don't be half-hearted, make it count.

Fighting talk

How about management and leadership styles? There's plenty of combative language in business; hostile take-over bids, aggressive pricing, the war for talent...Some of the best known businessmen are or were known for it. For Steve Jobs small arms fire wasn't enough. Towards the end of his career Jobs threatened "thermonuclear war" when Google launched Android in what he perceived to be an act of betrayal. When a delivery company let him down he said; "Just tell them if they f**k with us, they'll never get another f***ing dime from this company, ever." This incident occurred somewhere near the middle of Job's career when he had just resumed leadership of Apple, having been previously ousted by his own Board of Directors. And of course he began his career in 1974 by marching into the office of the HR Director of Atari video games and demanding a job. In fact he refused to leave the building until he had been given one. The owner of the company, Nolan Bushnell, saw past the beard, hair, sandals and lack of deodorant and decided to give him a chance rather than having him arrested. Jobs was constantly in conflict with the people around him, even including close family and friends. But first prize for raw aggression must go to Michael O'Leary of Ryanair who even hates his customers. "People say the customer is always right, but you know what - they're not. Sometimes they are wrong and they need to be told so," or even less ambiguously; "Nobody wants to sit beside a really fat bastard on board. We have been frankly astonished at the number of customers who don't only want to tax fat people but torture them." He appears even less sympathetic to his own employees; "I don't give a shit if no-one likes me. I am not a cloud bunny, I am not an aerosexual. I don't like airplanes. I never wanted to be a pilot like those other platoons of goons who populate the airline industry." Even his shareholders got an earful; "I'm here with Howard Miller and Michael Cawley, our two deputy chief executives. But they're presently making love in the gentleman's toilets, such is their excitement at today's results." Software tycoon Sir Alan Sugar has built an entire television series out of firing business trainees live on camera. A lot of his contestants are rather ludicrous and he has little apparent sympathy for their protests, particularly when subsequently played out in an industrial tribunal, as they were in the case of former show winner, Stella English. Sir Alan's show was of course picked up in the USA by a divisive leader.

It's enough to make an HR Director weep. The real question is whether those behaviours contributed to their success or whether, perhaps, they might have been even more successful if they had conducted themselves with more equanimity. Few people cited Steve Job's aggressive outbursts as being useful ingredients of his leadership and even O'Leary was beginning to show more respect to his customers before Covid emptied his planes. All things being equal, would a prospective pilot rather join the team of a passionate aviator like Richard Branson or that of someone who "doesn't like planes' and thinks you're "a goon"? Would a passenger prefer to travel with Scandinavian Airlines, who coined the customer concept of "moments of truth," or an airline that intends to put them in their place or worse if they wear comfortable trousers?

Duncan Bannatyne was a nineteen year old sailor in the Royal Navy when he was arrested for throwing an officer off a jetty. After a nine month stint at Her Majesty's pleasure, he bought an ice cream van from which he launched the "Glasgow Ice Cream wars" and subsequently ploughed the proceeds into nursing homes and later kindergartens and health clubs. He is now a presenter on TV's Dragons' Den, has been awarded an OBE for charity and written several best-selling business books. Net worth estimated recently at $645 Million. Other people might see him as a hard man but he had this to say; "People often think that success in business comes from being ruthless, but I don't think that's true: in my experience success in business comes from being tough. Tough enough to do the dirty jobs and tough enough to make the difficult decisions."

Interestingly, even some of the SAS legends weren't always admired for their aggression. If we return to Anders Lassen, some felt that he had a somewhat sinister side to him. As a boy he loved hunting with a bow and arrow and in wartime developed an affinity with the Commando dagger. On his first airfield raid he crept up behind a sentry and buried his knife up to the hilt in the man's neck and it had quite an impact on his companion, Corporal Ray Jones. There was a general feeling that this kind of hands-on warfare suited Lassen rather too well and that his pathological hatred of Germans sometimes clouded his judgement. He was killed at Lake Comacchio, leading an unwinnable assault against multiple German machine-gun bunkers and received a posthumous VC. Paddy Mayne was once criticised by Stirling for slaughtering a bunch of German pilots in a mess hut during an early desert raid. He wrote: 'It was necessary to be ruthless but Paddy had overstepped the mark. I was obliged to rebuke him for over-callous execution in cold blood of the enemy.' Mayne didn't adjust to the post-War peace easily. He returned to his legal practice but enjoyed too much poetry, Guinness and recreational fighting in bars and eventually hammered his car into the back of a tractor in the early hours of the morning with fatal consequences. In more modern times a dozen SAS officers have made General rank, reflecting both the growing importance of SF operations in conflicts like Afghanistan but also the calibre of the soldiers. The reality is that it is very hard for a contemporary officer to reach this kind of position of seniority without developing a pretty well-rounded skill set that includes managing multiple stakeholders in government, higher command or in friendly armies. So whilst it's fun to read about larger-than-life characters like Lassen, they are probably a slightly unrealistic example of peacetime leadership.

Leadership experts like Executive Search company Egon Zehnder place ever more emphasis on emotional intelligence, humility (again) and ethical leadership. Gurus like Deborah Rowland are going fully zen with qualities like 'Staying present, curious and intentional responding, tuning into the system and acknowledging the whole[53].' Aggression will only diminish in importance as more oestrogen finally enters the Boardroom. Listen to this quote from New Zealand's highly regarded Prime Minister Jacinda Ardern; "One of the criticisms I've faced over the years is that I'm not aggressive enough or assertive enough or maybe somehow, because I'm empathetic, it means I'm weak. I totally rebel against that. I refuse to believe that you cannot be both compassionate and strong."

   B *Have you learnt the art of Aggression-Discretion?*
   I *Have you thought about the difference between toughness and aggression? What does that mean for you?*

---

53   Still moving: How to lead mindful change, Deborah Rowland, Wiley 2017

Customer Delight & other Surprises

Surprise is the SAS's greatest weapon and probably the best example of this is the use of the ambush - something that's taken up quite a bit of my time. In Borneo we did a two day exercise, laying quite still, which turned into an Attenborough-style nature watch when various primates swung by including the famous orangutans. I even spent the night of my 21st birthday in an ambush in South Armagh. But the one that sticks most in my mind was another example of Aggression Discretion. My team had located an Armalite ammunition clip that had been positioned behind a concrete post, ready for immediate collection by an IRA courier or hit man. It was common practice for the IRA to deliver a weapon to one location, ammunition to another and then for the components to be separately delivered to a third person, the Trigger Man. This maximised security whilst minimising the amount of time the murderer actually had a fully loaded weapon in their hands. We lay in an ambush for two days and awaited the courier. In due course a female terrorist came along, collected the magazine and loaded it into her child's pram before sauntering off. We intervened and introduced her to some nice policemen. She was not gunned down by us, for the simple reason that it was neither necessary nor lawful. In showing restraint, two lives were saved; hers and the victim's. The point about the SAS is not that it is more aggressive or less aggressive but that it applies aggression more precisely and with a clearer sense of the outcome it wants to achieve.

Surprise is a powerful human emotion because it amplifies feelings, both good and bad. Consider the following heart-warming story; a homeless beggar called Billy Ray Harris was sitting on his pitch one February day in Kansas when a young woman called Sarah Darling strolled by and emptied the loose change from her purse into his Styrofoam cup.

It was only when she got home that she discovered, to her horror, that she had inadvertently dumped her diamond engagement ring into the man's change. Unsurprisingly, when she rushed back to his pitch she found Harris had vanished. However, two days later he re-appeared and when Darling approached him he knew at once what she wanted and handed over the ring without hesitation. She was so pleasantly surprised she established a tribute website for the man. In a few days he had accumulated $180,000! Evidently, the general public shared Darling's amazement and felt a powerful need to recognise his unexpected generosity. Without being cynical, the record will show that a penniless man made a quarter of a million dollars in a few weeks, simply by massively exceeding low public expectations. There must be a commercial lesson in there somewhere.

We've already seen how YUM CEO David Novak was so keen to wow customers that he declared 'The Year of Customer Mania' and re-branded his co-workers Customer Maniacs. Aside from the example of the waiter at a Puerto Rico branch of Pizza Hut who saw that a customer had left his wallet at the table and ran three blocks after him to return it, a veritable outbreak of Customer Mania has ensued. Another Pizza Hut waiter went outside the restaurant and fixed a customer's car that had broken down. YUM didn't have a monopoly on this kind of madness either. A US Army major called Shawn Fulker emailed his local pizza restaurant in Jacksonville, Florida from his base in Afghanistan. It was his wife Josephine's birthday and he wanted to send her and his five year old son Ethan a pizza and gift card. The Mellow Mushroom Pizza Bakery responded with admirable style. They cut a pizza into a heart shape, filled it with heart shaped pieces of pepperoni and delivered it to Mrs Fulker – all at no charge. Sticking with food and kids, a gentleman called Simon Niesler was shopping in his local Waitrose store with his two small children. He filled his trolley up with groceries until one of his brood decided to vomit over the lot! Waitrose staff swept into action. The child was cleaned up, a fresh trolley commandeered and replenished with the exact same inventory of (vomit-free) products and Mr Niesler was sat down with a cup of coffee.

All these stories have similar characteristics; a relatively small act of kindness creating a huge customer impact, simply by virtue of exceeding commonly held expectations. Nice surprises are also good for defusing anger or disappointment. An advertising business in Holland, De Telefoongids, went through a difficult period when customers became irritated by poor service. The CEO moved quickly to regain their trust. Customers were soon met at their doors by a brilliant bouquet of flowers. Strange as it may seem, customers who have complaints swiftly dealt with often become more powerful brand advocates than those that receive a seamless service in the first place. At times in my career I've been heavily involved with recruitment. There is nothing more disheartening, however much anticipated, than the proverbial job rejection letter; 'Dear Bloggs, thanks for your application…..good bye and good luck." When I have to send these kinds of letters I try to personalise them and add a little more information, for example citing the number of people who replied to a LinkedIn advert or referring to their own particular skills, so the recipient feels less of a sense of emptiness. Frequently I got replies that express both gratitude and surprise that I have done the candidate this small courtesy. When businesses have limited resources at their disposal they need to recognise the power of Surprise and to create situations where it can be effectively leveraged.

B *How often do you blow customers away by exceeding expectations?*

I *How urgently do you mobilise when any of your stakeholders get unwelcome surprises?*

L *How well do you use these opportunities to strengthen relation-ships and increase loyalty?*

L *How often do you go the extra mile personally?*

SAS = Speed, Aggression & Surprise		
Quality	SAS approach	Things To watch out for
Speed	Recognise the importance of speed as a key competence; speed to market, response to customer complaints etc.	Equate speed with danger and manage ponderously.
	Plan, rehearse & train so that mission execution is a variant of an "option" or routine. Could apply to product launch or customer service initiative.	Each new initiative is a re-invention of the wheel. Learning from previous initiatives lost, lead up to execution slow & awkward.
	Use pilot schemes to validate model & rule out bugbears before launch.	Unrealistic or non-existent pilot schemes leading to unnecessary mistakes.
Aggression	Appreciate Art of Aggression Discretion. No hesitation once things swing into action. Right or wrong, fully commit & make best of situation. Enjoy excitement of the roll-out!	Start questioning whether you're on the right track before you've even built momentum behind initiative. Cynicism or scepticism.
		Aggressive behaviour in the workplace.

Surprise	Leverage the power of surprise element to deliver disproportionate benefits, for example with respect to customers & employees.	No imagination. Lack sensitivity/ awareness towards stakeholders and their perceptions.
	Conversely, recognise powerful negative impact of nasty surprises.	

Chapter Six: Know the difference between vital and pointless.

This chapter is a lot about the Pirate/Navy conundrum. Hollywood movie-makers love the guy in uniform gone rogue: Jack Reacher the rogue military policeman, John Rambo the rogue Vietnam Vet, Jason Bourne the rogue gone rogue. There's something seductive about the idea of non-conformism within uniformed organisations. No one ever asks; "Why even volunteer for this shit if you don't want to wear a uniform, take orders or accept discipline? Why not be a games programmer-surfer?" But the genre has some basis in truth. Such characters have always existed, not least Stirling, Mayne and Lassen. I once took part in an SAS training exercise to capture an airfield with four C130s full of paratroopers landing in box formation. "It was all going so well", commented Ministry of Defense observer Colonel Andrew Pringle, "until this plane-load of buccaneers arrived, piling out in jeeps and motorbikes like something out of the Barbary Coast!" When the founder of Delta Force, US Captain Charlie Beckwith, started his secondment with the SAS he walked into a messy barrack room and said; "What we need to do is get this area mopped down, the equipment cleaned, straightened and stored and the tea brewed outside." "No Sir," replied Troopers Scott and Larson. "That's not what we want to do. Otherwise, we might as well go back to our old regular regiments. One of the reasons we volunteered for the SAS was so we wouldn't have to worry about the unimportant things."[54] It's cool to be an Eagle flying in formation. The question is: when is rule-breaking dysfunctional and when can freedom of action convey an edge?

Pirates of Penzance

When I first sketched out this chapter who would have thought the world would be working from home? With the change comes some huge questions about how work is best accomplished. For decades we lived largely according to Theory X[55], everyone sitting at allocated work-stations in office buildings, regulated and directly supervised. And in some ways that scrutiny was getting more intense. 'PropTech' gave ever greater insights into people's behaviour, both physical and digital. Arrival times, office locations, movements, phone calls, emails, keystrokes, even biometrics and retinal movement. In the name of productivity we surrendered all privacy. Covid confounded everything. Wrapped in duvets and sitting at kitchen tables people found they could get just as much done without the commute, the over-priced sandwich - or the presence of authority. They could incorporate work into more complex routines that - whilst not perfect - included childcare, exercise, home administration and leisure. And they could do it all from Cornwall. Why did it take a pandemic to focus minds on the power of independent working? And why are we so surprised that Theory Y - the power of personal responsibility - came out on top?

Let's get back to basics. The fundamental truth of military discipline is that much of it is imposed. There is a good reason for this. When confronted with a brutal and terrifying situation in combat, a soldier can't afford to hesitate when they receive an order. The hours spent on the parade ground are all about executing commands, precisely and without delay. Moreover, each soldier needs to know that they can count on their colleagues to play their part. No one will want to work

54   Delta Force, Colonel Charlie Beckwith, Arms & Armour Press 1984

55   Theory X and Theory Y, Douglas Macgregor, MIT Sloan Professor 1950s & 1960s

with someone who has second thoughts when lives are on the line. In the Army, everything has its place. Ammunition is always kept in the same place on the web equipment. Why? Because if someone is trying to kill you and you've just emptied a magazine, you can't afford to spend valuable seconds rummaging around in your equipment looking for a replacement. Even when the bullets are not flying, the same sort of principle applies. If it's dark, you're cold and wet and only have ten minutes to eat some food, you don't want to spend five of those precious minutes trying to remember where the heck you put your spoon. Every item lives in its own special place. But as Troopers Scott and Larsen pointed out, the trick is to know when rules and regulations are vital and when they are pointless - or even potentially dangerous.

Learn the rules before you can break them

The first phase of SAS Selection is a bit like a boot camp. 100 officers and NCOs line up on parade and address the Training Wing members as "Staff" (one thing that does ring true about the TV programme) as though they are raw recruits. Standing beside a line of trucks in the cold, dark predawn air the names of each man is called out. "Staff!" comes the reply. If there is no reply the name will be repeated. Still no reply and the man is off the course. He may be late for roll call for some complex reason. It doesn't matter. He's gone. Everyone has been given a kit list and a spring scale dangles somewhere in the barracks to make sure that Bergen rucksacks weigh the stipulated amount. In fact, it's wise to overshoot a little to allow for the water you will consume during the march which could bring the weight down below the required level. If that happens - and the directing staff catch you out - the penalty is the addition of a large rock. This is unwelcome when you may already be carrying 65 pounds - even more so when every march is timed and no allowance is made for this new burden. If someone is a little slow on a march they receive a warning - just one. If they're too slow twice they fail the course. There is no allowance for injuries. If they are minor you are expected to cope. If they are major you are invited to make a further attempt at Selection at some later point. There is a basic principle at stake; before the SAS recruit is given the freedom and independence that goes with special forces soldiering, they must first prove that they are capable of adhering to rigorous standards and self-discipline.

Closely associated with this point is the issue of individual calibre. In the first chapter I talked a lot about 'The Man is The Regiment' and it's a theme that tends to repeat throughout WDWiB. When you give people freedom you expect them to rise to the challenge - not exploit the opportunity. The calibre/freedom link is well signposted in the Netflix HR strategy. *Responsibility* is also one of the Five Principles of Mars. The concept of the Mars *Associate* is a further reinforcement of the idea that individuals must feel ownership of problems and never feel it's Ok to duck an issue, hide behind collectivism or pass it on to someone else - and Mars is very thorough with its recruitment process. But as we saw in the last chapter, high calibre isn't the same thing as highly educated or highly paid. A co-worker in a Puerto Rican KFC is no less capable of being an ambassador for a brand or applying the 'Man is The Regiment' principle.

Boots on - when detail matters

For the second phase of training, in the jungle, SAS soldiers live with their boots on. They sleep with them on, they wash with them on and for this there's a very good historical reason. In 1942, Mike Calvert was part of the British Army's desperate rear-guard action to slow the Japanese advance through Burma. He had been engaged in weeks of hard jungle fighting when he saw the opportunity for a brief moment of respite. A short distance from his bivouac position was a river that ran clear over a bed of smooth rocks. In the early morning sunshine it was an inviting scene. Peeling off his damp shirt he stepped out of the trees and eased himself down into the cooling water. Unfortunately, as the saying goes, great minds think alike. At the exact same moment, a Japanese officer with the same idea sploshed into the river beside him. There was no truce; the two men launched at each other and wrestled in the water, punching, gauging and throttling as both fought for their survival. For the next fifteen minutes they took turns strangling and drowning each other but Calvert had a useful advantage. The Japanese officer had allowed himself the additional luxury of removing his boots. As the two men tired, Calvert found that the additional grip his boots gave him conferred a certain advantage over his opponent, whose shoeless feet slithered frantically across the slimy rocks. Eventually Calvert managed to bear down on the man and pin him underwater for long enough to drown him. As the body floated off down the river, Calvert rushed back to his men and they fell upon the Japanese officer's patrol nearby, killing them all. When Calvert later took over the SAS he instigated the "Boots On" policy and it hasn't changed in more than 80 years. (In the story of Colin Armstrong's epic exfiltration from Iraq he describes removing one boot at a time to tend to his suppurating feet).

When soldiering in the jungle you are more or less permanently wet during the day through rainfall, sweat or both. To deal with this you have two sets of clothing, one of which is filthy, stinking and wet and the other is dry. At night you change into the dry set giving you the chance of a restful, warm night. But in the pitch dark before dawn you must change out of your dry kit and squirm back into the filthy set. No one ever gets used to pulling a stinking wet shirt onto their back. But if you are ever tempted not to do this you will suffer for every remaining night of the deployment. Once again, because you are performing this excruciating act in total darkness you must know exactly where each item is placed. If you are attempting to dry out spare boots overnight you must place them upside down on sticks. If you don't, prepare to share your boot with a scorpion. In the movies Stallone and Schwarzenegger patrol through the jungle with naked torsos and flak jackets to show off their physique. Special Forces soldiers roll their sleeves down, elasticate their ankles and wear floppy hats because they don't want to be bitten by mosquitoes, scratched by vines and have leeches gorge on their blood. Plus they prefer to be camouflaged so as not to get shot.

SAS lives are under-pinned by a framework of 'Standard Operating Procedures' (SOPs) that are based on combat experiences and dictate all sorts of things from equipment to emergency rendez-vous procedures. "Boots on" is, of course, a very low level example but it translates to a whole range of procedures and processes. So whilst an urban counter-terrorist siege, a jungle attack or a desert reconnaissance will be scrupulously planned and fine-tuned, they will be based on a template that has been designed by experts and endlessly rehearsed. In fact, the various CRW scenarios – releasing hostages from planes, trains, buses, buildings and so forth – are known in the regiment as "options".

Clean restroom

I've called this chapter 'Know the difference between vital and pointless' and the kinds of things I've described are 'The Vital'. Business has its equivalents. Unless you are unlucky, you will be pleasantly surprised by the cleanliness of the toilets when you visit a McDonalds restaurant. This is no accident. Market research revealed to the folks at the Oakbrook, Illinois HQ that customers equate what they see in the "bathroom" with what likely goes on in the kitchen. Disproportionate attention is therefore paid to this point. You may also see an employee mopping an area of the floor that appears to be perfectly clean. Also not an accident. That employee is communicating to you, the customer, that they share your love of hygiene in places where food is prepared and consumed. Seemingly innocuous details can be crucial and skilful leaders spot them when and where they occur.

When PepsiCo restaurants became an independent company it took a hard look at McDonalds. There was a 20% point difference in their profitability outside the US and the reasons were clear. McDonalds had figured out a way of doing business and codified it. They took this to extremes. For example, if a new restaurant was to be built, there was a manual available that stipulated precisely how many boards, nails and gallons of paint would be required to create a perimeter around the construction site. Restaurant procedures were highly detailed as were the operational obligations on franchisees. Pepsi people saw themselves as much more entrepreneurial but were collectively inefficient because each market spent too much time figuring out what mattered, where and how money needed to be spent. When the study had been completed and digested, Pepsi introduced a new operating system that focused on the things that mattered to customers: Cleanliness, Hospitality, Accuracy (of order-taking), Maintenance (of the establishment itself) and Speed of Service. Pneumonic CHAMPS. Two years and a lot of hard work later Pepsi enjoyed the same margins as McDonalds; an extraordinary example of the power of process.

In Pizza Hut UK, the baton of CHAMPS was taken up by a huge Texan called Jon Prinsell. Jon had been running the remainder of PepsiCo's European restaurant operations and he could have legitimately considered the Pizza Hut appointment a demotion. In reality, his appointment was PepsiCo's well-aimed sledgehammer, designed to crack the nut that was a strained relationship between the joint venture partners. Jon combined enormous strength with humanity. His father was a missionary in Africa and Jon and his family committed Christians. (Bizarrely for a Texan, he was also mad about cricket). In spite of an upbringing split between the bush and Bible belt, he never displayed a modicum of zealotry, or the sort of John Wayne school of behaviour that such a heritage sometimes produces. Six foot four in his boots, he never raised his voice, lost his sense of humour or treated anyone unfairly. But nor did he compromise. More than anything, Jon realised that success would only come about if the business made CHAMPS a reality through disciplined adherence to these processes and principles.

In his first year in office he visited every single restaurant (numbering about 350) and guzzled enough pizza to make the rest of us feel like our very limbs were stuffed with Mozzarella. He checked the underside of kitchenware to ensure that dishwashers functioned correctly, discussed "mystery diner" scores with restaurant managers and had after-dinner mints wrapped in foil because too many customers had a habit of going to the toilet and failing to wash their hands at the end of a meal. Our in-trays were endlessly full of copies of letters of congratulation that he had personally sent to high performing employees. On one occasion he invited all field-based managers to visit the head office, where they met the carefully named Restaurant Support Team, and to sit in the CEO's office and high-backed chair, where they were duly photographed for posterity. Two years after Jon's sizable boots slid under the table the company was breaking records for profit, customer satisfaction and employee motivation.

Processes can also be tackled from a functional perspective, rather than on Business Unit (BMU) lines. In Chapter three I mentioned Vodafone's Marketing University. The genesis for this institution is interesting. There was a large meeting of senior marketing executives and at a certain point the discussion turned to the subject of functional competence. Paul Donovan, an ex Mars and Apple man, posed a question to his peers; "If a top headhunter was looking for marketing talent, would they naturally go looking in Vodafone?" Everyone agreed that, at that time, they wouldn't. The reality was that Vodafone still operated a portfolio of brands, its pricing structures were unintelligible (along with the rest of the industry) and it had a very mixed approach to retailing i.e. some subsidiaries had a full retail estate, others had almost none. Out of sheer self-respect, the group decided that they needed to raise their game. A decision was taken to create a Marketing University in which a dozen key marketing processes would be developed by in-house thought-leaders. These would be turned into teaching modules and toolkits. All related marketing staff would then be required to attend workshops and, ultimately, comply with the new standards.

Two further influences came into play. The first was the decision to consolidate the brands within the Vodafone group into a single megabrand. Leadership of this process fell to David Haines, ex Coke and Mars, now CEO of Upfield, a sustainable foods business. My job, in parallel, was to help Chris Gent and his senior team establish a group-wide culture. It was the start of a very effective relationship. David oversaw the creation of the University and I ran it for him as a member of his team. So now we had a global brand, a global employee culture and a set of marketing processes and tools that turned both into a tangible consumer experience. The Vodafone brand is now worth about $20 Billion and I later went on to work with David in private equity.

The Pointless

Knowing the difference between vital and pointless must be baked into organisational cultures. SAS soldiers are not averse to discipline but they have a strong preference for self-discipline rather than the imposed variety and they are mature enough to distinguish between what matters and what doesn't. Perhaps this explains why SAS General Graeme Lamb surprised then Prime Minister Tony Blair by turning up in a pair of Bart Simpson socks when he visited Number 10 Downing Street! Of all the things in business life, I doubt that many executives would see policies and disciplines as a major point of organisational leverage. But businesses face the same sort of choices as the SAS about when and where to impose structure. Workers in food factories are required to wear hats or nets because consumers do not enjoy eating other people's hair. Airline pilots adhere to tightly controlled flying procedures because few passengers would be comfortable with their Captain attempting a loop-the-loop. However, there is an expansive grey area where rules and regulations aren't really about safety regulations. They may not even have much to do with money. For the most part they have to do with fundamental beliefs about whether imposed discipline or self discipline is the better approach and such decisions say an awful lot about the relationship between employees and their companies.

Netflix have a nice if slightly old-fashioned phrase in their HR strategy: 'Responsible people thrive on freedom and are worthy of freedom'. They continue with an even more ambitious vision: 'Our model is to increase employee freedom as we grow, rather than limit it, to continue to attract and nourish innovative people, so we have a better chance of sustained success.' This second, forward-looking point is hugely important. For many years US department store Nordstrom was cited as a highly progressive business. It restricted itself to an employee handbook comprising 75 words on a grey card;

'Welcome to Nordstrom. We're glad to have you with our company. Our number one goal is to provide outstanding customer service. Set both your personal and professional goals high. We have great confidence in your ability to achieve them. Nordstrom rules: Rule 1: Use best judgment in all situations. There will be no additional rules. Please feel free to ask your department manager, store manager or division general manager any question at any time. '

They pay above average wages and the only way to get a promotion is to work your way up from the shop floor. They have very few difficulties recruiting new people and adhere to some interesting organisational principles; 'Nordstrom sales people are empowered to make decisions and Nordstrom management is willing to live with these decisions – it's like dealing with a one person shop. Empowered employees are energised[56].' In the last ten years Nordstrom has been hammered by on-line retailing, even before the Covid crisis and stock returns have been very modest. But you could argue that their culture has allowed them to defend against a worse outcome suffered by many other bricks 'n mortar retailers.

This was the same sort of grown-up regime we ran at Pepsi-Cola. Admittedly I was part of a modest sized sales and marketing organisation but there literally were no policies beyond compensation and benefits considerations. As far as I recall, this never gave rise to any confusion and there were never abuses (beyond one Australian HRD who drank the entire contents of his hotel minibar in San Diego one evening - and this probably fell within Australian norms). Perhaps it is a fear of Australians that drives other companies organising elaborate no-expense-spared international meetings to then require attendees to pay for hotel "extras" themselves. In the course of a hectic meeting schedule, how many newspapers, brandy miniatures or porn films can a person attend to? It can't be enough to justify a tedious check out process that would otherwise be swept up by the meeting administration.

Life at Mars was very different but also not without its merits. Mars has a strong engineering and manufacturing heritage and I suspect personnel policies owed much to the thinking that goes with it. Certainly

---

56   http://en.wikipedia.org/wiki/Nordstrom#Employee_handbook

you couldn't rely upon the sales force to cater for this issue. (Question: How long does it take a sales manager to conduct an annual performance review? Answer: depends on the car wash). Engineers try to make sure that machines don't malfunction and when you apply that to personnel policies you end up with a singular result. Engineers need a system that works, no matter what variables are thrown at it. But the downside is that it creates an environment in which common sense is replaced by algorithms. Interestingly, when consultant Mike Walsh - modest job title CEO of Tomorrow - explores the concept in depth through his book 'The Algorithmic Leader'[57] he concludes with such battle cries as; "When in doubt, ask a human" and "humanize, don't standardise". The machines have their place.

As with so many things in business, it is not how many policies a company has, or even which ones they choose. What matters is that someone actually sits down and thinks about what kind of framework best supports their organisation and what cultural messages this conveys. Is there proportionality between the number and scope of policies and derived benefits? Most importantly, are we starting with a Theory X or a Theory Y baseline? Are we telling people that to be an employee of this company is to accept responsibility for most areas of personal and professional conduct? Rule-books and flow-charts lead to precise outcomes or, to put it another way, entitlements. Perhaps it is better to live with ambiguity knowing that, ultimately, all parties will need to come to a shared judgement of what is just and reasonable and what is not. Of course the hardest thing of all is to change from one type of rulebook to another but this is also where the opportunity to inject a catalyst for change exists. Tedious though the topic may be, policies are often more tangible manifestations of corporate culture than speeches from over-exercised senior executives.

B *Is there a strong baseline of self-discipline and are key processes in place? What's your "Boots On" equivalent?*

---

57   The Algorithmic Leader, Mike Walsh, Page Two Books 2019

I	*Is your business driven by empowered team members or a rule book (or even algorithms)?*

L	*Do people share a clear perspective on the things that really matter to the organisation? When was the last time a Sacred Cow got slaughtered?*

L	*Is there any ambition to grow Freedom within your business?*

Owning the Vital/Pointless problem

You can tell from my earlier examples that the SAS is not some crazy free-for-all that fights to a Hollywood script. In some ways, you could even argue that it is more repetitive in nature because the '10,000 hour rule' is applied to so many disciplines like close combat shooting. But it does differ from "the Green Army" in a few important cultural respects:

SAS soldiers have more freedom to act and are expected to use their judgement at all times. Typically, contact with HQ will be sporadic and over extended lines of communication (via HF transmission) so they will have to take the initiative without waiting for orders.

Similarly, they may receive detailed briefings and orders in camp but once deployed independence, self-discipline and intuitive teamwork prevail over order-giving.

They are expected to know when rules or procedures are critically important and when they can be de-prioritised. As a very crude example, boots must be "on" but they're unlikely to be polished to a parade ground shine (even in G Squadron).

There is an informal but ruthless set of checks and balances to ensure that freedoms are not misused.

SAS patrols routinely operate in isolation, miles from conventional support and command structures. In 1950s Malaya (now Malaysia of course) an SAS patrol set a new record by spending 103 days in the jungle, searching for Communist Terrorists. Resupply was infrequent and by helicopter. To give some idea of how isolating the jungle can be, I would like to share a fun anecdote. As I mentioned, my father was serving alongside the SAS in Malaya in the 22nd (CHESHIRE) Regiment, a line infantry unit. One of his brother officers was out on patrol and after two or three days radioed HQ to admit that he was utterly disorientated and needed rescuing. This is not as daft as it sounds because jungle maps have always been made using aerial photography and contour patterns are confused by the varying heights of trees. So, for example, a valley may appear as a flat area if the trees are unusually high and so forth. (There was no GPS in those days!) HQ staff instructed the officer to send up an orange marker balloon, the standard way to locate any patrol since it then becomes visible to helicopters. This is done by emptying crystals into a canvas bag tied under the balloon and then adding water. The chemical reaction creates a hot gas, which inflates the balloon and causes it to rise above the jungle canopy. The officer sent the balloon up and informed HQ. A few minutes later everyone in the camp was howling with laughter when they saw an orange balloon floating above the trees fifty yards outside the camp perimeter! In fairness to the officer he went on to win a Military Cross by rugby-tackling and capturing an armed terrorist.

In general, special forces rarely work in teams of less than four or five men. Just like Netflix employees, they are expected to speak up when necessary, to take ownership of problems. When a single individual has to make it on his own it's normally because multiple things have gone wrong. These types of scenarios spawn books and screen adaptations like 'The One That Got Away[58]' and the US Navy Seal equivalent 'Lone Survivor[59].' But every SAS soldier knows that the day may come when they are alone and have to rely on their own wits as Ryan (Montgomery) and Luttrell did. Each man is individually accountable and must be capable of functioning independently. Sounds like "motherhood and apple pie?" Think about the following group-think scenarios:

---

58   The One That Got Away: The legendary story of an SAS man alone behind enemy lines, Chris Ryan, Arrow 2011

59   Lone Survivor; The eyewitness account of Operation Redwing and the Lost Heroes of Seal Team 10, Marcus Luttrell, Little Brown & Company, 2007.

The Dangerous

On the 6th July 1988 the Piper Alpha North Sea oil rig exploded killing 167 men and inflicting losses of £1.7 billion on owner Occidental Petroleum (Caledonia) Ltd. We need not dwell on the technicalities of what caused the inferno but cannot escape some terrible "moments of truth" when well-intentioned employees contributed to the death of their friends because they lacked autonomy to act – even when it would have been common-sense to do so. The first explosion occurred around 10 p.m., bursting through firewalls that had been designed to withstand flame rather than explosive force. In time, the blaze on Piper Alpha would have burnt out and the cost in human life been avoided or minimised. Unfortunately, the rig was part of a three-way system that incorporated feeder pipes from the nearby Tartan and Claymore platforms. As the Piper crew abandoned their control centre and sought shelter away from an increasingly fierce blaze, the staff in the Claymore and Tartan platforms were afraid to shut down their pipes without some higher authority because the costs of doing so would have been extremely high and it would have taken three days to resume production. Instead they continued to pump thousands more gallons of burning fuel into the inferno that was consuming their colleagues. About twenty minutes after the first blast, Tartan's gas pipeline melted releasing thirty tons of gas per second into the blaze. It ignited instantly shooting flames hundreds of feet into the air. By now the men were sheltering in the fireproof accommodation awaiting rescue or instructions. None came and their refuge was utterly destroyed. The decision to keep, quite literally, adding fuel to the flames was by no means the only human error that night. But it is a heart-breaking vision of disempowered men killing their co-workers.

In the aftermath of the disaster the decision was taken to shift responsibility for enforcing North Sea safety procedures from the Department of Energy to the Health and Safety Executive. From one perspective this decision makes perfect sense. The government of the time was making the point that Safety was paramount and ultimate authority should lie with the department that "owns" safety, rather than with those who are measured on oil output. But let's dwell on this a moment longer. What that also means is that they *reduced accountability* for safety in the body that was *responsible for operations*. So now the Energy folks could concentrate mono-maniacally on output, secure in the knowledge that the buck for any future Piper Alpha would land on someone else's desk. I'm not sure that fits with the ethos of this chapter. In fact, it rather suggests a cultural opposite.

In 2010 eleven more oil men died when the Deep Water Horizon rig exploded and sank in the Gulf of Mexico with catastrophic environmental consequences. Once again there was a whole series of mistakes involving mud, gas, seawater, mechanics and poor judgement. The upshot was that most of the blame went to BP who were fined $18.7 Bn, the largest corporate settlement in US history and ten times the financial hit of Piper Alpha. Whilst the disaster still raged then-CEO Tony Heywood was filmed on a sailing trip with his son, adding a further PR disaster. But a review of the accident[60] by an industry expert contains telling remarks: 'Interior Secretary Salazar has announced a suspension of offshore drilling permits and an indefinite ban on new offshore drilling. This will have a profound economic impact on many thousands of rig and associated service jobs. The result will undoubtedly be new regulations. More regulation will accomplish little, however, if the underlying problem is a lack of critical thinking by the companies that drill oil and gas wells and the government agencies that oversee their activities'. Once again, the issue is not a lack of rules or even technical capabilities but an absence of joined up thinking.

Jump forward another 10 years and a third maritime accident killed 200 people, injured 4,000 and inflicted a similar amount of financial damage to the city of Beirut. Exactly what happened may never be known - it's thought welding equipment, fireworks or even ammunition may have triggered the explosion of a huge, unstable quantity of

---

60   What caused the Deepwater Horizon disaster? The Oil Drum, Arthur E Berman, May 21 2010

ammonium nitrate in a port warehouse that had been delivered seven years earlier by a barely sea-worthy ship called MV Rhosus. What *is* known is that Beirut was sitting on a home-made bomb for the previous six years and, in spite of pleadings from the port authorities, no one in a position of power felt it necessary to take any kind of action until it was too late. Nor were the port authority executives empowered to solve the problem themselves. Amidst mounting anger the entire Lebanese government then resigned but that would be little consolation for the population. Death and misery aside, only about 20% of the carnage was likely covered by insurance.

The root cause of these three catastrophes was slightly different in each case. With Piper Alpha people were anxious to overstep their authority. With Deep Water advice was ignored. With MV Rhosus there was a universal abrogation of responsibility. They all had elements of negligence, ignored warnings, lack of problem ownership and other ingredients that wouldn't, in the words of oil expert Arthur Berman, have been solved by simply having more regulations. What was needed was for people at different levels of seniority to step up and wrestle the problems to the ground.

Within the SAS, having personal freedom to operate – and accepting the accountability that comes with this – is a precious commodity. There is also a general recognition throughout the Army that the "man on the ground" is often best placed to decide how to handle a particular situation. For example, although Terry and I were relatively junior, we were allowed to get on with the management of the Droppin Well incident outlined in chapter three without senior management interference. This dynamic has changed a little with the wearing of "helmet-cam's" that allow live video streaming of SF operations, for instance in the case of the Navy Seal raid on Osama Bin Laden's hideout in Abbottabad. Whether this is a good thing is debatable. Personally, I wouldn't want the distraction of knowing that my actions - and potential mistakes - were being observed in real-time by the President of the United States. Gratifying when you get it right perhaps, not so nice when one of your stray rounds hits a civilian. Unimaginable would be if Obama or one of his top brass actually started issuing instructions in the middle of this kind of situation (as 'M' does to Moneypenny in the movie Skyfall, with the inevitable result that Bond gets accidentally shot).

B *Does the 'Man is the Regiment" principle apply, or do people feel ownership of the business lies elsewhere?*

I *Do you tend to "ask forgiveness rather than permission" or the other way around?*

L *Are mistakes handled in a good way? Are lessons learned and improvements made?*

L *Could a Piper Alpha equivalent ever happen in your organisation? How do you guard against this?*

The Sword of Damocles

If you are going to create an organisation that relies heavily on self-discipline and personal responsibility, it will be necessary to have some form of sanction to deal with people who exploit this situation to their own advantage. The SAS has a kind of two-speed approach to crime and punishment. Hanging above all SAS soldiers is the Sword of Damocles. Having taken months to secure a place in the regiment, it is quite easy to be ingloriously "returned to unit" if there is any major transgression or sign of under-performance. Minor infringements are dealt with via a kind of on-the-spot fine regime, which, as far as I could tell, had no recognisable tariff scale for misdemeanours. Someone would just be told to put £20 or £40 pounds into some regimental kitty and to argue would be to invite some ill-defined catastrophe. As a system, it worked pretty well. Of course the underlying message is; "we treat you like a grown-up and that's how we expect you to behave." And then; "If that doesn't work for you, go work someplace else."

It's quite interesting that companies that are seen as fun-loving and progressive do not shy away from this topic. Disney's mission statement has a lot to do with creating happiness in their customers and, for employees who can't relate; "If you don't enjoy our culture, take your happiness elsewhere!" Interestingly, Netflix also focuses quite a bit on off-loading people in their celebrated HR manifesto. It covers three outplacement scenarios: sustained 'B level' or adequate performance, not being seen as a key player within a team and valuing job security above outperformance. There's a kind of faustian pact at play, trading unlimited holiday for a sense of ownership and accountability.

Know the difference between vital & pointless		
Quality	SAS approach	Things To watch out for
Vital	Understand the critical leverage points, both big & small, within your business. Know what matters to you and your customers.	Assume that what matters to you is identical to what matters to customers.
Individual Freedom	Recognise the kinetic energy, initiative & responsibility that comes from the freedom to act.	Allow supervision, whether electronic or human, to come between employees and their work.
Process adherence	Identify critical processes with biggest impact on organisation & codify. Checks & balances to make sure they work.	Sloppy or absent processes, archaic processes that owe their origins to a situation that is no longer relevant.

Pointless	Ruthlessly expunge things that don't add much value to organisation.	Sacred cows, company rituals and red tape. Busy work, petty work, pointless work.
Self-discipline	Self-discipline, adherence to critical processes & procedures.	The opposite – lack of self-discipline, non-adherence to critical processes & procedures.
Checks & Balances	Combine toughness with an informal code of conduct, respected by all.	Expansive rules and regulations.

Chapter Seven:
Standing still makes you a target

Adapt or die, right? Unless you believe in the Six Day Creation it's pretty much accepted wisdom. And yet it doesn't come that naturally to us. Consider the following recent example: after six months of Covid lock-down the UK government urged workers to return to urban areas to support the bars, restaurants and other local businesses that depend on city life. Feels politically sensible. But if you applied ruthless logic the government would be saying; "you shifted to a more home-centric model of working. Now is the time to take the money you've saved on commuting and casual dining and to plough this money back into ergonomic home office furniture (maybe rent it through Fat Llama), improved wi-fi and cyber security. With more apparent leisure time you should rejoin your local gym." The concept of *returning to normal* is somehow the enemy of *moving on to the new reality.*

Design and future-proof

Let's face it, military analogies are not for everyone (thanks for sticking with me BTW) but it's really no exaggeration to say that the kind of existential crisis facing many businesses compares with the kind of melt down you're more likely to see in times of war. Healthy companies are in danger of becoming zombies; businesses that survive to service their debt but have no hope of moving beyond that point. Others won't even make it to B horror movie status. So what can the SAS tell us about pivoting to new challenges?

The SAS has lived in a state of almost perpetual reinvention. And there's a difference between tolerating a new reality and really going for it. The regiment has survived and prospered as an organisation by responding to changing needs in several ways:

Adapting – at the macro level to "market" requirements
Improvising – to cope with the immediate, tactical situation
Innovating – using grass-roots insights
– and doing so *at speed.*

By now you will have got comfortable with the whole *raison d'etre* and modus operandi of Stirling's wartime invention. So it's a great time to stick a spanner in the works and do our own mini-pivot! The oldest part of the current SAS is actually my grandfather's unit 21 SAS (Artists) (Reserve), rather than the regular regiment. It was raised in 1859 at a time Britain feared a French invasion. The founder was an artist named Edward Sterling (not to be confused with David Stirling, failed Pigalle artist!) and the regiment was filled with painters, artists, musicians and other creative types. With the French threat a distant memory, the regiment fought in the Boer War but in WWI it became an officer training unit and by this time included doctors, architects and other professionals. Its alumni included famous names like Wilfred Owen, Siegfried Sassoon, Noel Coward and dambusting inventor Barnes Wallis. In total, the men who passed through the Artists won 8 VCs and 56 DSOs between them, suggesting a very effective training regime. Inevitabley, they were eventually sucked into the trenches to fight (hence grandfather Horace's wound at Passchendaele) but essentially remained a training unit until the end of the Second World War.

For a lot of the regiment's history it was an elite organisation and the only way to get in was via a personal recommendation from an existing member. Briefly disbanded in 1945, along with 22 SAS, they reformed as the Malayan Scouts and then formed the backbone of the new 22 SAS in 1952. During the Cold War they trained as stay behind parties, a terrifying job that would have involved living for months in underground hides whilst soviet tanks rolled over their positions and then transmitting data back to NATO from behind enemy lines. Post *glasnost* the regiment fought in Iraq and Afghanistan, returning to their training heritage teaching the Afghan National Army and Police, as well as bodyguarding duties for the Secret Intelligence Service. 23 SAS (Reserve), the other TA unit, morphed out of wartime MI9. This was the unit that supported European resistance cells to exfiltrate downed pilots. They also subsequently fought in Afghanistan and elsewhere.

22 SAS, meanwhile, has reinvented itself numerous times. In the military context the Market Macros equate to the theatres and types of warfare in which the UK and its Armed Forces are engaged. When you look at a chronology of the regiment's history it runs something like: Desert - Europe - Jungle - Jungle - Desert - Desert - Europe/Arctic - Antarctic - Urban - Desert - Europe - Desert - North-west Frontier. In reality, members of the SAS regiment have been simultaneously involved in operations in all of these theatres of war throughout, sometimes pulling off their snowshoes after winter warfare training in Norway and plunging into the steaming jungles of Borneo, Africa or Central America with no more time to acclimatise than a long airline flight. This requires physical fitness but also a ready-for-anything mind-set that embraces the challenge and excitement of such disparate tasks. It also requires organisational mobility; resources that can be moved around quickly to where they are needed.

These attributes are not automatically true of all elite military units. For example, the Royal Marine Mountain and Arctic Warfare cadre are an excellent outfit but with a pretty self-explanatory purpose and a bunch of Skidoos that aren't much use if the snow melts. In recent years the Special Forces Directorate has gathered the Royal Marines Special Boat Service (SBS), the Special Reconnaissance Regiment (formerly 14 Intelligence company) and elements of the Parachute Regiment to create a greater critical mass of this kind of more flexible expertise. What commanders need are organisations that can be confronted by all sorts of scenarios and respond to them effectively with minimum notice, moving resources to where they are needed most.

Below the regimental level, the SAS is divided into squadrons and each squadron has four troops: Air, Mobility, Boat and Mountain. L Detachment began as a parachute unit (motto 'Descend to Ascend'?) but learned to fail fast and rapidly reinvented itself as a unit that relied on motor transport. The regiment's 'pink panther' jeeps and land rovers have existed ever since. Motorbikes were added and then more recently All Terrain Vehicles and quad bikes - anything that can be described as a motor vehicle. Each vehicle is adjusted, new weapon systems and other technologies added. Air Troop came back into its own with the use of HALO (High Altitude Low Opening) and HAHO (…high…) parachuting, helicopters, Osprey fixed wing aircraft and experimentation with detachable aircraft pods. Boat Troops owe their origins to the Special Boat Section of WWII. At the time Lassen and the Greek Sacred Squadron disguised themselves as fishermen and sailed around in caiques. Over time these have morphed into rubber dinghies, semi-rigid raiding boats and dismantlable canoes. Underwater SCUBA gear was replaced by oxygen rebreathing apparatus, mini submarines and even submarine pods.

To some extent you could argue that these things represent nothing more than the onward march of technology. But the SAS has always preferred to be on the front foot, training and preparing for emerging scenarios. One of the greatest quotes on anticipation came from the Canadian ice hockey champion Wayne Gretsky. When asked about the secret of his success he said; "A good hockey player plays where the puck is. A great hockey player plays where the puck is going to be." In many ways that personifies the SAS. Whereas the average infantryman accepts the equipment, strategy and tactics he is given, the special forces soldier is more intellectually curious about future needs and creative possibilities. There is a small R&D team in 22 SAS specifically dedicated to this topic. Without exaggerating the point, it may not be a coincidence that the SAS's early DNA included sculptors, architects and designers or that Stirling himself had these leanings. You could argue that it is a trend extended by some ex-SAS and SBS people who are making a good living from TV shows, novel writing and promoting literacy in general. These are not the activities of people with closed minds who sit at home waiting for the world to happen.

Facing reality

There is, of course, no silver bullet. But a good start point is to acknowledge the pivot and start fighting according to the new landscape. There will be no "return to normality". We are moving at breakneck speed to a new reality and businesses that can't or won't adapt will succumb. Let's think about imperiled high street retailers. According to John Gildersleeve, well qualified as a Tesco veteran and Board Director of both retail and real estate businesses, Bricks 'n Mortar retailers can't simply blame the internet for their misfortunes. In his view, many retailers made themselves vulnerable by selling poorly differentiated products with indifferent customer service. The internet merely put a magnifying glass over this fact. When consumers see no experiential upside of visiting a store they prefer the simplicity of an at-home transaction. Covid has now forced consumers to trial digital solutions and the question will be whether cash-starved high street retailers can up their game in the hope of luring shoppers back into stores when it all ends. Others may explore alternatives like dark store concepts, where physical premises are basically order-fulfilment units. Nobody will get anywhere by simply hoping that things recover.

Retail landlords, meanwhile, have been hammered by tenant CVAs (a form of voluntary insolvency), store vacancies and the added burden of a set of emergency government measures that prevented them from taking legal action against non-paying tenants in the normal way. At the low point less than 14% of quarterly rental receipts were collected. Once again, the government is pandering to politics, oblivious to the fact that many landlords are "dividend stocks", producing a steady income for ordinary investor-pensioners, whilst some of the non-paying retailers are owned by unscrupulous billionaires with large cash piles.

As a compromise, the industry has come up with a voluntary code of conduct to help it navigate out of the mess. However, one inevitable consequence is a move away from upwards-only rent reviews towards a turnover-based, shared risk model. This is making many property investors nervous. And yet it's no different to 99% of industries where a supplier's fortunes are broadly tied to those of the customer. Real estate's model of entitled prosperity, regardless of the customer's success, is pretty unique and it relates to history and the lack of liquidity of their assets. Change is inevitable. And whilst the high street sorts out its mess, the on-line retailing community won't stand idle. Companies like Fat Llama and Fjong (#coolgirlsrent) in Scandinavia, to pick a couple, are challenging traditional purchasing models in favour of the shared economy.

What about commercial office-based real estate? This has its own version of the existential double-digital-Covid crisis. The serviced office has been around for some 30 years and the biggest player is IWG, brand name Regus. The sector has had its ups and downs but gradually expanded to around 3% of the global office footprint and, along the way, spawned some very decent medium-sized businesses like Industrious, Convene, TOG (The Office Group) and Brockton Capital's Fora. However, the sector went nuclear with the meteoric rise of WeWork. WeWork has all manner of issues, not least a $50Bn leasing obligation, but its stellar growth had the effect of forcing both landlords and occupiers to embrace the concept of space-as-a-service (SAAS). This focus on the end-user customer was a huge departure from the traditional landlord model of collecting quarterly rent and having nothing to do with a tenant's employees. Property-related technology massively reinforced the concept. Then came Covid. WeWork's ex-CEO Adam Neumann was lampooned for his mission statement: "To raise the World's consciousness" but, in a sense, this is exactly what the pandemic has done. Having worked more or less effectively from home for months, both businesses and employees are demanding a better explanation for the role offices play in commercial life. Not many people believe "the office is dead" but just about everybody thinks it needs to be deployed more thoughtfully around company culture, meetings and other value-added activities. There is discussion of a "Hub & Spoke" office model and people like IWG's Mark Dixon, once a hotdog salesman now a Monaco-based billionaire, are rubbing their hands. No one's voting for cubicle life, Dilbert-style.

The rise of flexible offices has caused consternation amongst the professionals who make a living from valuing commercial property. When we buy our domestic homes we pay what we think is right for the local market, guided by Zoopla, aggregator sites and Estate Agents. Increasingly, we might also calculate the price per square foot/meter as a useful way to judge whether we're getting value-for-money. Commercial valuers see office buildings differently. They see an office as a business with a revenue stream. They apply a multiple to this revenue (although they don't express it that way) and a valuable building is one that has a well-covenanted tenant with a long-lease. Just like any other business, they value a secure, profitable future. Then came the SAAS movement and the observation that, in an age of uncertainty, businesses don't necessarily want to be tied into long leases. They may expand, contract, move location or simply prefer something different. Accounting rules also changed to force businesses to carry their leases as a liability on their balance sheet. As a result of these things, lease lengths have been gradually dropping. Property valuers marked down accordingly. But then people like moustachioed Giles Fuchs of OSIT (Office Space In Town) gamely produced his "Fuchs formula", pointing out that strong cash-flows associated with SAAS more than compensated for this lack of certainty. The valuers sucked their teeth. In due course, they concluded that they could agree to this type of approach but would need years of data to prove that it worked. In very crude terms; "if you want us to value SAAS like a 7 year fixed lease, we need 7 years of trading data". In other words; "We will value your apple like our pear - but only once it looks, tastes and smells like a pear". *We need to get back to normal.*

To anyone coming from a consumer-facing background, the idea that a product is *less* valuable because it's *actually what your customer wants* is anathema. Financial people joined the discussion and thought about how they could bake future and option value into space-taking as a way to make sense of the new reality. But when Amol Sarva, ex CEO of Virgin Mobile and now Founder of flexible workspace business Knotel, began observing these arguments he voted instead for a complete new crypto-currency that threw the entire rule book out of the window in favour of a ledger of real-time transactions. He just wasn't buying the whole industry mumbo-jumbo. Amol is a highly successful businessman and, like his chairman Edward Shenderovich, is a UC Berkeley Philosophy major. This may explain his questioning approach and reluctance to buy in to accepted wisdom. It's a quality that will be in much demand in the months ahead.

Intrapreneurs & death of the Sacred Cow

True entrepreneurs have no corporate safety net to rely upon but they do at least have the freedom to stand or fall by their own decisions. But many business people are part of some broader corporate framework that is laden with sacred cows. And herding these sacred cows into the office car park and slaughtering them is every bit as hazardous as the vision suggests. (Even more chaotically zoological when combined with Elephants in the Room). This calls for the "Intrapreneur," a person who exhibits all the creative problem-solving flair of the entrepreneur but does it whilst taking account of corporate legacy systems, hierarchy and all the other paraphernalia of big business. Steve Jobs alluded to such people when he said; "The Macintosh team was what is commonly known as intrapreneurship… a group of people going, in essence, back to the garage, but in a large company.[61]" The consulting group Bain had a helpful way of visualising the problem with the terms 'Engine 1' and 'Engine 2'. Engine 1 is the traditional business, a reliable source of profit, Engine 2 the upstart but one which will eventually become a large part - if not a total replacement - of Engine 1. The transition is where the pain lies.

Being an intrapreneur is a hazardous business. Pinchot Gifford III,

---

61   Steve Jobs, Newsweek interview 1985

inventor, entrepreneur and founder of USA's first 'Green MBA' program, wrote a set of rules for successful intrapreneurship[62] and Rule 10 was: 'Come to work every day willing to be fired'. When you think about Stirling, already on a disciplinary charge, breaking into Cairo HQ to launch his organisation, you can see how literally he took that mantra. In the early days the "Top Brass" were highly sceptical of his plans and couldn't wait to see him trip up. Even Field Marshal Montgomery once remarked; "The boy Stirling is…quite mad." Gifford's first rule was no less illuminating: 'Work underground for as long as you can - publicity triggers the corporate immune system.' In some ways this explains how the SAS "got away with it" for so long, a maverick unit within an organisation - the British Army - that has existed since Cromwell commanded in 1660. Nowadays the SAS is homed in an ex RAF base, before that in a campus that resembled a red-brick business park (apologies Sir David) but when I first visited Bradbury Lines many years ago it was a bunch of snow-covered nissen huts hidden away behind multiple layers of fencing in a quiet corner of Hereford, itself an understated west country town famous only for its cattle market. Very few visitors were permitted, even amongst senior military ranks and when they came it had to be for a specific purpose. There was no tourism.

The rest of Gifford's manifesto reads like an SAS play-book:

Work underground for as long as you can - publicity triggers the corporate immune system

Remember it is easier to ask forgiveness than permission

Do any job needed to make your project work, regardless of your job description

Follow your intuition about the people you choose and work only with the best

Circumvent any orders aimed at stopping your dream

Find people to help you

---

62   Pinchot Gifford III intrapreneuring: Why you don't have to leave the corporation to become an entrepreneur (New York, Harper & Row)

Never bet on a race unless you are running it
Be true to your goals but realistic about the ways to achieve them
Honor your sponsors
Come to work every day willing to be fired

I can personally relate to these principles, starting with Rules 1-4. When I founded a flexible workspace business I began by gathering a group of a dozen co-conspirators into a basement meeting room in a Covent Garden hotel. I already knew everyone - although not everyone knew each other. They were a great mixture of characters with diverse skills and, most importantly, a can-do attitude and a sense of humour. We worked largely underground for six months before bursting onto the scene with a new brand. As things became more complicated Rule 6. became important, along with pretty much all the others. Of course there are some much better known examples of intrapreneurship. A skunkworks on the periphery of W.L. Gore resulted in the creation of the world's #1 string for acoustic guitars. Searchable Gmail and the Sony Playstation are other celebrated examples of where co-workers developed products with very little permission or resources. Some years ago I attended an elaborate dinner that involved taking a course at several different venues in the Fort Lauderdale area and travelling by boat along canals between each one. Along the way we saw jaw-dropping superyachts and houses. One giant waterfront pile was the property of an intrapreneur who, when working at 3i, developed yellow Post-it notes.

Local Improvisation

The SAS are masters at improvisation. They can conjure a lethal explosive device from some diesel, fertiliser, a battery, a couple of wires, two can lids, a bit of plastic and some 'shipyard confetti" (nails, nuts and bolts etc). The Taliban are not the only people who can do this sort of thing. During combat survival training I once raided a builder's skip for a length of copper piping, a bit of discarded hardwood and a small lump of polystyrene. Ten minutes later I had a blowpipe and dart that would have made an Iban headhunter proud. Readers of Lofty Wiseman's legendary SAS Survival Handbook[63] will know that soldiers can feed themselves by "strangling, mangling or dangling" living creatures or, for the vegetarians amongst us, harvesting comfrey, berries, nettles, mushrooms and other edibles. Of particular importance is correct fungi identification. If you get this one wrong there is rarely a remedy, even with access to sophisticated medical facilities. We were taught this particular discipline by an older lady who resembled an escapee from a Harry Potter film and who, by her own admission, had managed to kill her husband by once getting it wrong!

Of course improvisation is also about tactics; responding flexibly and creatively to an unfolding situation. In Iraq a group of SAS were alerted to the intentions of a would-be suicide bomber. With little time to react, they donned Arab clothing, piled into a bright pick-up truck, Sarah Palin style, and intercepted the bomber before he could martyr himself at the expense of the good people of Baghdad. The overall commander at the time, US General Petraeus, was interviewed by The Times in 2008 and commented; "The SAS have helped immensely in the Baghdad area, in particular to take down the car bomb networks.......they have exceptional initiative, exceptional skill, exceptional courage and, I think, exceptional savvy. I can't say enough about how impressive they are in thinking on their feet.[64]" A quarter century before these events, the Pebble Island raid, described in Chapter Four, moved from intent to action in a heart-beat. The moment my predecessor, the D Squadron Boat Troop Commander, had discovered eleven Argentine aircraft on the airfield he called in the attack that same night. The soldiers had to think, design solutions and execute simultaneously like the proverbial jazz musician. This is the essence of improvisation.

The importance of improvisation as a way to deal with business uncertainties has increasingly been recognised. Companies like

---

63   SAS Survival Handbook: The Ultimate Guide to Surviving Anywhere, Lofty Wiseman, William Morrow & Company 2014

64   Times August 11 2008, Deborah Haynes

PepsiCo, Procter & Gamble and Capital One have all teamed with business schools such as UCLA's Anderson, Duke's Fuqua, MIT and Colombia to work with concepts of improvisation. When Five Year Plans and conventional leadership models don't seem to be working, managers need to take a more "situational" perspective, gathering whatever resources are available to them and making the most of the prevailing circumstances. This can take many forms. Sales and marketing managers may need to make decisions with only 80% of the information that they would normally require for a given program. This may be because the money isn't available for more thorough research, because time is of the essence or simply because the data doesn't yet exist. IT staff may need to do improvisational "work-arounds" in response to pressing operational needs. When that's not possible, Finance and HR staff may need to use Excel spreadsheets whilst more elaborate solutions are being conjured. Line-managers monitoring sickness-absence of smaller teams may even need to use scrap paper and pencils (a long forgotten art).

To this latter point, I once had an interesting encounter with John Mars, one of the two famous Mars brothers. I was part of a small team that was in the throes of setting up a multi-sales operation in the former Czechoslovakia. Mars' incursion into Central Europe was of particular interest to the brothers and they worked their way around each of the markets; Russia, Poland and so forth. Our job that day was to present the annual operating plan and, as always with such "Royal visits", a good deal of preparation was done beforehand. At a certain point in the proceedings I was showing a slide on labour costs and pay and John wanted to know more about how I had arrived at my conclusions. As it happened, I had literally scribbled some calculations and rough bar chart sketches on a used A4 envelope and hadn't yet tossed it in the bin. I pulled it out of a drawer and began to refer to it when a large hand snatched it out of mine and John engaged in the conversation with a whole new degree of intensity. Exhausted by so many highly orchestrated Powerpoint presentations, he was delighted to enjoy a "real" conversation using imperfect data to explore the possibilities of a new market. For a few precious minutes, Co-President of a $40 billion enterprise was having some improvisational fun with some scribbled notes.

B *When was the last time a sacred cow got slaughtered?*

I *What does the "new normality" look like for you? How can you pivot and take advantage?*

L *Does the whiteboard get well-used in your organisation or are you quickly bogged down with Powerpoints?*

L *Are you willing to be fired - or at least stick your neck out - for your biggest ideas?*

Bottom-up innovation

Innovation in the SAS is entirely different to the top-down, linear procurement process that operates in conjunction with the military-industrial complex to deliver weapons systems and technology to the rest of the Armed Forces. Military procurement is often criticised for running over schedule and over budget but it probably deserves even *less* credit than it claims! To begin with, top down requests for kit haven't spawned many of the breakthrough ideas. According to John Chambers in the Oxford Companion to American Military History[65]: 'None of the most important weapons transforming warfare in the 20th century—the airplane, tank, radar, jet engine, helicopter, electronic computer, not even the atomic bomb—owed its initial development to a doctrinal requirement or request of the military.' Once the top brass have written down their Christmas list, however unimaginatively, the armaments folk demand a "Cost-plus" pricing structure, which basically gives them *carte blanche* to be as wasteful as they like because their profit margins are guaranteed regardless. They then begin a tortuous and sometimes politicised process of product development.

Aside from the elongated timelines and costs of top-down

---

65   Oxford Companion to American Military History, John Chambers, OUP USA 2000

procurement, the approach is sometimes weirdly disconnected from what soldiers on the ground might actually want. Between 1954 and about 1985 the British Army had the Self Loading Rifle (SLR) as its main infantry weapon. The SLR is a powerful piece of kit but rather heavy, both in terms of the weapon itself and its 7.62mm ammunition. It is also long barrelled making it unwieldy in urban environments and lacking the fully automatic capability of the US M16 Armalite and Soviet AK47 Kalashnikov. The Army's response was the now familiar SA80 rifle. As SAS troops we were amongst the first to be given the new weapon and were immediately unhappy with it. When you tucked the weapon into your hip it was all too easy to depress the magazine release catch, allowing your ammunition to drop to the ground. Failure to spot such a mistake could be annoying, expensive and potentially fatal in a combat situation. The weapon also made no provision for left-handers. They would get an ejected cartridge case in the face if they fired from the left shoulder. The working parts of the weapon were rather fiddly. The great thing about the M16/AR15 and AK47 are that they are deliberately idiot-proof. They have few working parts, are easy assembled and disassembled and relatively tolerant of dirt. The SA80 felt a little over-engineered. It was also designed to be used with a telescopic sight which grated a little, given that we received the weapon when we were about to deploy in the jungle where combat tends to occur at point blank range and you need to be able to fire shot-gun style. At the other extreme, the Household (Guards) Regiments disliked it because it looked awkward when used in ceremonial drill. More than any of these points, we felt as though the weapon had been designed by some strange men in brown coats somewhere on Salisbury Plain, rather than being the product of grass-roots infantry requirements. Of course, for political (national security) reasons, it also had to be a British manufactured weapon when the French, Austrians, Swedes and others already had perfectly well developed bullpup style rifles like the SA80 that could be purchased off the shelf without a penny being spent on R&D (the route pursued by Australia, New Zealand and Canada).

The SAS have their own skunkworks that prototypes new products and ideas. This doesn't cater for every requirement because things like communications equipment are too complex for non-specialist development, beyond end-user requirements. However, the SAS don't wait for Land Rover to come up with a new lightweight dune-buggy with a pintle-mount for their machine-guns, if they need a nifty desert reconnaissance vehicle. They just get on and proto-type it, giving it a run for its money in the field. These days SAS soldiers have access to sophisticated 'Red Eye' laser sights but at the time of the Iranian Embassy they couldn't wait for such things. Instead that developed a metal bracket that enabled them to attach a torch to an MP5 and learnt to synchronise the torch beam with the fall of shot at a given range. The various types of Flash-bangs were largely dreamt up in someone's kitchen. Boat troops experimented with underwater delivery vehicles that attached to submarines and Air Troops looked at fixing two-man detachable pods to the wings of aircraft. Mechanical claws were designed to enable CRW assaults to cling onto the smooth fuselage of aircraft and "Harvey Wallbanger" charges designed to blast localised holes in walls or armour-plated windows. As we know, Jock Lewes' experimental bomb-making in 1941 was all about finding a way to remotely detonate a device, giving SAS teams time to get well clear of their target. None of these things went through a NASA-style nine step process, nor were they authorised via an NPD manual, MOD Whitehall or Brown Coats. Soldiers acted on the "necessity is the mother of invention" principle and just got on with it. The same is inevitably true of the SAS's potential enemies. Bomb-makers in Iraq and Afghanistan have become masters of the Improvised Explosive Device (IED). Hezbollah flew a home-made drone deep into Israeli territory in 2012. A US domestic terrorist, Rezwan Ferdaus, was intercepted before he could fly a model aircraft packed with explosives into the Pentagon. Innovation at the grass-roots level is increasingly part of asymmetric warfare.

For a sense of what this might look like in industry, consider the challenge set by ABC, the US television channel, to Ideo. Ideo is a Palo Alto based innovations company and it was given the task of designing a new type of shopping trolley that would be much more functional than the traditional kind and much less likely to end its life in a canal or up a tree. (The cost of lost trolleys in the US has been estimated at $175 million per year!). Ideo has built a reputation for innovation based on a bewildering range of products from Apple's first mouse to the mechanical killer whale in the movie *Free Willy*. The idea of the TV company's challenge was to take a mundane product that no one thought very much about and see if Ideo could develop a new break-out design. The team sprung into action and their work was characterised by phrases such as; *"It's not organised, it's focused chaos,"* and *"trying stuff and asking for forgiveness."* As each iteration was produced, the lead designer Peter Skillman asked himself; *"What needs should they optimise their solutions to?"* Skillman and his team were focused on making the shopping trolley a more ergonomic and practical device for shoppers whilst denying would-be trolley thieves the big basket that made conventional trolley's such tempting targets for horseplay. What they ended up with was a modular product with separated, stacked mini baskets incorporated into a frame, a barcode scanner, wheels that enabled the trolley to crab sideways and hooks for carrier bags. This addressed both objectives simultaneously.

In order to accomplish the task in the five days stipulated by ABC, the team went through a few short steps, starting with ethnographic market research. This included interviewing and observing users, as well as talking with purchasers and repairers of shopping trolleys to form a general picture. Once again, the designers didn't talk to the manufacturers at Shopping Trolley MegaCorp Inc. they talked to the men who gather and stack trolleys in supermarket parking lots, to mothers who try to balance baby seats on them and everyday shoppers. They also took hundreds of photographs of what actually goes on in stores including young children surfing on the backs of trolleys and shoppers (without babies) who were strangely reluctant to let go of their chariots. What they needed was bottom-up feedback, grassroots intelligence.

Brainstorming sessions used "Hot Teams" and the interesting thing about these teams is that they comprised an eclectic mix of engineers, MBAs, Marketeers, a psychologist and even a Medical School drop-out. You get a clear sense that the creativity of the group came from its disparate nature. Skillman himself is a Stanford graduate, selected for the task of team leader because of his group leadership skills rather than functional know-how. Beyond this relatively informal role there was a total absence of hierarchy – on the basis that, just because someone might be a Senior Vice President, that wouldn't make him or her a shopping trolley expert!

Fast prototypes were developed, elements of which were incorporated into the final design and demonstrated at a grocery store. To ensure "the chaos" stayed "focused" the group imposed a set of working principles upon itself:

One conversation at a time
Stay focused on topic
Encourage wild ideas
Defer judgement
Build on the ideas of others

The rules also included some practical constraints, such as designs had to be capable of manufacture in a single day to meet the challenge requirements. As the work evolved the team broke into sub-groups and came up with four different prototypes, each one of which had a different set of features and benefits.

The final task before manufacture was to combine the best ingredients of each idea. There was no reliance upon a sole genius. Once a prototype had been developed they circled back into a store, seeking validation and feedback from store workers. It's probably no accident that they chose the forward-thinking Whole Foods, whom we met in Chapter Two, for this phase of the challenge. Some of the trolley features can now be found in mainstream food retailers like Tesco.

To watch the group in action, clad in their blue jeans and T-shirts, it all looks quintessentially Californian but they were largely following a protocol established by the great Prussian scientist Hermann von Helmholz a century before this experiment:

Preparation: study of the problem and learning about ideas that might be relevant.

Incubation: Unless the problem is trivial, a solution will not be apparent by direct study. The creative mind needs time to make subconscious associations between the widely differing kinds of ideas that might be combined. (I guess the justification behind WDWiB).

Inspiration: occurs at some point, seemingly without effort and the novel solution appears.

Elaboration: the last stage is where the new idea must be subjected to scrutiny and developed to make it useful.

Service innovation is just as important as product innovation. The SAS's namesake, Scandinavian Airlines (SAS) pioneered the concept of a customer-centric, grass-roots view of service. The expression "moments of truth" is now commonly used in business but it originated in SAS where airline staff pinpointed the various key moments in a passenger's experience where things could go well or badly depending on how the company's people and systems behaved. As with so many things in this book, it all begins with a general philosophical perspective that innovation actually matters. When you look back through the company's history, it's clear that innovative thinking has shaped a lot of what the airline has accomplished.

When commercial airlines started the "Jet Set" were an elite of wealthy people who formed the bulk of passenger lists. SAS broke the mould by making a Tourist Class available to transatlantic fliers in 1952. It proved so popular that they extended the formula to all flights two years later and other airlines quickly followed suit. Next they introduced a round-the-world ticket, followed by a multi-city ticket called the 'Extra City Plan' that allowed US fliers to visit various European cities at no extra cost. They were the first to introduce SASCO, a Europe-wide instant booking system and, when technology permitted, the first to utilise a biometric check-in. If SAS were the first airline to make air travel accessible to the masses, they were also the first to provide separate check-in and lounge facilities for business travellers. In 1992 they introduced an innovative "Eurosleeper" bed on longer flights. For a modest sized airline it is a formidable list of accomplishments. The airline also showed an innovative approach to employment. Turi Wideroe became the first female pilot of a European airline and was quite a celebrity of her day. Some years passed before Swedish pilot Lena Lindeberg became the first female Captain and in 1998 an entirely female crew took a SAS plane from Stockholm to Dublin.

Like many airlines, SAS suffered huge financial pressures from carrier consolidation, budget airline discounting, fuel prices and other factors. Eventually in 2012 the airline teetered on the brink of bankruptcy. All eight Trade Unions involved with the company approved a draconian package of employment and pay measures that saved the business. It's doubtful that a company with a less forward-thinking mentality would have survived. Now of course in 2020 SAS is again battling with the impact of Covid and demands from non-travellers for ticket refunds. It will be a further test of the company's culture.

Standing still makes you a target		
Quality	SAS approach	Things To watch out for
Values Anchor	Stay anchored to core values whilst adjusting to new market realities.	Try to reinvent yourself and, in so doing, walk away from natural strengths of the organisation. Forget "who you are".

Adapt	Mind-set, organisation and mobile resources allow responsiveness to change.	Allow Fixed assets and debt to dictate strategy – even when it makes no sense in the longer term.
Innovate	Develop new competencies. Continually experiment with new routes to market, tactics & techniques. Learn to adapt quickly to changing situations.	Wait until things start to go wrong or until competitors have a head-start before investing in new capabilities.
Improvise	Creatively deal with local issues, thinking outside the box & conjuring new ways to win.	Adhere to conventional working practices even when ill-suited to a local situation.

Chapter Eight: Dare to ask for help.

No one gets to serve in the SAS unless they can back themselves. If ever there was an example of a man on his mettle it has to be the story of Colin Armstrong MM, *nom de plume* Chris Ryan, on-the-run survivor of infamous patrol Bravo Two Zero. The title of Chapter 4 of his book[66] is: 'Down to One' - by which he means he is accompanied by one other patrol member, an ex Australian dentist by the name of Stan. But Stan refuses to kill a passing goatherd, he is compromised and captured. Armstrong is truly now down to one. He starts the next chapter: '...*A wave of loneliness swept over me, as I realised I was utterly alone. I thought, "This can't get any worse." I was hungry, wet, tired, cut off from all communication with friends, and still far inside a hostile country.*' After a week of dodging Iraqi military, with no water let alone food, he staggers into Syria barely alive.

And yet quite often the story of the SAS is about accepting help from useful third parties rather than rejecting it. Indeed when Armstrong gets to Syria he is passed along a bewildering chain of farmers, para-military police, British Embassy officials, Army officers and even their wives before he eventually meanders back to his unit in Saudi Arabia. At the regimental level, strategic help of different sorts has been critical to the unit's success throughout its history - starting after the very first abortive raid.

---

66   The One That Got Away, Chris Ryan, Century 1995

Daring partners

Stirling woke up to find blood trickling down his face and his body being dragged across rocks and gravel by his parachute, inflated by the sandstorm. He punched the quick-release button and the canopy flew madly off into the dark night. In the howling wind he tried to find his colleagues.

They had taken off in five Bombay Bristol aircraft from Kabrit, Egypt and had bucketed around in storm clouds for some hours as they made their way towards the enemy targets in the Tmimi area of Libya. When the pilots of 216 Squadron descended to smoother weather beneath the clouds, the Italians and Germans over-compensated with flak and small arms fire that hit several of the aircraft. It must have been a relief when the paratroops finally got the green light and threw themselves out into the night air. One of the aircraft, carrying the team of Eoin McGonigal, simply disappeared and no trace was ever found of it, nor bodies buried or retrieved.

For the next two hours Stirling waved his torch and shouted in the wind as he tried to gather his men. They were a sorry bunch. Out of a dozen men there was at least one broken arm and no one had survived with less than multiple cuts and bruises. More importantly, the equipment containers had disappeared and the group was left with a handful of Lewes bombs but no fuses, a few blankets and one day's food. In terms of offensive capability they only had their revolvers and limited ammunition. Stirling tried to salvage something from the situation by doing a reconnaissance but even this proved of no consequence and the whole party then trudged fifty miles through the desert back to the *rendezvous* with the Long Range Desert Group (LRDG). Thankfully, it rained or they might have all died on the march from dehydration because they had precious little water. When the LRDG column finally moved off, only 21 of the original 62 SAS participants in the raid were present. The remainder had been killed or captured.[67]

---

67   A History of the SAS Regiment by John Strawson, Secker & Warburg 1984

David Lloyd-Owen and his Long Range Desert Group had been pursuing their own brand of warfare rather successfully when the remnants of Stirling's mob stumbled into his camp at dawn on 20th November 1941. The LRDG was a reconnaissance unit that drove far behind enemy lines and monitored the movement of men and armour, vital intelligence for the Eighth Army. Like the SAS, it had suffered birthing pains at the hands of intransigent staff officers but finally got going. The key to its operations was concealment and the ability to travel up to 2,000 miles across Libyan sands. This, in turn, was only possible with lightly armoured vehicles. Anything heavier would have consumed too much fuel, requiring more transportation.....a circular logic that went nowhere. The consequence was that LRDG columns were very vulnerable to air attack. Stirling, on the other hand, intended to leave his calling card as far and wide as possible. And now his shambolic group had imposed itself after its abortive first raid, drawing unwanted attention and showing very little promise. Lloyd-Owen could have been forgiven for sending Stirling packing. Stirling, meanwhile, had been selling the idea of parachute insertion to his sponsors and wasn't necessarily in a mood to listen to anyone who doubted his ideas. It might have been an unhappy meeting.

What actually happened was that the two men sat down on a rocky outcrop at the top of a wadi and shared a mug of tea and started to talk. Lloyd-Owen was impressed by the fact that Stirling seemed completely unfazed by his failure and was already talking about his next outing. Perhaps, he suggested, his unit could provide a taxi service for Stirling's raiders, avoiding the need for parachutes, good weather and available aircraft? Stirling was a little doubtful. He wasn't sure whether his new brainchild could be put in the hands of this other group that would have to be masters of navigation, concealment and long range communication to succeed. But by the time the two parties had driven back to Siwa, with what he perceived as nonchalant ease, his mind was made up. In spite of the fact that the two units had contradictory goals, (the LRDG to remain hidden, the SAS to blow everything to pieces) they formed an unshakeable alliance. It is fair to say that the SAS could not have achieved its North African objectives without the LRDG and indeed the use of "Pink Panther" style vehicles has stayed with the regiment ever since.

At face value, his abortive first raid showed very little promise and indeed drew unwanted attention on the LRDG. But Lloyd-Owen could see advantages in working closely with Stirling's new group, namely the handy combination of surveillance and an executive arm. He was careful to ensure his new alliance worked. He loaned his ace navigator, Corporal Mike Sadler to Stirling to ensure that the SAS stayed on track. Stirling promoted him to Lieutenant and made him his personal driver. He was also less dismissive of the Staff Officers in Cairo. Stirling regarded such people as REMFs but Lloyd-Owen had a more balanced perspective; "Provided the separate aims of each (organisation) were not allowed to clash, there was no reason why they should not co-exist happily. In the event I think this was achieved pretty well, due in some measure to the tactful handling by the Operations Staff at GHQ."[68] What the SAS/LRDG example shows us is the overriding importance of having two leaders who have an unselfish interest in making their alliance work and of two cultures that share similar values.

Such complex partnerships exist in business and they need careful handling. According to the Harvard Business Review between 70% and 90% of mergers fail, when measured against some standard criteria such as shareholder value creation[69]. There are various explanations according to David Garrison, CEO Profitable Engagements, but all tend to have a very human dimension:

Hubris fuelling false beliefs
Lack of understanding of the company's success factors
Absence of a people inventory
Unclear social compact between leadership teams

---

68   Providence their guide, David Lloyd-Owen, Harrap 1980

69   Most Mergers Fail Because People Aren't Boxes, Forbes, David Garrison, June 24 2019

Around the Millenium I was the CEO of a News International Internet company called Revolver.com. Initially I worked for a lady called Susan Boster, who had already made a very good living from Barnesandnoble.com, the Internet arm of the US bookseller. In our group was also an auction site called Firedup.com and Page3.com, a celebration of The Sun newspaper's Samantha Fox and friends. Simply stated, Susan's vision was to eat the lunch of News International's print advertising department. Thirteen years later, print advertising revenues worldwide have declined dramatically and recruitment websites like Revolver proliferated. At the time, it was an uneasy alliance because, whilst relationships within News were civil, the unavoidable fact was that our P&Ls were inversely linked, rather than being mutually beneficial. The extent of our synergy was little more than Revolver's purchasing, at cost, of newspaper print advertising to push our wares to a less Internet-aware nation. In time we combined print and Internet propositions but by then the bubble of 2000 had burst and the moment lost. Balancing the needs of the two parties were News bosses Les Hinton and Camilla Rhodes, both of whom were very helpful to me in ensuring that the two parties kept things on an even keel. Over the last twenty years I've talked to many CEOs who have attempted to combine start-ups or skunkwork businesses with large commercial motherships and these kinds of problems are far from unusual. Just as with the SAS/LRDG partnership, they require two bosses who assume positive intentions on the part of their opposite number and a little help from senior sponsors.

There are, of course, many much better known examples in business of two companies trying to form a strategic partnership that leverages the best of what each party has to offer. The collaboration between Disney and Pixar is a case in point. Disney had been stuck in a rut creatively and needed access to the advanced animation skills used by Pixar. For Pixar, as well as a financial lifeline, the deal offered access to Disney's sophisticated distribution network, a factor that can so easily make or break a movie. Disney turned Pixar into a household name and Pixar gave Disney the means to move into the future with enhanced and visually striking animation.

When the $26 million deal was struck in 1991, Pixar was to produce three animated films, it worked well for a period. However, the two companies were only part way into the three part deal when the cracks began to show. Following the success of Toy Story, the two parties had disagreements over the production of Toy Story 2. No one had really thought about sequel rights in the initial discussions and Pixar didn't feel the on-going distribution deal was fair. Steve Jobs, the combustible Apple founder who also headed Pixar, also wasn't happy with the Disney-dictated November release dates, preferring the more school-holiday friendly summer months, followed by DVD release for Christmas. Eventually what had been a profitable relationship became unmanageable. Disney took ownership of Pixar in 2006 for a hefty price tag of $7.4 billion and in doing so it ironically also made Jobs Disney's single biggest shareholder.

The Disney-Pixar tie-up was hardly a disaster. Toy story 3 grossed $1 billion and all of Pixar's other animations sit in the top fifty movies of the category. Between them they have earned twenty-seven academy awards. Nonetheless, it was not a marriage made in heaven. In Walter Isaacson's biography of Jobs he paints a picture of two clashing person-alities, Disney CEO East Coaster Michael Eisner and West Coaster Jobs. Neither man appeared overly interested in each other's opinion. In fact, in 2002 Jobs talked to Roy Disney, Board member and nephew of founder Walt, and said that he wouldn't continue the relationship with Disney as long as Eisner stayed at the helm. Eisner hit back with rather ill-advised criticism of Pixar's next movie, *Finding Nemo*, that found its way into the Los Angeles Times. In due course Jobs and Eisner went their separate ways and we need not dwell on their deteriorating relationship. However it's interesting to note that, whereas the Stirling/Lloyd-Owen partnership worked well in spite of potentially conflicting aims, the Jobs/Eisner relationship was fraught when they so obviously had so much to benefit from each other.

But conflict is not inevitable. Contrast the Disney/Pixar battles with Cisco, a company that has made around 200 acquisitions and reckons that c.87% of key employees were still with the company two years after the various mergers. Although a technology business, Cisco has always recognised that it's acquisitions are more to do with people and their creative competencies than code.

Daring sponsors

For most of its history the SAS has been blessed with unambiguous support at the highest level. Although Stirling was a junior officer when he founded the SAS, he probably received more attention than he deserved from General's Ritchie and Auchinleck because of what might be termed "the old boy network". Ritchie served in the Black Watch regiment and would have been acquainted with Stirling's father, Brigadier Archibald Stirling. David's cousin was Lord Lovat, a celebrated Commando leader, and a fellow Scots Guards officer. Lovat was four years older than Stirling but they both attended Ampleforth School. You get the sense that, whilst separated by some distance in rank, all these men were part of a Scottish officer aristocracy that looked after its members.

In the 1980s the SAS had some impressive patronage. Margaret Thatcher was a big fan after episodes like The Falklands War, Iranian Embassy Siege and Peterhead prison. When the IRA attempted to murder her in Brighton in October1984 she was only too happy to have the SAS seeking out her would-be killers in Ulster. In the months that followed there were vigorous SAS operations against an IRA team planting an IED, two groups planning the murders of off-duty Ulster Defense Regiment soldiers and others returning weapons to a large cache. By February of 1985 seven IRA men had died in these operations at the cost of one SAS casualty, Alistair Slater, a man who had previously been a minor TV star in the documentary series 'Meet the Paras'.

Perhaps the most controversial SAS operation of all, Operation Flavius, occurred in Gibraltar in 1988. Three members of an IRA team planning a bomb outrage in the colony were intercepted by the SAS and shot dead at the reconnaissance stage of their mission. Questions arose when it was discovered that the terrorists were unarmed and hadn't yet driven their car bomb into the area but the soldiers made their risk assessment and acted upon it. When Thames Television produced a documentary on the affair called 'Death on the Rock' Mrs. Thatcher was outraged, saying: "If you ever get trial by television…that day, freedom dies." Her loyalty to the SAS and military in general was unshakeable. When Thames lost its franchise in 1991 at least one senior executive thought this a reflection of her ire.[70]

Meanwhile, HRHs Prince Charles, Princess Diana, Princess Anne and even The Queen were occasional visitors to the "Killing House" and familiarized themselves with how the SAS would likely attempt to liberate them in the unfortunate event they were taken captive by terrorists. Charles took it in good humour and handed the troops a piece of headed notepaper saying; *"Should this demonstration go wrong I, the undersigned Prince of Wales, will not commit B Squadron 22 Special Air Service Regiment to the Tower of London. Charles."* Which was just as well because Diana's hair got singed when a stray pellet from a flash-bang landed on her head! If anyone ever doubted the stoicism and resolve of The Queen they would have been persuaded by what occurred in the Killing House. As part of CRW training, SAS soldiers sometimes pose as live hostages, sitting between terrorist targets inside one of the range rooms. The reason for this is so that they can experience what it's like to have a flash-bang thrown in their vicinity and to have troops burst in and engage targets either side of them with live rounds. This gives them a better appreciation for how hostages will likely react to an assault. It's pretty hairy and it occasionally goes wrong. A colleague of mine received burns to his face from a grenade and, on one tragic occasion another was fatally injured when he received a round to the back of the head from a fellow assaulter. When The Queen visited the Regiment she insisted on going through the exercise and, whilst she didn't get a stun-grenade in the face, she did sit quietly whilst two men burst into the room in the full black kit and fired a dozen rounds at four hundred meters per second into two targets either side of her. She didn't flinch.

---

70   David Elstein, Our Kingdom 2009

The Queen's personal bodyguard was also trained by an SAS VIP Protection expert. This particular area of expertise endeared the regiment to a host of domestic and foreign VIPs who felt safer for their services. Not only did SAS soldiers protect visiting dignitaries in the UK but exported their expertise via training teams to a whole range of police and local VIP protection units in the Gulf States and elsewhere. US President Bush was delighted when a team abseiled onto the roof of a building in Kandahar, Afghanistan and liberated a CIA agent held captive by Al-Qaeda, who would otherwise have met a terrible end. The controversial US Special Forces general Stan McChrystal built a strong rapport with SAS commander Richard Williams throughout his period in Afghanistan and was hugely supportive of SAS operations. Of course in Operation Desert Storm, the first Gulf War, the second in command of Allied Forces was general Sir Peter de la Billiere, my gym buddy and himself a career SAS man. He ensured the regiment a prominent role and their actions were later publicly lauded by the overall commander, Marine General "Stormin'" Norman Schwarzkopf. The SAS has always had powerful friends.

The benefits of high-level support are obvious; leaders feel encouraged, resources are made available, value is added to strategy and mistakes used as learning opportunities rather than reasons to fire people. However, in order for this support to be fully effective, it is also necessary for sponsors to have a good understanding of the people and organisations they are involved with. When Harold Wilson ordered the SAS to patrol the streets of Belfast in their open-top Land Rovers in 1976, he was demonstrating an appreciation for their deterrent value but a negligible understanding of how the SAS best operated or, indeed, how the terrorists would likely prosecute their own nasty brand of warfare. According to well-placed sources, Wilson was also concerned at the time that he and his government were being threatened by a military putsch because of his left-wing leanings. This was said to involve MI5, elements of the Army and possibly Lord Louis Mountbatten. To be fair to Wilson, he volunteered for wartime service but was deemed more useful in the Civil Service working on issues like the Trade Cycle and

Unemployment. Consequently, for a man of his era, he had a rare lack of understanding of warfare and no taste for getting involved in things like the contemporary US adventure in Vietnam.

In business, sponsorship comes in different shapes and forms; private equity investors, lenders, Board Chairmen and Non Executive Directors. There are also "anti-sponsors" like activist shareholders, or hedge fund managers taking short positions because they don't like what a company is doing or looking to a sale, purely as a way of dramatically enhancing returns. In Fortune/FTSE businesses senior managers often spend a lot of time trying to win such people over. But this is very unlike the SAS who "just get on with it" and tend to win friends through their actions rather than extensive schmoozing. I once worked in a private equity portfolio company for Cornel Riklin, a CEO who had previously been a partner on the investment side of PE (TPG) which gave him a dual perspective. It was interesting that, whilst we held Board meetings in the usual way, he had a strong sense of owning business strategies and limited appetite for "upwards delegation" of decision-making. The conclusion is that senior sponsors are there to give support, encouragement and advice too but they are not a substitute for on-the-ground leadership (unless things have gone wrong). On the flip-side, if I were to pick out a great Chairman I have worked for it would be Paul Walker, now an establishment figure but originally one of the first four employees of Sage, the £8Bn software company. There's no substitute for "combat" experience.

Force Multiplication

Sometimes governments send their troops into combat but quite often they prefer to fight wars by proxy. There are a couple of advantages to this approach. The first is that a government may wish to achieve a strategic outcome but distance themselves from the war itself, for political reasons. The second is the "force multiplication effect" of getting a third party to do the bulk of the work for you. For example, neither the US nor UK governments were very happy about the Soviet invasion of Afghanistan in 1979 but they weren't about to escalate the

Cold War by sending large numbers of "Advisors" 'into the country to help the Mujahideen. At first a team of CIA and MI6 officers used ex members of the SAS to provide the Mujahideen with guidance on how to attack a Soviet air base that housed twenty-four Mig 21 fighters[71]. They studied aerial photographs and detailed maps and effectively gave the Afghans an attack plan. Four weeks later all but one of those Migs was a smoldering wreck. In time, a group of ex SBS men started to operate in-country but they were ambushed by the Russians, their pack horses were shot up and they barely escaped with their lives. Finally – and this is not a very comforting thought – a group of Mujahedeen were brought to Britain and trained by more ex SAS men in a country estate in the Home Counties, all paid for by some shadowy third party. As you could imagine, the fighters were highly motivated but lacked organization, tactical understanding and communications skills. The SAS men developed these skills in them but also attended to other needs. The Afghans were malnourished and vitamin deficient and these things were addressed. They were also taken up for helicopter rides so that they could appreciate the limitations of the Soviet Hook and Hind aircraft, for example in terms of ground surveillance. In short, they were shown how to defeat a large, modern well-equipped army using guerrilla tactics. As the war escalated, they were subsequently supplied with British Blowpipe and US Stinger surface-to-air missiles, some of which have never been accounted for – and all of which are more than capable of bringing down a civilian airliner. On the other hand, it may allay concerns to know that these fighters were in the employ of Ahmad Shah Mansour, the "Lion of Panjshir", who was no friend of either the Taliban or Osama Bin Laden (with whom he had acrimonious dealings) and he was generally a force towards democracy and reconciliation as he became Vice President of post-Soviet Afghanistan. Whatever the political ramifications, there's no question the ex SAS men did their job rather well.

In business there are basically two ways of exercising the force

---

71   Ghost Force; The Secret History of the SAS, Ken Connor, Phoenix, March 2006

multiplication principle; the first is franchising, the second outsourcing. Outsourcing is the preferred solution when someone outside the organization has superior expertise, a concentration of resource or a specialty skill set that isn't economic to retain and hone in-house. So, for example, there are specialist helicopter and Hercules C130 pilots who support SAS operations but they are not "badged" SAS soldiers. It is better to rely upon the RAF to keep on top of this particular capability. All sorts of activities get outsourced in business but prominent amongst them are various types of IT. It's important for businesses to recognise the limitations of their own competence. I once worked for a business that needed to build websites and asked a third party supplier to produce them, incorporating some features that we thought were rather unique. The supplier agreed but insisted they be allowed to sell the enhanced products to others rather than giving us exclusivity over the intellectual property. Neither side could agree so we took the problem in-house. Six months and a couple of million pounds later we had a mess and the supplier was already selling a product incorporating our requirements in the open market. Ouch!

Franchising is much more analogous to the Afghan experience described above and it has two big advantages from the point of view of the franchisor. The first is that it allows a company to expand its brand footprint without having to commit excessive resources. In Afghanistan that means getting the Mujahedeen to do your fighting for you, in the High Street it means asking franchisees to put somewhere between about $500k and $1.5 million of their own money into their business, depending on which particular brand we are talking about. (7 Eleven is the world's most prolific franchisor). A by-product of this "skin-in-the-game" commitment is that franchisees will typically be highly passionate about making their investment work. Once again you could draw a comparison between a Western soldier posted on a tour of duty in Afghanistan who will doubtless do their best but unavoidably has less at stake than the indigenous population. It's instructive to think about the kinds of support the SAS hosts provided to their "franchisees";

Strategic direction (on the Mig airbase attack)

Training in core processes and skills (guerilla warfare techniques)

Key market insights (in terms of benefits and limitations of enemy helicopters)

Logistical support (such as missiles)

Welfare support (food and medicine)

On the ground support to get operations going (local SF team)

When you look at this list, it's not a bad framework for a commercial franchise operation. What's striking is that the "franchisees" of Mansour were being prepared and equipped to support the UK's foreign policy objectives but, when the SAS men thought about what was needed to accomplish this task, they sought a real understanding of the Mujahideen's on-the-ground needs and provided accordingly. You can also be sure they did this with humility and a real empathy for a group of people who had suffered invasion. This was not high-handed imperialism (although one could question this given all that has subsequently happened). Contrast this with a common complaint of franchisees in many of the world's major franchise systems, namely that they are forced to comply with strict operating guidelines, pay hefty monthly fees but receive remarkably little in return. It's also unfortunate that when companies like Forbes rank global franchisors they tend to take a largely financial perspective, citing average costs of store opening and the proportion of units that fail within a given timespan. We know, for example, that you need about $1.5 million if you fancy yourself as a McDonald's franchisee (of just one store) and that, statistically speaking, you have a 97.4% chance of still being in the business three years later. We also know that, on average, you will be provided with 840 hours training and linked to the Golden arches supply chain. So points 2, 4 and initially 6 above seem well covered but less is said about the other three considerations.

Around 1997 I had the task of rolling out the new YUM/Tricon culture and core operating processes to a range of franchisees from Latin America to Singapore. The previous year the company had run a survey for franchisees to gauge their satisfaction with the support they were receiving. The response was highly critical. Consequently, I was anticipating a cynical reception from many of the franchisees when I came to their markets peddling my wares. It's worth bearing in mind that, as with McDonalds, the cost of a franchise start-up is significant and consequently the smallest of my "Mom 'n Pop" customers was pretty financially successful. The larger ones included companies like Hong Kong based Jardines that were huge corporations in their own right. I thought they would probably send me packing. In the event I got the strong impression that the franchisees felt this more intimate support, even including discussions on company culture, was a very welcome departure. It was a pleasant surprise and an interesting corollary to the rest of this chapter; it's important to dare to *offer* help as well as receive it!

Expert Advice

Special Forces in modern Afghanistan now have an array of technology at their disposal; remotely controlled drones that can recognise faces or number-plates, phone tracking devices, satellite surveillance and even DNA testing, as deployed in the hunt for Osama Bin Laden. But none of this is entirely a substitute for human intelligence, small numbers of well-informed guides or local partners with an in-depth knowledge of the population and this has been a feature of SF warfare for a long time. In Chapter Three we heard about the crucial role the Iranian Embassy caretaker took in briefing the SAS before the assault. Back in 1953 a Troop of B Squadron were heavily reliant upon a trio of Iban headhunters as they patrolled the Pahang area of Malaya. A group of nine soldiers entered the Telom Valley area and soon bumped into one of the locals, complete with blowpipe and poisoned darts. He led them back to his longhouse where their translator asked the local headsman if he knew of any Communist Terrorists (CTs) nearby. He politely suggested they make enquiries across the other side of the valley – or at least that is how they interpreted the advice. As they crossed the valley they found an established path and were about to proceed into the village when they saw a well-dressed individual approaching. The lead Iban scout instantly shot the man with his Tommy Gun and the group withdrew to cover. It was just as well. They were about to stumble into a major camp of over one hundred enemies! For all the SAS's arduous jungle patrolling, it was the first "kill" they had had in twelve months but it wasn't a British soldier who took the scalp but an Iban headhunter.[72]

B *Who are your most important business partnerships? How mutually beneficial are they?*
I *What sacrifices would you be willing to make to help your partners be successful?*
L *How clear are you on what you bring to the party? Does your partner share your perspective? How open are you about your mistakes or short-comings with them?*
L *How do you feel about "placing yourself in their hands"?*

If the SAS patrol hadn't availed itself of local expertise it would likely have been annihilated. To get to that point, four steps were necessary. The first was to acknowledge the limitations of their own "market understanding" and not to muscle into unfamiliar territory, hoping to win purely on the basis of Speed-Aggression-Surprise. The second was to select a group of helpers whose goals were aligned with those of the SAS soldiers. In Malaya, the Communist Terrorists (CTs) were largely Chinese and their allegiance was to the expanding post-War Communist Bloc, not the indigenous population of Dayaks and Iban. Consequently, the Iban guides were as keen to see the CTs defeated as their British paymasters. Thirdly the guides needed to have genuine, detailed local knowledge, rather than being, say, opportunists out to make a quick buck at the soldiers' expense. The final prerequisite was for the troops to treat the Iban scouts well, to respect their customs and let them do their job. In any theatre of war, where any one of these steps are missing it can quickly have fatal consequences, as the coalition forces have found out to their cost in Afghanistan.

---

72   An Adventure with the SAS, Tony Beveridge

Acknowledge limitations of own market knowledge

Identify helpers with aligned objectives and a genuine ability
to deliver competitive edge

Respect the helpers' expertise and let them do their job

The selection and use of experts is an important feature of business life. Mars always tried to avoid importing consultants, preferring to rely upon its own expertise. At least one company I have worked for seemed positively addicted to them. Perhaps what matters is not whether outside experts are used more or used less but whether they are used *correctly* according to the criteria above. The genuine alignment of interests can be problematic territory. In business most professional services firms have developed billing models that reward quantity of work and expansive timesheets, rather than getting to the overall objective as quickly and as cheaply as possible. In the longer term, of course, they will need to be seen to help the client achieve their outcome but, if we live with the analogy a little longer, they are quite happy to lead the patrol around the jungle for a couple of extra weeks before they locate the CT camp if it means a bit more pay. A spectacular example of this phenomenon sometimes occurs with financial restructurings. A whole group of advisors, bankers and lawyers gather round the trough of a company that needs a new balance sheet and gorge themselves until they can see that any free cash is sitting comfortably in their bellies. (To avoid being sued I won't cite examples!) They are unlikely to be bullied into a fixed fee based on an agreed outcome. The purchase of Information Technology (IT) expertise can also leave companies vulnerable and particularly where projects are not being paid for by shareholders but by powerless tax-payers. When the Commons Public Accounts Committee looked at the National Health Service's IT program (hilariously christened Nipfit) they reckoned at least £2.7 billion of the total £11.4 billion bill was utterly wasted. The program was eventually abandoned, which rather raises a question mark over the remaining £8.7 billion!

Of course not all experts are greedy or incompetent. Most are well-intentioned but they may also have a tendency to try their hand at tasks that sit outside their core area of competence if they see a good opportunity and think that a dose of common business sense will see them through. This can be a false economy. To quote legendary American fire-fighter Red Adair; "If you think it's expensive to hire a professional, wait until you hire an amateur." Similarly, managers that hire consultants sometimes do so as a kind of insurance policy rather than because they need a special type of expertise that lies outside their department. Either situation is low value-added. Experts must be carefully chosen, aligned with the businesses interests and not allowed to obstruct the 'Lead/Follow/Get out of the Way' imperative.

No man is an island

It is an irony that an organisation that places so much emphasis on the independence and accountability of each individual soldier must also be consummate at leveraging all sorts of help from third parties. If you are trying to do something very difficult and original with only limited resources, it stands to reason that you are going to need some help and the SAS is no exception.

> B *Are people in your organisation loyal to each other or is it a case of "every man for himself"? Can you be counted on?*
> I *Are sponsors engaged and informed enough so that they can give the support they would wish? Do you ever conceal bad news from them? Is that smart?*
> L *Do senior bosses have your back - in good times and bad?*
> L *Do you ever get addicted to advisors? Do they rip you off or cost you more than they save?*

Daring to ask for help		
Quality	SAS approach	Things To watch out for
Sponsorship	Capture the imagination of senior sponsors & harvest their support.	Contrarian relationship with investors, Board members or other senior figures.
Partnership	Identify strategic partnerships, sometimes in the "co-opetition" category. Develop symbiotic relationship that benefits both parties.	As market dynamics change, drift into new competence areas that company is ill-equipped for, rather than seeking effective partners that can accelerate acquisition of new capability.
Force Multiplication	Use franchising to extend & multiply impact. To do so effectively requires empathy for franchisees' goals & other management skills.	Treat franchisees as second-class citizens, less valuable than own employees. Lack expertise or credibility in their eyes.
Expert advice	Recognise critical value of experts steeped in local knowledge who will help you avoid what – to them – are obvious mistakes.	Commercial imperialism – one-size-fits-all approach when this clearly wont work in certain circumstances.

Chapter Nine: If you're not learning, you're becoming a liability.

The SAS exists in two states;

Learning to fight

Fighting, followed by learning

There is a principle at stake and it applies as much to business life as it does to the SAS. With technology and market or battlefield environments changing at an exponential rate, it is only through continuous learning that individuals can hope to keep up, let alone set the pace within their organisation. There is an "inter-connectedness" in the world today that wasn't there before - things can happen in a far away place or sector that have unexpected impacts on our own organisations. Technophobia, false pride in established methods and complacency have no place. Nor is there an age limit on learning. One of the things that has surprised me about my own career is that I would consider periods in both my forties and fifties to be amongst the richest learning opportunities of my life, something I wouldn't have anticipated in my youth. 10,000 hours is no more than a milestone along a journey that has no end.

Badged - Learning to Fight

The SAS has a term "to be badged" which literally means receiving the coveted sand-coloured beret and "winged dagger" cap badge, a mark of acceptance into the regiment. But it also means that a baseline of training has been achieved. Basic training includes navigation, jungle warfare, escape and evasion, resistance to interrogation, parachuting and anti-terrorism. (In the Appendix to WDWiB I enclose an article I wrote for Huffington Post, in the wake of 3 deaths on Selection, questioning whether training methods need to better reflect a technology-based battlefield.[73] I hope this demonstrates an appropriate lack of complacency.) Once "badged" the soldier undertakes whichever specialist training pertains to the method of entry into hostile terrain practiced by his Troop. My own troop was Boat Troop, which meant being wet a lot of the time and training with the Royal Navy and Royal Marines. I learnt to dive with a closed-circuit oxygen rebreathing apparatus and, specifically, how to avoid getting oxygen poisoning by diving no deeper than nine meters, whilst simultaneously avoiding being run over by the Isle of White Car Ferry. On other occasions I practiced a hair-raising technique which involves zooming around in a Gemini inflatable and then making a rendezvous with a submarine using a sonar device before manoeuvring onto the ship's deck without getting sliced in two by the hydroplanes. Such moments are memorable.

Each troop had its speciality. Air Troop members would face their own "Car Ferry Conundrum" when required to parachute from the altitude of a commercial airliner, at night and carrying heavy equipment, only opening the chute two or three thousand feet above the ground. This technique is known as HALO (High altitude low opening). A variant on this is HAHO, where soldiers drop from the same extreme height but deploy their chutes early and glide over huge horizontal distances to their target. This was a technique that was used in a live combat situation in the Anbar region of Iraq in 2008. An isolated farm was the home to a counterfeiter who was literally printing money for Al-Qaeda. Members of B squadron jumped from a C130 Hercules and used HAHO to land silently in the vicinity of their target. They dumped their rigs, moved in on foot and adequately laundered the problem.

Training could be miserable, fun or even funny. Miserable was a

---

73   Huffington Post, Has the SAS Gone Soft? The Author, 11 Aug 2015

resistance to interrogation program that left me with a muscle spasm in my lower back and frostnip in my toes that stopped me sleeping for weeks. I couldn't take painkillers because I spent most of the day running around with a HK MP5 submachine pistol with the safety catch off and drugs wouldn't have been sensible. Fun was parachuting into the sea with a gentle splosh instead of the usual bone-jarring crunch on land. Funny was watching my good friend Miguel developing his Hollywood-style get-away driving technique. In the movies you see stuntmen reverse a car at high speed and spin it through 180 degrees before roaring off in the opposite direction. It's quite a difficult thing to do and the stuntmen often cheat by having a modified gearbox. Without this you have to spin the wheel, yank the handbrake and then release, change gear and synchronise it all with the accelerator pedal. It's not easy, as Miguel discovered. He did all of the above but only managed a 90 degree spin before charging headlong into a ditch, which left the car standing vertically on end and Miguel scrunched up against the windscreen. It's the only time I saw an entire SAS troop cry with laughter.

For the incorrigibles who actually want to do these types of training, the world (Covid aside) is now a place of limitless opportunity. You don't need to volunteer for the *Who Dares Wins* TV programme or even join the TA to access paramilitary experiences. Ultra fitness, previously centered on an Ironman formula, now includes a global calendar of adventure racing in deserts, jungle and even Arctic terrain. Less time-consuming are Tough Mudder courses, Barry's Boot Camp and other forms of military fitness. With the parting of the Iron Curtain it's now possible for civilians to attend a Tactical Field Firing Course in Poland where students fire the Glock 19 pistol, AK 47, HK MP5 and US M4 in a variety of simulated anti-terrorist situations. An IT manager who worked for me recently visited a supplier in Ukraine and was taken on an excursion where he fired the main armament of a tank! If you don't have time to learn to parachute but want the free-fall sensation, you can do a tandem-jump or visit Airkix in Manchester or Milton Keynes where you can float above a column of air in an indoor simulator. Or if you want to emulate Miguel and do some stunt-driving there are several places you can do it such as Stunt Drive UK in Gloucestershire. More hard-core are pre-deployment courses for people like journalists and NGO workers or VIP protection training. And then of course there are the usual local rock-climbing, canoeing and SCUBA clubs. Adventure training has never been more accessible (and happily to a broader section of society).

Beyond Technology

Whatever you want it's now pretty much there. But of course this book is not about mobilising business people or turning everybody into members of the SAS. The "Badging" principle has more to do with establishing a baseline of competence and delivering it via a comprehensive series of training interventions. Stirling's nemesis Ernst Rommel once said; "The best form of welfare for soldiers is training – and plenty of it." In the context of a wartime army it makes total sense. A more highly trained soldier is more likely to survive the battlefield. You could argue that exactly the same applies in business. For example, sections of the Financial Services industry see many roles as being prone to replacement by AI in the medium term. As a consequence, several of the banks now require their junior staff to develop coding skills, presumably so that they can create the robots rather than become their victims.

It's not just junior staff that require training. In fact the "training dividend" is likely to be much greater when senior managers are involved - particularly if they can be invigorated with fresh thinking. When European Directories, a print advertising company, were confronted by the need to adapt to new Internet-based realities they began by recruiting Simon Greenman, an executive who had founded a digital mapping company and understood concepts like SEO/SEM[74]. A Brit, Simon was based in Colorado and held an MSc in Artificial Intelligence combined with a Harvard MBA. In due course the company also poached Ben Legg, COO of Google Europe, and an alumnus of various organisations

---

74   Search Engine Optimisation/Marketing

including Coke, McKinsey and the Siege of Sarajevo. Between Simon and Ben they had a formidable list of Silicon Valley contacts. A plan was hatched to take the Chairman, all the CEOs and functional leaders on a 3-4 day field trip into Silicon Valley, the objective of which was not merely to learn about what companies like Google did in more detail, but to start to give everyone a visceral sense of what it feels like to operate like the "co-opetition" (companies that can either compete with, or compliment your own offering).

The program began for most people with a 6 a.m. jog around the campus of Stanford University. If that sounds like Boot Camp, it was a very apt wake-up call. The brightest brains on the planet were already doing laps of the pool and the athletics track in the early morning sunshine and these were exactly the people who were going to eat their lunch, before my group usually even sat down for breakfast. The next few days were a whirlwind in a minibus. The first person the group met at Google was Francoise Brougher, VP Business Operations. She talked about everything from strategic business challenges to utilising satellites to alleviate Third World problems. After lunch at Google's giant warehouse canteen we rushed from on-line video start-up Ooyala to SME software provider Intuit where they met founder Scott Cook, a man with spectacular wealth and wisdom in equal measure whom we met in Chapter three. They had dinner with Sierra Ventures and breakfast with bankers from Jefferies. They visited Skype, Marketo and stumbled around office buildings until they found the new home of mobile App's provider XAD. By now they were in San Francisco and after breakfast on the third morning climbed the stairs into a quintessential warehouse office of Branchout, brainchild of Rick Marini, a man who had already made a fortune from Superfan and Tickle, which he sold to Monster for $100 million. These people were all very different; some calm and thoughtful, others spontaneous and charismatic. All of them had a sense of purpose and urgency and one thing became very clear; either print advertising people could learn from these folks, adapt to their ways and work with them, or they could watch them effortlessly obliterate the industry. It was both sobering and uplifting at the same time. Did the program make a difference? Lessons were learned and valuable insights shared but it would be naïve to think that a seasoned group of CEOs would experience an overnight conversion to Silicon Valley thinking after only a few days in California. But, somehow the group had turned a corner and, from here, there was no going back.

B *If you are in a leadership position, what training and formative periods have you had that qualify you for this unique role? Is there a match between your job title and your leadership expertise?*

I *Is development in the organisation aligned with the needs of the company strategy?*

L *Are training programmes stretching enough?*

L *"Don't be intimidated by what you don't know". (Sara Blakely, Founder & CEO Spanx) How bravely do you tackle the unknown?*

Beyond Profit

Talking of turning corners, the world is no longer driven by economist Milton Friedman and the God of profit. ESG - Environmental, Social & Governance - issues are now an absolute prerequisite for senior management and insisted upon by Millennial and other right-thinking staff. But is it possible to *train* executives to think more dynamically around this subject? The Times columnist Patrick Hosking is sceptical[75]. He quotes a hedge fund manager, Dan Loeb, who is concerned about; "… the move towards pleasing ill-defined stakeholders" allowing managers "simply to camouflage their own incompetence." Hosking believes that the profit motive is in danger of getting replaced by 'cant, hypocrisy and muddle.' Is he being too cynical?

Unfortunately, I think he may be right. How could Bernie Madoff successfully con so many intelligent, prominent people out of billions

---

75   The Times, Greed may be dead, but who says the new corporate creed is any better? Patrick Hosking, 22 September 2020

of dollars when the respected fraud investigator and forensic accountant Harry Markopolos had already spelt out to regulators, in graphic detail, what he was up to? Did it never occur to anyone that the sprawling banking business of Texas financier Allen Stanford couldn't legally make the guarantees on investment returns that it did or that it was odd, to say the least, that such a wealthy corporation should run its affairs from an office above a fish and chip shop? Both Madoff and Stanford were subsequently convicted of massive ponzi schemes which cost their victims millions. Far from learning a collective lesson, Goldman Sachs executives positively embraced the overtures of Jho Low, a 27 year old financier who fleeced the Malaysian people of billions of dollars in what became known as the 1MDB scandal[76], whilst living an impossibly lavish lifestyle. Interest has waned in the convicted paedophile Jeffrey Epstein after his suicide in a New York prison but, sex and trafficking crimes aside, no one seems very clear on how he accumulated such astonishing wealth in the first place. Similarly, how could so many intelligent people in the financial sector allow the subprime bubble to expand so catastrophically without contemplating the consequences? And how is it possible that Enron, Global Crossing, Kmart, Worldcom and the rest could succumb to complex accounting scandals? The banks were just as bad, as Lehman, Barings and Anglo Irish have proved. The answer, at least in part, is because an awful lot of people focused on their near-term objectives and rewards and chose to somehow ignore the towering black cumulo-nimbus that had already covered most of the sky.

Fast forward to the present and the world is being hammered by two new ESG-related threats. The catastrophe that is Covid19 was entirely predicted by the hugely informed figure of Bill Gates in 2015. Gates locks himself away for days at a time in his luxurious man-cave in his Medina home Xanadu 2.0 (!) and studies medical issues and the science that surrounds them. In a Ted talk Gates explained exactly how

---

76   Billion Dollar Whale: The Man who fooled Wall Street, Hollywood and The World, Tom Wright & Bradley Hope, Scribe 2019

an epidemic might unfold and put forward a five point action plan:

Strengthen health systems in poorer countries
Create a medical reserve corps
Pair with military logistics and mobility
*Do simulations "germ games" (last done in 2001 - with very
    disappointing outcomes)*
Conduct advanced R&D on diagnostics and vaccines

Gates concluded that time is not on our side but the ebola outbreak should serve as a clear early warning signal to get cracking immediately. In fact he only got one thing wrong. He estimated that an epidemic would likely cost c.$3 Trillion. The World Economic Forum is now estimating a Covid cost of $8-16 Trillion.

How about the environment? I once sat at a Board dinner with a wealthy, powerful figure who told me that he had studied climate change at university (in 1970 when?) and was convinced that the change was part of Earth's natural cycle rather than a man-induced problem. (He also believed Gary Linneker should be prime minister. Since my wife was friends with the mother of Linneker's four children, who he dumped for a lingerie model, I wasn't enthusiastic about this latter suggestion). There is a proportion of climate scientists who would support his view. The other 97% don't. And yet this man is a highly numerate financier. If someone came to him with an investment proposition with 97% of experts advising that - even if not conclusively proven - he was *at least likely* to lose money he would laugh in their face. To be fair, he was in favour of climate change management, whatever the causes, but the logic of my observation stands.

So maybe Hosking has a point. If you take the three letters E, S, & G businesses track record is not simply dodgy but lamentable. But what sort of training would actually have an impact? People have different learning styles. For some the most impactful training may come in the form of a scientific paper. But this book is an "SAS book" and the SAS has a strong bias for action-based learning. I happen to share that tendency.

Vanishing trees and ice-sheets

To the extent that it matters, my own perspective on sustainability has been shaped through practical experiences. There is plenty of data on deforestation in places like Kalimantan. It's graphically described, for example, in Leonardo DiCaprio's documentary 'Before the Flood'. But my exposure to deforestation was more personal. As a jungle warfare instructor I often looked for areas of terrain that would be good for navigation training. On one occasion I found an area that would be testing for my students. It was an alluvium plane, a flat area either side of a meandering river with multiple smaller tributaries. In the jungle rivers are the highways but on this occasion the many streams would lead the soldiers all over the place unless they paid close attention to their compasses. I walked the course, returned to base and then awaited the arrival of my students who would fly in from Hong Kong in two months time. When the day came for the navigation exercise I briefed everyone in detail, explained the challenges and urged the guys to be thoughtful at every turn. We jumped in the Hueys and flew to the area about half an hour away from camp. I was too shocked to be embarrassed. The entire valley had been stripped to sand. Barely a leaf remained. And for what? A handful of hardwood trees.

Some years later I travelled to Antartica with environmentalist Robert Swan, the cousin of my SAS Squadron Commander. Once again you didn't need to read the scientific papers to understand what's happening in the polar regions. You could observe the Larsen B ice-shelf falling to pieces in front of us. Do trees and icebergs matter? I recently completed a stint as governor of St Mary's Bryanston Square Primary School in Marylebone. It was a great school but with one unwanted distinction. A survey showed that its playground air was the most polluted of any school in the Greater London area. To give Sadiq Khan his due, the Mayor spent a whole morning at the school and imposed a 'no idling' ban on the road beside the playground. Things improved a little. My two youngest children, students at UC Berkeley, woke up a few weeks ago to an orange sky. California was on fire. There's just too much eye-watering (literally) evidence to argue the point any more. Air, land and sea are a mess and business leaders need to acquire a whole new sense of urgency. It's no accident that I now sit on the Board of Inventure, a Los Angeles based executive search firm that focuses on hiring for green energy and other advanced technologies.

Action-based learning - in the Antarctic

My friendship with Rob Swan began some fifteen years before that trip. Around 1990 I was tasked with organising a leadership conference for the top 100 managers in Mars Europe. This was no easy mission. They were an ultra high-achieving group with a lot of self-regard and Mars' in-built scepticism towards anyone who sat outside the organisation and claimed to know better. In desperation I went to the Deputy Director of the Royal Geographical Society, Nigel Winser, and asked if he knew anyone who could cut through a very thick layer of corporate ice. He immediately volunteered the name of Robert Swan. The conference assembled some weeks later in a hotel in Bonn. By this time I had designed the program and multiplied my exposure to the Robert Factor manifold by deciding to break his presentation into three short sections, using these as catalysts for discussion throughout the day. Not to put too fine a point on it, if Robert screwed up, the whole event would be a disaster.

In the event, Robert's speech was, quite simply, the most charismatic story I had ever heard. Its impact on my hard-boiled audience was little short of astonishing. In brief, Robert is the first man to walk unsupported to both North and South Poles and he has become a UN Goodwill Ambassador and an environmental evangelist. However, more important for our story, is the dexterity with which he linked his expeditionary lessons with business life. One of many lessons was the importance of combining a good mix of complementary skill sets when assembling teams. Even before they set out, a shy and awkward member of the team had proven invaluable when he pointed out certain short-comings in the expedition's logistic arrangements. When they arrived on the ice Robert's team included navigation experts, logisticians and doctors. However, more subtly, his groups comprised optimists like himself, cautious types, hard men and humorists. It was a mixture that kept them alive in some very trying circumstances. He talked about the importance of individuals taking care of themselves and exercising self-discipline since to do otherwise was to jeopardise the team. At the half-way point of the man-haul to the South Pole the group had to decide whether to press on with what supplies they had left or turn back. It was an entirely unsupported expedition (i.e. no radio or facility for aircraft rescue) and, as Robert said to his spellbound audience; "I'm sure in business you talk about "Commitment". Well I can tell you it was quite a moment to be committed" (to what was effectively a life or death decision). He explained that each day the party had to cross hundreds of crevasses and the person on point would therefore be entrusted with his colleagues' lives, over and over again. Robert politely wondered about how much delegation people feel comfortable with in business. Above all, he emphasised the need for effective communication between team members. There was no room for silo thinking or negativity in a group that was pitting itself against the coldest place on Earth. Since those days I have used Robert many times to energise leadership conferences around the world and he has always been tremendously effective. He was a keynote speaker at a PepsiCo conference in Austria that concluded with the management team going down the Olympic bobsleigh run. He spoke underneath The Shed at Chelsea Football Club to a European Directories leadership audience.

(In a hopeless attempt to out-gun Robert I followed up his talk the next year with a lecture from one of the world's most experienced astronauts, Mike Foale, who had been at Cambridge University with my brother. The verdict? Too much of a "me too" event. After all... *what is 374 days in space beside the challenge of selling candy bars?*)

After a 15-year friendship, Robert finally insisted that I get involved with one of his frozen junkets. He had built a program with the help of SAS man Bronco Lane (Mount Everest partner of Brummie Stokes, Chapter One) called 'Leadership on the Edge,' which involved taking groups of executives on expeditions to Antarctica. In the space of three weeks these groups sail from Ushuaia at the southern tip of Argentina, across Drake's Passage, to the frozen southern continent. On arrival they combine exploration with leadership training and, specifically, development of environmental strategies for the companies they represented. In the months leading up to the trip the CEOs of each of our subsidiary businesses selected high potential managers and a group assembled in London. It was a great trip full of icebergs, Force 9 gales, wildlife, glacier climbing, camping under the stars and other adventures. A few years later I organised for a second group to expedition with Robert and the experience was just as impactful. Since the first trip in 2003 the program has delivered training to some 640 managers of all ages and nationalities and attracted some heavy-hitting sponsors like BP and Coca-Cola.

Were these trips game-changers? Ask Annika Boberg, the Swedish sales manager from Halmstad. When she returned home she was interviewed by the local newspaper and her story occupied a double-page centre spread with lots of colour photographs. Her teenage son was flabbergasted and shared it with all his schoolmates. "Mum!" he exclaimed excitedly when he got home, "my mates can't believe what a cool mother I have!" That, my friends, is priceless currency.

The S in ESG

So much for the Environment - what about the "Social" ingredient of ESG? Building enthusiasm for this topic can be no less exciting and enjoyable. It may be a cliché but a good way to cope with life's setbacks and disappointments is to compare one's travails to the hardships of others. The whole area of CSR (Corporate Social Responsibility) is fertile ground in this respect. Vodafone, for instance, had a partnership with the United Nations Foundation which sees company employees providing communications support in disaster relief situations in trouble spots around the world. Trinity Mirror (now Reach) used to send employees into deprived areas of London to improve the literacy skills of under-privileged youngsters. More recently I was involved in a project that involved sending a team of high performing employees to an inaccessible part of Africa. The program was triggered by a chance meeting with an ex-Paratrooper called Chris Short. Chris and I had been Army friends but we hadn't seen each other for decades before I bumped in to him in London. Chris told me about his company, *Far Frontiers*, that ran expeditions to some quite exotic places including, at the time, Syria. His clients were mainly independent travellers and school children in search of adventure but by the end of a good lunch we had designed a program for high achieving leaders in my company. Fifteen kilometres north of the Ugandan town of Masaka is the Kinyerere Church of Uganda Primary School. This school serves a very poor rural community and many of the young students walk long distances to and from their villages to attend class each day. The school building itself was of rudimentary construction with a dirt floor and corrugated iron roof. Chris had befriended the school and suggested to me that we send a group of high potential leaders to combine adventure, community service and leadership. All we needed was an expedition leader.

Before entering the world of politics full time, Tim Gordon (who became CEO Liberal Democrats) was our Group Strategy Director. Tim had previously spent a gap year teaching students in Zimbabwe. He was the perfect candidate. I bought the cheapest airline ticket I could find and dispatched him by some barely legal airline to Entebbe airport, famed only for Operation Jonathan, the spectacular attack by Israeli Special Forces in 1976. Tim and his team rumbled in battered trucks for hours along dirt tracks to the school and immediately set to with shovels, cement mixers and trowels, laying a new classroom floor and plastering walls. When they weren't hard at work, they were teaching a fun-loving crowd of kids how to play cricket and visiting the local game park.

Although the incentive lasted only a few days, the participants were incredibly moved by the experience, some welling up with tears as they returned to their businesses to tell their story. They also noted that many of the children had to make do with a single bowl of food per day. So when a second team returned to the school the following March under the leadership of Norwegian CTO (and Scout Leader) Tor Gisvold, they built a poultry house and filled it with over 100 chicks. This provided the children with food but also enough surplus eggs to bring in a little income from the neighbouring community.

I continued my friendship with Chris and - with a different company and a different group of high potential managers - tackled a new project in the High Atlas mountains of Morocco. This involved a Womens' refuge that was in need of refurbishment and once again generated a whole new set of powerful life experiences for the team members. Unfortunately my final program with Chris unravelled. We had lined up yet another project, this time involving the repair of a kraal for working elephants in Nepal. At the last minute Nepal suffered a severe earthquake and the group had to divert. Such programmes might seem expensive, time-consuming and less relevant than a functional training course. But in every case the participants were required to return to their companies and give presentations to all employees on their observations and lessons they had learned. Many created blogs and other social media to promote their ideas. Some visited schools and talked to the kids. If such activities can build genuine, deep ESG competence in our best, up-coming managers perhaps business won't continue to pollute, be ravaged by viruses, disrupted by conflict and fleeced by the likes of Bernie Maddof. If so, the costs will have been trivial by comparison.

B *Have you fully explored the areas of ESG as a potential source of employee development? What cool ideas have you had?*

I *If you like the idea of outdoor training but weren't interested in abseiling, what might you do that paid higher dividends?*

L *How often do your employees describe company training interventions as truly life-changing? Is that a realistic aspiration?*

L *How early in the year does the training budget get pruned? Is that OK?*

On The Job

In Spite of my enthusiasm for these adventures and training programmes, I'm inclined to agree with Netflix's core belief around development: 'We develop people by giving them the opportunity to develop themselves, by surrounding them with stunning colleagues and giving them big challenges to work on'. But this doesn't mean companies can't give people a gentle nudge. There are plenty of ways to give people rich learning experiences without leaving base camp. A good way to engage managers with the principle of recruiting for raw potential is to involve them directly in the selection and development of graduate or management trainees. At Vodafone we built an intensive trainee programme in conjunction with Henley Business School (now part of the University of Reading) and had the active sponsorship and involvement of our then-Chairman Sir Ian Maclaurin. Ian participated in panel interviews and took a personal interest in which of the aspiring managers would secure precious places on the programme. It was a bit like Sir Alan Sugar's Apprentice, except that nobody got fired! With Ian's leadership secured, it was relatively easy to persuade a whole caste of other senior managers to make themselves available for selection panels, group assessments and the subsequent workshops and MBA classes that followed. In doing so, they were forced to think a little more deeply about the characteristics of the types of people they wanted to assume key leadership positions within the future company. Of course, a subliminal by-product was that they also had plenty of time to reflect upon their own leadership behaviours.

In the last chapter we explored a range of opportunities: sponsorship, partnership, force multiplication and expert advice. Similarly, these may be matched against a whole host of on-the-job learning interventions that can improve skills in this area. Senior managers may better understand the role of sponsors by volunteering for Non Executive Directorships in other companies or by chairing working groups outside their functional area. They might also seek out senior mentors who will challenge their assumptions about the company or working life in general and provide coaching. Secondments to other functions, business units or even suppliers are a powerful way to build a better understanding of what partners do and empathise with their objectives. At the very least, it is important to regularly visit suppliers and listen to what they have to say. Working with franchisees, as I described in the PepsiCo/ YUM example, can also be professionally rewarding. There are many opportunities to seek help and managers may be both surprised and gratified when they see what happens when they do.

So much for "learning to fight".

Fighting, followed by learning

Reflecting upon what has gone right and what could have gone better is a neglected competence in business only addressed - at best - by the often hated Appraisal round. To the SAS it is a rich source of wisdom and the importance of this discipline is thoroughly explored in Mathew Syed's book Black Box Thinking.[77] Syed is a fascinating character; Olympic table tennis player, newspaper columnist and someone with a deeply enquiring - and somewhat contrarian - mind. Much of Syed's book (hence the title) focuses on the contrast between what goes on in the aviation and medical industries. The aviation industry has developed a rigorous process that forces every pilot, without prejudice to themself, to unambiguously document any accident or near-miss event. The principle is that each new failure should be examined and fine-tuned to ensure that the same problem cannot arise in the future. By contrast, deaths through maladminstered medical treatment only receive this kind of scrutiny where lawsuits are concerned and, even then, it's often a matter of an insurance based, out-of-court settlement. There is no sense that every death is a unique learning opportunity to be examined

---

77   Black Box Thinking, The Surprising Truth About Success, Mathew Syed, John Murray 2015

until every last learning has been eked out. Adopting this discipline is a fundamental building block of the learning organisation.

When you examine what happened with Stirling's first raid and Bravo Two Zero, certain clues start to emerge that signpost the possible origins of failure. As we know, Stirling's SAS ideas met with considerable scepticism and he had enjoyed thumbing his nose at his detractors when he conducted successful dummy sabotage runs on RAF airfields. He had made a bit of an exhibition of himself by bursting into the offices of the Top Brass in MEHQ Cairo on crutches and must have been excited when they backed him. In the weeks that followed he had run a stringent selection and training process with Jock Lewes and persuaded the L Detachment recruits that they were part of something special. He was probably also conscious of the fact that to-date he hadn't accomplished that much with his own life, either in or out of uniform. When you add these factors together it's pretty clear that the pressure would have been mounting in Stirling's mind to get on and prove his case to himself, his backers, his detractors and, most importantly, the soldiers under his command.

When the time came for the first raid, the weather conspired to exploit Stirling's one weakness; his reliance upon parachuting and his lack of expertise in this area. Stirling's immediate boss put no pressure on him to go and in fact suggested that he probably shouldn't because wind speeds were too high for jumping. Long after the war the view of surviving "Originals" (L Detachment members) was that, if they hadn't gone that night, the whole idea of the SAS might never have got off the ground, so to speak. But the evidence suggests otherwise. Even though the raid was a catastrophe, Stirling was allowed to continue with his project. So why would HQ have pulled the rug from under his feet, simply because he had opted for a short delay? In truth, Stirling had a brilliant idea, but it was nearly destroyed by an overwhelming desire to succeed in the short-term whilst ignoring the storm clouds that were, quietly literally, gathering overhead. As we saw in Chapter eight, without David Lloyd-Owen's far-sighted offer of partnership it might all have finished then and there. There is a famous book called 'On the

200

psychology of military incompetence[78]' and its title is self-explanatory. The SAS's first raid doesn't feature in it but what the book explores is exactly how these kinds of mental pressures can force leadership errors that, on the face of it, make no sense.

Happily, Stirling kept away from the HQ naysayers, rebuilt and re-purposed his team and went back into action. This time, he learnt his lesson and used long range desert vehicles rather than parachuting. On the next raid they destroyed 24 enemy aircraft, three weeks later a further 37 and six days after that, on Christmas Eve 1941, 28 more. As always, it was not without a price; on the last raid Lewes, effectively co-founder of the SAS, was strafed by a Messerschmitt 110 and killed. But Stirling had achieved his objective; the SAS concept was fully vindicated.

Less psychologically complex was the story of Bravo Two Zero, although the protagonists don't necessarily agree with each other on exactly what went wrong and why. There were problems with concealment, communications and emergency rendezvous procedures. The one thing that does tally with Stirling's experience was that senior commanders had, far from pressurising Mitchell, suggested that he might make life easier for himself by taking vehicles. Instead he forged ahead with his plans for a foot patrol which necessitated the group carrying so much equipment that they had to move it by shuttling backwards and forwards between the helicopter drop-off point and their destination, a forward observation post. By doing so, the patrol lost its essential mobility, a key attribute for SAS forces. Mitchell attributed his failure to the paucity of intelligence, others pointed to a lack of attention to key detail like radio frequencies and a failure to heed advice. Whatever the explanation, it is clear that intense pressure can focus minds but in doing so screen out other important decision-making factors.

After each mission the SAS stage a Post Operation debrief. Everyone on camp convenes in a lecture theatre and the participants run through what happened; what went well, what got screwed up, what they would

---

78   On the Psychology of Military Incompetence, Norman Dixon, Pimlico, 1994

do differently next time and the lessons learnt. It is an open, honest, no-blame discussion, the objective is to avoid repeating the same kind of mistakes in the course of future operations. Measuring the rate of return (IRR) on a commercial project and reporting this in a financial document is a common enough occurrence in business. However, I can't recall sitting in a room very often, listening to business people describing the errors and assumptions they had made that proved incorrect, the consequences and suggested learning points. More typically, the dogs bark and the camel train moves on. Sometimes the dogs even fight over the bonus scraps and bite each other.

Many successful people have said something along the lines of; if you're not failing from time to time, you're not trying hard enough. This doesn't make failure a virtue. The real question is what you do with it and, in particular, whether you use it as a learning opportunity. For example, Sir Stuart Rose, ex Chairman of M&S said; "If you only ever make one mistake, you are not pushing the boundary. The trick is not to make the same mistake twice." Self-examination takes self-confidence. As pancreatic cancer took hold of him and he faced death, Steve Jobs was keen that a biographer would record his life, neither praising nor excusing, but documenting the totality of his experience. Books, films and other testaments to Jobs' life are already proliferating, but of course the real monument to him is the multitude of Macbooks, iPhone, iPads and iTunes that sit in the homes and offices of the world.

Fail quickly and move on

Another key lesson in the realm of mistake making is to embrace the concept of "fast failure". This is endemic in the Internet space because the cost of web-based start-ups is so low that entrepreneurs can afford to try various new ventures without taking too much financial pain. You don't read many Business books about failure, which is perhaps understandable, and yet what leaders do with failure is incredibly important. Some sectors of the business community get this more

202

than others and American business people tend to be better than the British in this respect. The British seem firmly wedded to the notion that failure is something you are, rather than something you do. When I visit Silicon Valley in Northern California I meet entrepreneurs and Venture Capitalists (VCs) who consider failure a statistical inevitability and hence a factor to be baked into financial plans. All of this requires a working assumption that the experience of failure will not deter people from picking themselves up, dusting themselves off and trying again. In fact many VCs are serial investors in specific leaders and their loyal teams, sharing in their successes and allowing them room to experiment and, if necessary, fail. The archetypal entrepreneurial story is full of triumph and disaster, oscillating between a lavish lifestyle and unimaginable levels of debt but ordinary business life has more than its fair share of trauma in these straightened economic times and being able to manage this with equanimity is an important leadership competence. When things start to go wrong, it's very easy for a business boss to start wondering why their subordinates are struggling to implement their strategy. Much harder is self-examination.

The most damaging mistakes come from neglected values

After the Second World War, the SAS was disbanded, along with a number of other "private armies". The country was in the mood for peace and in any case the SAS now comprised both French and Belgian, as well as British troops, and they had to adjust to their new national realities. Stirling was liberated from Colditz and that might have been the end of the SAS adventure. During the war in the Far East a unit known as Force 136 had done a very good job of training Chinese guerrillas in Malaya to fight against the occupying Japanese forces. The group called themselves the Malay People's Anti Japanese Army. At the end of the conflict the same group now turned their attention to the returning British colonial masters. They saved on stationary by re-christening themselves the Malay People's Anti *British* Army! What followed was something that became known as the Malayan Emergency and, after some discussion, a long range patrol unit known as the Malayan Scouts (SAS) was formed to deal with the insurgency.

An ex-Burma Chindit and jungle warfare veteran called Mike Calvert was called in to create the unit – you may remember him from Chapter six ("Boots on"). Calvert successfully argued the case for the resurrection of the SAS but, when they formed, they did not share Stirling's cultural tenets. This posed the greatest threat to the survival of the SAS as a concept. Calvert was under pressure to get results and he wasn't particularly fussy about whom he recruited. There were veterans from the wartime SAS, SOE, Force 136 and Ferret Force but also a rag-bag of Foreign Legion deserters and other undesirables who drank too much, threw grenades at their officers ("fragging") and generally behaved in a way that drew no admiration from people like my father, who was serving as a regular infantry officer in Malaya at the time. A few of his men deserted and, when Calvert discovered that prostitutes were asking for payment with bullets and grenades, he doctored a few munitions and encouraged his men to "plant their devices"! Once again the regiment experimented with parachuting and, once again, the casualties piled up as they discovered how impractical it was to crash into the canopies of one hundred foot tall trees in primary jungle. Overall (not just parachuting) the SAS lost 28 men during the course of the Emergency out of an Army total 519. When 21 SAS moved in to support the unit they were singularly unimpressed.

Calvert was nicknamed "Mad Mike," both for his fearlessness, his skill with explosives but also his general behaviour. In 1951 he was sent back from the Far East to an administrative post in Soltau, a sleepy garrison town in Germany and it is here that his troubles really began.[79] Most probably gay, he invited a group of 17-20 year old youths back to his flat where he allegedly attempted to grope and kiss one of the men. He was found out, court-martialled and his life then spiralled out of control. Before long he was a down-and-out living on

---

79   The Shaming of A Hero, The Independent, 5 May 1999, Ann Treneman

the streets of Australia in a state of total inebriation, eventually selling his medals to survive. In the 1950s, homosexuality laws aside, there was very little in the way of a safety net for someone like Calvert. One hopes he would have fared better today and in fact towards the end of his life he was encouraged back to Remembrance parades by SAS veterans and died in Richmond, aged 85, a little more at peace with himself. This anecdote is not to suggest that Calvert's sexuality was somehow incompatible with SAS values. Although inconclusive, Stirling's biographer Alan Hoe quizzed him about his lack of female company and Ben Macintyre was even less circumspect when it came to Paddy Mayne. His "conflicted sexuality" was all but confirmed by journalists Martin Dillon and Mary Kenny, whose brother Carlos had been a drinking partner[80].

Nonetheless, in Malaya the regiment established useful new principles, like the application of "Hearts and minds" operations to woo local support and extended patrol durations to a record-breaking 103 days. In time, the weaker performers were weeded out and new officers brought in. Amongst them was Stirling's driver, Johnny Cooper, who ended up a Major in charge of B Squadron and Brian Franks. Men like Cooper and Franks drew the regiment back closer to its wartime roots and the more the unit realigned with its founding principles, the more resilient it became once again. Had they not done so, it is likely the regiment would have folded because it was reduced from four squadrons to two and its future relevance questioned by Whitehall.

When you are guided by a very clear set of principles you know what to do and when you ignore them you quickly get into trouble. Uber billionaire Travis Kalanick was on a roll until accusations of sexism, disputes with drivers and local authorities forced him out of office and ruined the company's reputation. Uber's "Bro-like" culture became increasingly inappropriate for a company of that scale. Similarly WeWork's credibility was damaged when Adam Neumann was accused of smoking dope on his private jet, hard-partying and

---

80   @MaryKenny4., Irish Independent Newspaper, 10 October 2016

other misdemeanours. It's not always bad behaviour that catches companies out, sometimes it's a focus on money that starts to eat into other important considerations. An article appeared in the Financial Times suggesting that blue chip accounting firm KPMG's obsessive focus on client billing was starting to make it an unattractive company to work for. Companies like retailer Bed, Bath & Beyond have been accused of corrosive cost-cutting at the expense of brand values. Julian Dunkerton, founder of fashion retailer Superdry, stepped away from daily running of the business and felt that his successor had little understanding or empathy for the products, customers and accompanying social media. Shares dropped like a stone. Dunkerton has now resumed control of the business and is hoping to get back to the core ethos of the brand.

The lesson from these organisations is not that culture alone will support a business and help it grow, but it is the key to its resilience. You still need to manage cost and capital, introduce and market new products and all the other things that keep a company competitive. But, if you want to sabotage a business, permanently and irrevocably, abandon the principles that made it successful in the first place. Wise companies react quickly when they think they may be making these kinds of mistakes. The first principle of Mars is *Quality*. Simply stated: "don't sell crappy products or cut corners". When some marketing managers thought they could squeeze margins a little by being measly with the chocolate coating on the Mars Bar, they got an instant wake up call from customers. There is a certain sensation when you bite into a Mars Bar and if the "bite height" changes it's just not the same. The Mars Bar was quickly restored to its former glory. Coca-Cola famously launched its New Coke product in an ill-advised attempt to improve upon what is arguably the most loved flavour on Earth. The initiative failed spectacularly and had to be reversed.

B *What psychological factors might force you towards a big mistake in your work area?*

I *How regularly do you review your mistakes (formally or informally)? Have you really learnt from them?*

L *Do your team members feel like they can make mistakes without getting s**t?*

L *Do you ever "sail close to the wind" on company values to get stuff done? Is that smart?*

The Training dividend

The purpose of this chapter is not to advocate less "business-y" development. Over the years I have worked on a number of programs with the IMD Business School in Lausanne, Switzerland, and found them to be particularly good at tailoring programs to the specific needs of different businesses. But even they also favour the use of analogies as a way to communicate core business principles, for instance by studying the Apollo 13 space mission or Leonard Bernstein's production of West Side Story on Broadway. No one is suggesting that trips to the Antarctic or Uganda or even are a substitute for group-working on business issues. But for those managers who want to stretch the envelope, to explore new avenues of leadership, I hope this small sample of suggestions will help or, better still, inspire some original new training ideas.

If you're not learning you're becoming a liability		
Quality	SAS approach	Things To watch out for
Leadership	Play close attention to fundamentals of leadership at all levels. Ensure basic training for all managers.	Equate size of pay-check with leadership capability and allow senior managers to set poor example.

Competence framework	Think carefully about strategic priorities and the competences that will be needed to deliver. Shape development agenda accordingly.	Flavour-of-the-month training, random distribution of available resources.
Budget	Ring fence the development budget. Have enough resources to cover stretching programmes.	Start nibbling away at the training budget, seeing it as a "soft target."
Sponsorship	Involve senior management extensively in graduate trainee selection and development	Graduate programmes left largely to HR to organise.
Training	Experiment with new and challenging approaches to leadership development incorporating ESG, multiple programs, tools and techniques that really stretch.	Off the shelf training solutions, psychometrics and abseiling.

Chapter Ten: Learn to bounce-back.

One afternoon I was doing unarmed combat training in the gym and we were all flailing away at punchbags. My own exertions were rather pathetic but the man beside me was walloping his bag with a great 'KAPOW!' that would have graced any comic book. Ex Irish Guards, he was one of the Army's top boxers and you wouldn't want to get anywhere near his right hook. Each SAS soldier has a specialism. His was demolitions or the use of explosives. The following week he was learning to make improvised explosive devices (IEDs) and was handling a trigger device that had unfortunately seen better days. As he set the trigger it caused the IED to explode prematurely, blowing his arm off and blinding him in one eye. A second man was injured by his body parts. He was rushed to surgery and G Squadron colleagues later visited the hospital to check that he was okay. They returned the following evening to monitor progress but found that his bed was empty. After some concerned searching by orderlies they found him - in the rehabilitation gym doing dumbell curls with his remaining arm.

No Option

When I wrote the first edition of WDWiB the world had largely rebounded from the effects of the financial crisis. The stock market had climbed back above the levels achieved before the crash and the previous low of the Millenium dotcom bubble. Things seemed to be back on track. People were drawing upon their courage and resilience to get back into the game (whatever it was for them) and green shoots of recovery were evident. Risk-taking had come back into fashion. Now, writing in 2020, even the most consevative, risk-averse businesses have taken a Covid-pounding. Whole sections of industry are reeling from lockdowns, travel restrictions and other medically-driven precautions and politicians have prioritised public health above near-term economic prosperity. If you live in Britain all this is going on at the same time as Brexit, a dislocation with European markets that many businesses didn't welcome. Other parts of the world are even worse off. So bouncing back is no longer something you opt into, a by-product of embracing risk. Our backs are against the wall. There is no option but to fight back.

Beating the clock

Standing in the SAS barracks is a grey, portable clock tower with the names of the Regiment's fallen soldiers inscribed upon it. To survive a mission, in SAS parlance, is to "Beat the clock". The simple truth is that those "Who Dare" can't "Win" every time. That's the law of probability. SAS soldiers have been killed and wounded in almost every post-war conflict, often without their families knowing where they have been deployed. The very first SAS operation in 1941 was an unmitigated disaster, just as the bureaucrats at Middle East Headquarters had predicted. But this was by no means the last time that the SAS would taste the bitterness of failure. Ironically, another disastrous operation became the SAS's best known, thanks to the astonishing success of Andy McNab (Steve Mitchell)'s best-selling book *Bravo Two Zero*. As nearly two million readers know, Steve led a patrol during Operation Desert Storm, the objective of which was to sever a communication link between Baghdad and North-Western Iraq. The patrol got into difficulties and, after a series of fire-fights, three men were dead. Bob "Mumbling Midget" Consiglio was shot in the head, "Legs" Lane died swimming the Euphrates River and

Vince Philips succumbed to hypothermia whilst trying to exfiltrate. As we know, a fourth man Colin Armstrong famously "got away", leaving Steve and three colleagues in Iraqi custody. What followed was beyond imagining. Mitchell was beaten with planks, whips and a thing like a medieval mace, his teeth were yanked out with pliers and he was made to eat faeces. He was kicked, punched and spat upon and endured weeks of bitter cold, terror and filth. By the time his Iraqi captors had finished with him he had hepatitis, a dislocated shoulder, scars, burns, ruptured muscles and lost sensation in his hands. His colleagues fared no better. Cruelly, SAS death's are rarely publicly acknowledged and grieved in the normal way, for reasons of security. When sniper Matt Tonroe was killed by an IED in Syria it only became public knowledge when US media identified a US special forces operator killed alongside him.

The pressures of SAS service are as psychological as they are physical. TV's *Who Dares Wins* star Jason Fox describes his battle with PTSD in his candid memoir *Battle Scars*[81] which resulted in him leaving the service. Other SAS soldiers were reported in the Mirror newspaper as suffering PTSD from a "wheel of death" lifestyle,[82] afraid to seek counselling in case it resulted in them being forced to quit the regiment. Amongst them was Commanding Officer of 22 SAS, Richard Williams. For some it proved too much. Frank Collins who left the Army to become a priest took his own life as did Charles "Nish" Bruce, one of the world's most experienced freefallers, who took his last journey to earth without a parachute. Guilt at surviving is sometimes a feature of PTSD and it can last a very long time. Mick Williams was one of few survivors when an SAS Sea King helicopter plunged into the South Atlantic during the Falklands War killing 14 comrades. With the blackest humour imaginable he was nicknamed "Splash" by his wartime colleagues. 25 years later he broke cover to confess his angst. SAS soldiers occasionally land in prison like sniper Danny

---

81   Battle Scars, War And All That Follows, Jason Fox, Bantam Press 2018

82   Mirror newspaper 29 Sept 2018, Sean Rayment

Nightingale, jailed for possession of an illegal pistol. SBS celebrity Ant Middleton did four months at Her Majesty's Pleasure for assaulting two policemen in a nightclub brawl in Essex. Steve Mitchell originally joined the Army from youth custody. Others wind up homeless, like Iranian Embassy veteran Bob Curry.

Perhaps cruellest of all are the fates of men like John McAleese, another Iranian Embassy siege-r and Bob Horton, a man with whom I served personally. Both were exceptional soldiers who inspired their sons to follow in their military footsteps, only to witness their deaths in combat. It's an unimaginable cocktail and it is widely believed the death of his son contributed to McAleese's fatal heart attack, aged 62. McAleese's wife took her own life on Remembrance Day eight years later. Colin Armstrong describes the heartache of casualty Vince Philip's family after the Bravo Two Zero patrol, convinced that the Army were somehow concealing the facts of his death. SAS families in general carry a considerable burden and it is interesting that David Stirling emphasised the need for "regimental wives" to support each other, regardless of their social class. The life of an SAS wife was well documented by Jenny Simpson in her memoir *Biting the Bullet*[83], in which she describes fearing for her own life as well as her husband's. She also notes that her husband acquired flecks of grey in his hair and the wrinkles of an older man before his thirtieth birthday. The wife of my own Best Man, then an SAS officer, battled with advanced breast cancer and heroically conquered the disease but it took a toll on them both and he had to step down from service. The MOD have a curious, even callous term for this kind of situation where they classify the officer as "Non-Effective". Another SAS officer friend of mine left the military to spend more time with his children but also because he was mentally exhausted by having to meet with so many SAS families to grieve and talk through the circumstances of their sons' deaths.

When you look at all these human stories you quickly come back

---

83   Biting The Bullet: Living with the SAS, Jenny Simpson, Harper Collins 1996

to the whole point of Selection which I describe at the start of the book. Selection is not about brute physicality or "proving yourself". It's about whether a person really wants to sign up to a life that will be tested physically, psychologically, domestically - or even foreshortened. This is not a decision to be taken lightly. And there's no turning back. Yes, a soldier can voluntarily leave the unit or the Army altogether but SAS service leaves an indelible mark, one way or another. This is an organisation where resilience and the ability to rebound is not an option - it's a core competence. If the SAS had a patron saint it would be Saint Ignatius with his; "to fight and not to heed the wounds; to toil and not to seek for rest; to labor and ask not for reward...".

During my own SAS training I remember performing rather badly in a reconnaissance exercise and being heavily criticised by my instructor, the late *Jock Harris*. I became most depressed at this because I ran a real risk of failing the course, which meant having to relive the nightmares of Selection if I wanted to continue with my dream. My fears were well founded. I did eventually fail the course and had to endure months more of the same exhausting assessment before finally taking my place in the regiment. However, it was not my failure during the exercise that really got me into trouble, but my apparent self-recrimination. Jock, veteran of many battles, impressed upon me that SAS life would be full of setbacks and disappointments, some of which would be very hard to stomach like the loss of fine comrades. What mattered, in his learned view, was not that mistakes could never be made, but that the aftermath must be managed with fortitude.

History proves him correct. A lesser man than David Stirling might have thrown in the towel after the first abortive raid. He didn't. On the contrary, the setback just seemed to spur him on to try even harder to succeed with his idea and that was almost certainly what persuaded Lloyd-Owen to support him. In reality you could pick almost any chapter from the SAS playbook and you would come across the same rebounding pattern. Hitler became so angry with the SAS he ordered them murdered when caught and the SS were only too willing to oblige. An abortive mission with the French resistance in the Vosges region resulted in 2 SAS deaths and 31 captured. Amongst the captured, the wounded were finished off with lethal injections, the others beaten to death or hung upside down over an open fire. Those who escaped the melee were back destroying roads and railways in the area within days, driving Hitler into a blind rage. The SS might have tortured and killed some soldiers but they singularly failed to demoralise the unit.

The Fight Back

Some, but not all, of the stories I mention on the previous page have a happy ending, apparent proof of the bounce-back principle in action. Steve Mitchell was originally vilified for his kiss-and-tell war story but in time became something of an establishment figure, talking to large groups of soldiers with the blessing of Top Brass and championing literacy in general. He also supported a "Suited and Booted" programme to help soldiers succeed in civilian life and of course has so far published around 50 books. Hollywood beckoned and he consulted in the Miramax movie *Heat,* coaching Robert de Niro, amongst many other ventures and was awarded a CBE in 2017. Fellow patrol member Colin Armstrong is also now up to about 50 novels (perhaps they're competing?) and has done various TV shows. Jason Fox's story of PTSD is ultimately uplifting as he works through his demons, shrugs off a corporate life he doesn't want and settles into adventurous training and TV presenting. My Hereford lodger, Ken Hames, hosted various TV adventure programmes like CH4's 'Desert Darlings' and 'Jungle Janes' in which he put military wives through their paces. VC winner, Australian Ben Roberts-Smith, has gone on to be General Manager of Seven Queensland, a TV station.

However, not every ex-SAS soldier seeks their fortune via storytelling or the media. Some 14 security companies are based in Hereford and some 32 others employ ex-SAS. A few ex SNCOs are now multi-millionaires as a result, with the Guardian newspaper complaining that Britain is becoming a global capital for mercenaries.[84] For those who give up the gun, risk management and related insurance products provide employment. De-militarise altogether and adventure travel beckons. The highly regarded Trailfinders travel company was founded in 1970 by SAS Officer Mike Gooley and has prospered for half a century. But others, like myself, have moved beyond anything that remotely resembles military life and settled into more conventional civilian careers. Amongst others, I know of at least one ex SAS officer who worked at McKinsey, the elite management consultancy, and another who became a FTSE 100 HR Director. Perhaps the best-known officer of my generation is Jamie Lowther-Pinkerton, the aristocratic ex Eton, Irish Guards who mentored Princes William and Harry for much of their young lives. (He's left it to their wives now). He's currently involved with Venture Capital and technology. Henry Gow, who once said of the bullying he received during recruit training; "To be honest, it was so bad it drove me to the point of suicide," pursued a career that included the SAS, RUC and a stint as a South African mercenary before gaining a legal education and becoming a high-powered barrister.

There are various resources available to support SAS soldiers when things don't go so well. Most directly aligned is the SAS Regimental Association,[85] an organisation staffed by veterans who well understand the work and lives of SAS men and whose mission is to intervene when welfare support is needed. Combat Stress takes the lead on issues like PTSD. A friend of mine, Gary Burns, fundraises for Combat Stress and told me that the special forces were not over-represented amongst their clients. On the contrary their numbers were no more than proportionate which, given the tasks assigned to them, suggests an above average capacity to process and cope. Perhaps the

---

84   Britain is at center of global mercenary industry, Richard Norton-Taylor, Guardian 3 Feb 2016

85   *(If you would like to help with the work of the SAS Regimental Association, any member of the public can donate via their website: www.marsandminerva.co.uk.)*

most powerful of all weapons in the SAS armoury is simply humour (one of Stirling's founding principles) - generally of the dark variety. Steve Mitchell began his memoire with; 'I had never known my real mother, though I always imagined that whoever she was she must have wanted the best for me; the carrier bag I was found in when she left me on the steps of Guy's Hospital came from Harrods.' It sets the tone. Humour can even be deployed tactically. When Captain Gavin Hamilton was shot dead in the Falklands War, his signaller Ron was captured by the Argentinian forces. From the equipment he carried, they surmised he was a member of the Special Forces and began to interrogate him accordingly. The man is dark-skinned and managed to play to who-knows-what prejudices by persuading his captors that he was not SF but a coolie employed by them to carry their heavy kit! The ruse worked and he spent a few uncomfortable days sitting out in the cold and the rain, but otherwise unmolested, as he awaited the liberation of Port Stanley. When SAS soldiers are killed in action their mates try to provide for their next of kin in a unique way. The deceased's possessions are auctioned amongst the Troop and everyone ludicrously overpays for whatever bric-a-brac they fancy. "A battered old Mexican Sombrero from a holiday in Cancun? That'll be a hundred quid to you Sir!" The money is gathered and handed over to the family.

The SAS are also not so preoccupied with their own challenges that they have nothing left to give anyone else. An interesting fact came to life when ex-SAS Colonel Henry Worsely died as he attempted the first unaided solo crossing of Antarctica. With only thirty miles to go at the end of a thousand mile journey Henry succumbed to peritonitis. The expedition itself was in support of the Endeavour Fund, a charity set up by the Royal Princes Harry and William to support injured servicemen. Less well-known was his support for prisoner rehabilitation. Whilst serving with the SAS Henry had taught himself to sew to calm his nerves. He then visited Wandsworth Prison where he passed the skill onto inmates, presumably also to help them achieve a calmer equilibrium. My friend Ken Hames got involved with the Community

Self Build Agency and helped ex servicemen and struggling families with over 140 home self-build projects. He also took wheelchair-bound youngsters on expeditions to Nicaragua, The Andes and Africa as part of his 'Beyond Boundaries' series.

A Bit Good

There are many examples of businesses that have foundered and somehow staged heroic recoveries drawing upon the courage of their leaders. Steve Jobs famously got into heated arguments with the Board of Apple and was effectively kicked out of his own company in 1985. He took such blows very personally and yet he capitalised on the opportunity. In a later speech to students at Stanford University he described his firing as a liberating experience that somehow forced him to reconnect with his creative side. The period following the financial crisis of 2008/9 is full of recovery stories. But in fact - and entirely by coincidence - I don't need to draw upon analogous examples to describe what businesses need to do to stage a post-Covid fightback. Because my family was *there* the last time this happened.

In 1912, a young man called Walter Mawer was orphaned and inherited a furniture business which he ran with his cousin. They had a large shop and manufactured on-site in Silver Street in the cathedral city of Lincoln. (In those days "manufacturing" was a half a dozen apprentice carpenters and a foreman rather than a sub-assembly operation somewhere in Thailand or Sweden.) But before he had got to grips with the business, he was called to the Great War where he served first in the Lincolnshire Regiment and then the Machine Gun Corps. He somehow survived the war, returned home and picked up where he had left off. If it sometimes feels as though we have barely recovered from the financial crisis, only to be hit by Covid, imagine the sensation of taking part in the carnage of WWI (20 million deaths) only to run straight into a Spanish Flu epidemic which would infect a third of the world's population and take 50 million more lives before it ran its course. There was no time for self-pity.

The Lincolnshire Corporation published its six precautions[86] for dealing with the flu:

> 'Overcrowding ... in unventilated rooms and places of entertainment should be avoided'.
>
> 'Aggregation of large numbers of persons in one room, especially for sleeping is dangerous'.
>
> 'Alcoholism or over-strain favour infection, and complication by pneumonia is especially fatal among immoderate drinkers'.
>
> 'Dirtiness whether personal or of living and working rooms, and dusty conditions, favour infection'.
>
> 'Indiscriminate expectoration (gobbing on the pavement) is always a source of risk of infection'.
>
> 'If every person ... took all possible precautions, the present danger and mortality from such Epidemics would be much reduced'.

Looks familiar? As a joinery specialist it wasn't difficult to get his coworkers to start manufacturing coffins and the biers (stands) that they rest upon. Sensing an opportunity, he extended his business to include undertaking. He must have also realised that dead people leave houses full of unwanted furniture because he then began auctioneering. New incumbents to these vacated properties wanted a fresh start. Walter obliged by sourcing wallpaper and soft furnishings to add to his joinery offering. Although he would never have used such grand terms, he had effectively created a vertically integrated manufacturing and service company to address the needs of a market place in shock. But this was not the end of his challenges. His warehouse and shop were themselves made from Lincolnshire brown oak and in 1922 an electrical fire in the basement burnt his premises to the ground. He had no insurance. Undeterred, uncomplaining he rebuilt the business from scratch. There was no furloughing of staff. They were deployed on the reconstruction process. As the business matured he began to

---

86   Social History Society, 6 April 2020

have three day team excursions to a modest hotel on the edge of the Peak District some two hours away. It was an opportunity to drive his Rover car, a source of some pride. These events were no more "off-sites" than his business was "vertically integrated". Three days of hearty eating (they all came from Lincolnshire farming stock and knew a good pie when they saw one) and bracing walks in the countryside where interspersed with business talk. When profits spilled over he diversified again by buying a pheasant shoot. Eventually, in the 1960s when age had finally caught up with him, Walter sold the business on for a decent sum.

By all accounts my grandfather, Walter (not to be confused with my 21 SAS (R) grandfather Horace) was a gentleman, much loved by his customers. His catchphrase "That's a bit good" says much about his understated demeanour. When MBA students look for solutions to the current crisis their first thought may be to look to Silicon Valley, the land of Unicorns, fast successes and fast failures. But we are not the first generation to face tough times and sometimes it is better - and this comes naturally to cultures the West considers primitive - to listen to the voices of our ancestors.

Ticket to Basingstoke

And finally, what of my own story? My use of autobiography in this book is mainly to ensure authenticity and perhaps the odd moment of reader amusement. I don't claim to have a heroic story or that anybody would cite me as a great example of what the SAS is all about. On the contrary, the SAS dispensed with my services before I was ready to call it a day and this all happened whilst I lay in a military hospital bed receiving two courses of chemotherapy, to deal with a tropical illness I had picked up on SAS operations in Central America. (My ultra fitness has never returned). Whilst digesting this news I further learned that my father had weeks to live due to prostate cancer and, for good measure, my illness had resulted in my attendance on a scheduled Staff Course being postponed. It's fair to say I had reached a low point. When I had my final discharge medical the Army doctor asked me how I was. "Fine," I replied. She looked doubtful.

But if the SAS had taught me anything it was the importance of bouncing back. At first I considered working for a security company in Washington. It felt like a pale version of what I had been doing. Instead, I embraced a second SAS principle, namely the need to reinvent myself according to opportunity, to develop new skills and to avoid self-pity. So I sold my ceremonial uniforms, got myself "suited and booted" with the proceeds and committed to an entirely new career as a businessman, starting by working for a company that made vending machines, the least glamorous product imaginable. Then I bought a one-way ticket to Basingstoke.

> *If you can make one heap of all your winnings*
> *And risk it on one turn of pitch-and-toss,*
> *And lose, and start again at your beginnings*
> *And never breathe a word about your loss;*
> *If you can force your heart and nerve and sinew*
> *To serve your turn long after they are gone,*
> *And so hold on when there is nothing in you*
> *Except the Will which says to them: 'Hold on!'*

(Extracts from *If*, Kipling 1909)

Postscript

Thirty-five years after the terrible events at Ballykelly I returned to Northern Ireland for the first time on a golfing week-end with some Australian friends; the Chairman of a Childrens' Hospital, his son and a well-known Sydney newspaper cartoonist. Against my advice, when they arrived in Belfast the three of them checked into an AirBnb on the Shankhill Road. Let's just say it was an education. The next morning we drove together to the north, a golfer's paradise with Royal Portrush, Portstewart and Castlerock courses lined up along the beautiful coast, interspersed with interesting beaches and watering holes. As we drove through the villages I noticed that kerb stones were still painted red, white and blue and - more provocatively - Parachute Regiment flags fluttered from a number of lampposts. After the golf my friends continued into Donegal and, before I headed home, I decided to visit the Ballykelly war memorial, the Droppin Well and to lay a few ghosts to rest.

I guess I was hoping to find a tranquil oasis but reconciled to the possibility that I would find it banal, an anticlimax. It was neither. The Inn had been rebuilt in the same sort of format as before with a chemist above ground level and a pub/restaurant below. The grassy bank of horrors had also been restored, a little steeper now, wrapped around the whole. I parked up, stood on the bank but there was a noisy, dusty road works opposite and contemplation was impossible. I looked for the entrance and instead found a long white, clinical corridor that ran from ground level to somewhere far below and to the rear (presumably the service ramp for the chemist). Walking round to the side I found the entrance and stepped into the bar. There were three men and a woman drinking - who sinks pints at 4pm on a Monday? As I approached I heard one of the men making racists comments of the worst kind and topping it off with; "There aren't many places you can still talk like that," as though we should all enjoy the privilege. I eased past and looked into the restaurant area where the carnage had taken place so many years before. The room was entirely dark except for three vertical, yellowish shafts of light that shone down over the grassy bank and through narrow opaque windows, casting shadows amongst the tables and chairs. I felt like I'd stumbled upon a hellish portal to December 6th 1982. Pure Stephen King. Shocked, I stepped out and poked my head into the kitchen, hoping to find the owner and reconnect with the present. "You can't go in there!" barked one of the drinkers.

I left the bar staff a fat tip. Some form of kindness was well overdue in this place. Afterwards and strange as it might seem, I extended the trip for another night and 36 more holes of golf at Castlerock. It rained most of the day but I drove, chipped, putted, bunkered, drove, putted, chipped until I felt normal again. In the evening, with the rain now bucketing down, I returned to my old haunt, the Harbour Bar at Portrush and had a couple of Bushmills - I prefer the Black. I was born in Northern Ireland when my father was garrisoned there. He also played at Castlerock and once said to me; "The folk here will only be happy when they spend less time thinking about their grand-parents and more about their grand-children." He was a wise man. As for me, I now have dual Irish/UK citizenship because I'm not interested in celebrating a divided country, Brexit or any other device that pushes people apart when they should be coming together to solve the real problems of the world like healthcare, the global economy and climate change.

Appendix -
Huffington Post, The Author, 8 Aug 2015

Author's Note: I have included this article to reflect the principle that the SAS never allows itself to become complacent and should therefore always be open to new ways of working

Has SAS selection just got softer - or simply less relevant?

The SAS Aptitude Course - better known by its more sinister name "Selection" - hasn't changed much in 40 years. And to the best of my knowledge, about a dozen men have lost their lives in the course of this training process. The most common causes of death have been illnesses brought on by extremes of temperature combined with intense physical exercise. In medical terms, they either died of hypo- or hyper-thermia. (Hyper is the hot one.) Others have suffered gunshot wounds in simulated close quarter battle conditions, had parachuting accidents or similar. Is that a lot of deaths for Britain's most demanding military training programme? It's a matter of judgement. 125 British servicemen have lost their lives in training over the past 15 years, suggesting that it may be no more than proportionate.

However, given political pressures, it must come as no surprise to anyone to read in The Times over the week-end that "Selection" is to be modified in the wake of three recent deaths in training. Test marches are to be curbed in extreme weather conditions and more support provided in the form of water stops. But these are just the latest in a series of safety improvements. Since the 1970s SAS trainees have carried emergency equipment including high-viz panels, first aid kits, water and radio beacons - rather than the pile of numbered bricks that used to fill Bergen rucksacks! Winter marches are commenced well before dawn in order to allow helicopters more daylight to rescue wayward trainees if such a situation arises. Back in the 1980s, when I did the final 64 kilometre "Endurance March," it was stopped after twenty hours of blizzard conditions for safety reasons. More modern technology has allowed these measures to be supported by GPS tracking devices. Nonetheless, SAS alumni are now debating whether Selection is going soft and, specifically, whether this makes sense in a world in which SF soldiers have spent more than a decade charging around with heavy equipment under a blistering Iraqi or Afghan sun.

Let the old sweats argue the point over a beer at the Special Forces Club in Knightsbridge. But perhaps a more useful question is whether it even makes sense that SAS Selection remains so true to its rhythm, after so many years and so much geo-political change. SAS Selection begins with three weeks of basic fitness and navigation training. The ability to map-read was always a key military skill, as much for an infantryman as an SF operator. However, these days the average housewife can pinpoint a teenage party in a barn in the middle of pitch black countryside at two in the morning by simply plugging a postcode into the GPS system in their Volvo. It's a diminishing currency. The infamous fourth 'Test Week' combines map reading with an escalating series of physical challenges, involving traversing mountain ranges at speed and with heavy loads. This certainly plays to the experience of recent campaigns but it does little credit, either to the military-industrial complex or SF tacticians, that soldiers still drag themselves around the battlefield carrying exactly the same amount of clobber as their forebears at the Battle of the Somme a full century ago. Boffins have started to experiment with a load-bearing military exoskeleton but it all seems a long way off. In the meantime, the Taliban will continue to refer to Western soldiers as "plodding donkeys".

After the joys of the Brecon Beacons SAS recruits head to Brunei, on the island of Borneo, to hone their jungle warfare skills. This owes its origins to the post-War recreation of the SAS as the Malayan Scouts during the "Emergency" in the 1950s. Other SAS rainforest campaigns followed; the Borneo "Confrontation" with Indonesia and the Brunei "Revolt". However, these campaigns were successfully resolved before my first birthday. (I'm now 53). Setting aside a smattering of anti-narcotics operations and the odd rumble in the African jungle, it all amounts to a slightly nostalgic take on modern SF soldiering. The main argument for this continued arboreal focus is that the rainforest provides for a good test of basic SF disciplines. Perhaps that's a little post-rational. You would have thought the time might be better spent on cyber and other forms of leading-edge warfare. It seems strange that in a world ruled by technology, sheer physicality is still such a prevalent SF competence.

With Brunei a leech-infested memory, it's back to Wales to learn combat survival, enabling recruits to take their place amongst Bear Grylls, Ray Mears and other TV pundits who show us how to knit a cagoule from an alligator's scrotum and drink your own pee, (even when there is a three star hotel less than a day's march away). There's no question that the ability to think positively and improvise your way out of tricky situations is - and always will be - a critical SF skill. However it would be interesting to document how frequently UK SF members have ever actually subsisted on edible plants, fungi and wild animals in a genuine combat situation. I suspect the answer is almost never. The combat survival phase of training ends with a resistance-to-interrogation programme and this is clearly relevant. The UK seems to make a habit of tackling regimes that go in for whole-scale torture, as experienced by celebrated SAS writer Andy McNab when he was caught by Saddam Hussein's forces. Whether it's actually possible to resist anything when you're being physically dismembered is debatable, but at least you know what to expect.

The penultimate phase of SAS training is the anti-terrorist package and there is no question that this is entirely relevant and will remain so as long as people like ISIS, Al Qaeda and even the IRA are at large. The final phase of SAS training involves the standard Army parachute course. I've always enjoyed parachuting and Airborne soldiers the world over like the prestige of wearing a set of embroidered wings on their tunics. However, in a world that now includes helicopters and Osprey fixed-wing, it is a somewhat redundant form of battlefield arrival. Soldiers from my own SAS Troop parachuted into the sea during the Falklands War, rendez-vous-ing with a submarine, and a group from B Squadron used the more exotic HAHO (High Altitude High Opening) glide technique to sneak up on an armed money launderer in Iraq. But in both cases the usefulness of parachuting was debated. The last major UK military parachute drop was in Suez 1956.

So whilst the SAS agonise about whether it makes sense to make "Selection" a little less dangerous, perhaps it would be better off spending time asking the question of "What", exactly, is it selecting its soldiers for? Is it a slightly nostalgic world of colonial wars, steaming jungles full of Iban head-hunters and dare-devil parachute jumps or a fragmented battle field of shape-shifting enemies, mutating objectives, surveillance, drones and technology prevalence? Should it even be necessary for the SAS soldier of the future to be capable of lugging his own body-weight in kit over Pen-y-Fan at a quick jog or are there other competencies that will better ensure his performance and personal survival on the battlefield? Happily, the SAS has always been good at re-inventing itself, whilst other elite units have run their course, and hopefully it will now take this opportunity to think about the attributes it requires, to ensure a further seventy years of success.